W9-BQS-719

Entrepreneur
MAGAZINE'S

ULTIMATE

GUIDE TO

DIRECT

MARKETING

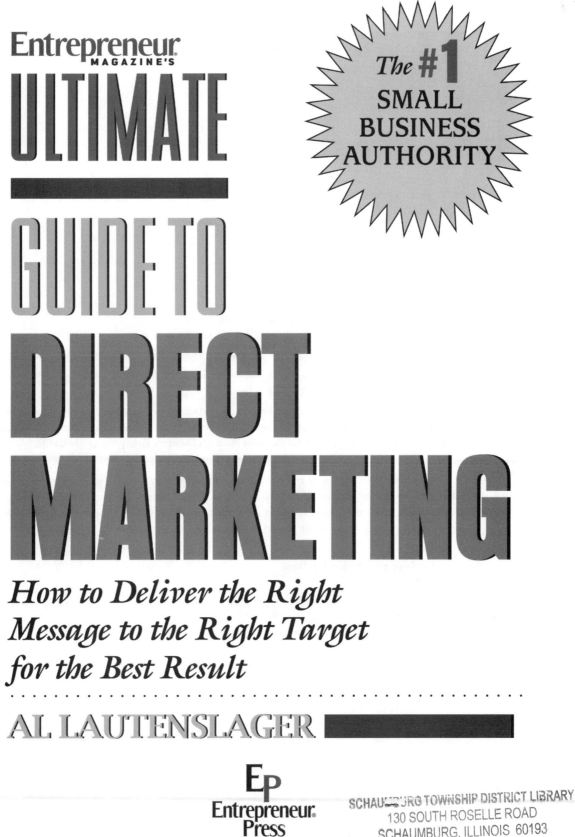

Entrepreneur
MAGAZINE'S

ULTIMATE

GUIDE TO

DIRECT

MARKETING

How to Deliver the Right
Message to the Right Target
for the Best Result

AL LAUTENSLAGER

Ep
Entrepreneur.
Press

The **#1**
SMALL
BUSINESS
AUTHORITY

SCHAUMBURG TOWNSHIP DISTRICT LIBRARY
130 SOUTH ROSELLE ROAD
SCHAUMBURG, ILLINOIS 60193

658.872
LAUTENSLAGER, A

3 1257 01666 5357

Managing editor: Jere L. Calmes
Cover design: Beth Hansen-Winter
Composition and production: Eliot House Productions

© 2005 by Entrepreneur Media, Inc.

All rights reserved.

Reproduction or translation of any part of this work beyond that permitted by Section 107 or 108 of the 1976 United States Copyright Act without permission of the copyright owner is unlawful. Requests for permission or further information should be addressed to the Business Products Division, Entrepreneur Media Inc.

This publication is designed to provide accurate and authoritative information in regard to the subject matter covered. It is sold with the understanding that the publisher is not engaged in rendering legal, accounting, or other professional services. If legal advice or other expert assistance is required, the services of a competent professional person should be sought.

Library of Congress Cataloging-in-Publication Data

Lautenslager, Al.
    Entrepreneur magazine's ultimate direct marketing guide: how to deliver the right message to the right target for the best result/Al Lautenslager.
        p.   cm.
    ISBN 1-932531-71-8
    1. Direct marketing. I. Title: Ultimate direct marketing guide. II. Entrepreneur (Irvine, Calif.) III. Title.
    HF5415.126.L37 2005
    658.8'72--dc22   2005004987

Printed in Canada

10 09 08 07 06 05   10 9 8 7 6 5 4 3 2 1

Contents

Dedication

I continue to have a personal mission to help as many small businesses and organizations as I can through my speaking and writing. Those that benefit are included in this dedication. This book also honors those who not only believe, but who set their sights high and reach their goals. As Henry Ford once said, "Whether you think that you can, or that you can't, you are usually right."

I also dedicate this to the memory of my mother. She was the one who encouraged me to watch every space launch and any other historic moment that came on the public airwaves. There was always a lesson and a push associated with each viewing. Many of those inspire and encourage me to this day. Thanks, Mom. Of course, I couldn't dedicate this to my mother without including my father. For so long, it wasn't just Mom or just Dad. It always seemed like it was Mom and Dad as one. I couldn't depart from those thoughts now. Thanks, Dad.

Acknowledgments

WHILE NOT MANY PEOPLE PICK UP books and rush to the author's acknowledgment section, a lot of thought goes into it. As entrepreneurs, we often can't do things alone. Writing books is in that same category. First and foremost, it takes the support of family. Much love and many thanks go out to my wife, who has cheered me on in my endeavors, supported me in every way, and is part of everything I do in one way or another. Thank you, Angela. To my daughter Allison, you continue to make me proud to be your father. Much love to you also.

My publishing success could not have been possible without the investment Jere Calmes, managing editor of Entrepreneur Press, has made in me. Thank you for your leap of faith and continuing confidence in my writing and ideas. Leanne Harvey, also of Entrepreneur Press, is one of the most brilliant marketing minds in the business. I am blessed to be associated with her and fortunate to benefit from her marketing savvy. Thanks, Leanne.

Thanks is also extended to the many people who have shared the company stories, successes, trials, and tribulations that are documented in this book. You are all generous with your information, and I wish you all success.

A big thank-you and high five to Jay Conrad Levinson, who allowed me to tag along and join him as coauthor of *Guerrilla Marketing in 30 Days*. He continues to be a mentor, friend, and inspiration. Finally, there are so many people locally and nationally who have lent their support to me with this publishing project and others. Thank you for your time, your support, and your encouragement. I look forward to thanking many others as my writing continues to contribute to the successes of many.

Preface

I T IS A GIVEN FACT THAT THERE ARE MORE MAR-
keting experts, more marketing books,
and more marketing information today
than ever before. Even within the whole
category of marketing, there are a plethora of
subcategories. As a small business owner,
consultant, coach, and speaker, I see much of
this marketing in practice and at work. I find,
however, that with entrepreneurs the marketing budget sometimes is limited. Because of
this, getting the biggest bang for the marketing buck is imperative. Direct marketing can
provide that bang.

Early on, in my marketing training and
then during my own business ownership, I
became hooked (no pun intended) on calls to
action. I quickly found out that prospects and
even some customers liked to be told what to
do, what action to take. Direct marketing is
very action oriented and motivates a prospect
or customer to take that necessary action.

Awareness marketing, advertising with no
calls to action, and branding campaigns are

certainly abundant and all around us every-
day. To the average entrepreneur, however,
these campaigns and initiatives take time,
take big budgets, and don't provide a quick
enough return on marketing dollars spent.
Direct marketing does if you have the right
message delivered to the right target in the
right way frequently enough.

It is these four points that are the foundation of the *Ultimate Guide to Direct
Marketing*:

1. The Message
2. The Vehicle
3. The Target
4. Timing and Frequency

The Ultimate Series by Entrepreneur Press
is a series of how-to business books designed
for all levels of entrepreneurship. It consists
of fundamental subjects pertinent to business
start-up, ownership, operations, growth, and
related supporting business concepts. The titles
have been well accepted by the entrepreneur market. This book is integral to the series. Direct

marketing should be part of any entrepreneur's business plan.

All marketers want to get their message out. Yet messages are not always seen or acted upon. Direct marketing stimulates that action and provides the return on investment that entrepreneurs are interested in. Sales increase, and profits grow as a result. The goal of this book is to increase your profits.

Today with the internet as a major marketing tool, online marketing is quickly becoming a major component of all marketing arsenals. Never have there been more appropriate vehicles for direct marketing than the internet and e-mails. Responding to a message is much easier when replying to an e-mail or clicking a link. Response is the primary objective of direct marketing. The internet also allows for testing of marketing in a more efficient way. Testing is very important in direct marketing. This book includes an updated section on direct online marketing.

Direct marketing has often been described as one of the most cost effective ways to sell products and services to target markets. This book contains tips, methods, strategies, tactics, plans, and techniques that produce results from the use of direct marketing. It has expanded coverage of direct online marketing. Not only planning but also testing and idea generation is covered. Because I learn by real company examples, I have decided to share these with you so you can learn as well. Lots of up-to-date examples bring these concepts and tips to life. An updated glossary and other resources makes this the direct marketing reference manual of choice for marketers of any size business.

Throughout this book, you will learn techniques of direct marketing, how to increase response rates, and what kind of marketing is best suited to your business. All of this is aimed at the main points in the direct marketing process:

- Identify a likely customer.
- Create a compelling offer for that likely customer.
- Create, design, and write a letter, package, or other marketing vehicle that will grab the attention of the likely customer and evoke a response of some kind.
- Sell and fulfill products and services quickly and directly.

That's essentially what MasterCard did during its tremendous growth phases. Direct marketing strategies and the use of direct mail were instrumental in its growth. It established offers, identified the audience/target it wished to go after, and communicated to that audience in a language that persuaded people to respond, or in its case, apply for credit services.

That's all there is to it. Each of these steps represents a critical point in the direct marketing process. Ignoring any one of them is a ticket to sure failure. Studying, employing, and completing each is the path to direct marketing success.

The vision of pundits like David Ogilvy and Lester Wunderman has become a realization; and that trend will only increase in intensity. This book was written to help you keep up with that trend. Happy Marketing!

Direct Marketing Basics

YOU ARE ABOUT TO EMBARK UPON A DIRECT journey. Yes, that pun was intended; direct as in a direct marketing journey. I will let the context from here forward fix the proper usage of that sentence and intent in your own mind. Before jumping right into that direct path, I am offering a bit of perspective first. Mind you, this is without the background, foreground, technicalities, definitions, etc., of what you are about to learn. I lead with it because it is something most readers will be able to identify with and something that sets the stage for that direct journey you are about to embark on.

Let me introduce to you to one of the most prolific perspective pontificators of the past and present century—Yogi Berra. With permission from Dean Rieck of www.directcreative.com, I present his rendition of Yogi Berra's Tips on Direct Marketing:

> Lawrence Peter 'Yogi' Berra is a 15-time All Star. He won the American League Most Valuable Player award three times, played in 14 World Series, and set a number of baseball records, any one of which would assure a lifetime of fame and fortune for most people. But what is Yogi best known for? His slips of the tongue—which is understandable, if you go around saying things like "It's déjà vu all over again!" and "I'm as red as a sheet."

> On the surface, his off-kilter pronouncements are just amusing mistakes. But look a little deeper, and you will find profound lessons. Here are a few favorite Yogi-isms and the admittedly liberal interpretations for direct marketers:

> - *"We made too many wrong mistakes."* Do you think Edison invented the modern light bulb on his first try? He endured failure after failure before arriving at the solution. But his mistakes were "right" mistakes. Each taught him something and brought him closer to his goal. If you're not making lots of

mistakes, you're not learning anything.

- *"A nickel ain't worth a dime anymore."* People aren't logical about the way they perceive money and value. That means you have to test not just prices, but price presentations. Which is best, $24 per year or $2 per issue? How about $7.50 per month or 25¢ per day? I recently had success presenting a $149.95-a-month internet service as "less than 1/2¢ per minute."

- *"Slump? I ain't in no slump ... I just ain't hitting."* Sometimes things just don't go the way you plan. A test flops. Sales fall. And you just can't explain it. Usually it's temporary. The point is, don't panic and change your entire marketing strategy based on short-term results. And never, ever discard a control until you have something that tests better.

- *"Why buy good luggage? You only use it when you travel."* When you get right down to it, an envelope is nothing more than a container for printed matter. It carries your message to the destination and then gets ripped open. So while it can be a four-color masterpiece, it doesn't have to be. Many times a plain old #10 is all you need.

- *"We're lost but we're making good time."* Never confuse activity with progress. You need to map out a measurable strategy before launching any marketing campaign. And you need to execute your strategy carefully and methodically. If all you're doing is slapping together one ad after another, you'll get nowhere fast.

- *"If you can't imitate him, don't copy him."* There's no substitute for experience, expertise, or talent. If you don't know what you're doing, you won't solve any problems by producing carbon copies of your competitors' promotions.

- *"Ninety percent of the game is half mental."* I'm forever amazed at how little thought people put into the creative process. Personally, I spend at least half of any given project on gathering information and brainstorming. When you think things through first, copy and design are a lot easier and usually far more successful.

- *"I wish I had an answer to that because I'm tired of answering that question."* Your customers know the difference between BS and information. So don't try to shovel a pile of one to cover up for a lack of the other. Give details. Answer questions and objections. Provide a means for customers to easily find out more (a web site is good for this). People often make buying decisions based on a single feature.

- *"You can observe a lot by watching."* Look at the numbers. Do surveys. Run focus groups. Talk to your phone operators. Your customers will tell you everything you need to know if you just open your eyes and ears.

- *"It ain't over till it's over."* You can guess and estimate and reason and calculate, but you really don't know anything until you run a test. If there's one thing that's for sure in this business, it's that nothing is for sure.

Of course, Yogi also said, "I really didn't say everything I said." Maybe. But who cares? Coming from anyone else, quotes like "Pair up in threes" or "I usually take a two-hour nap from one to four," would seem stupid. Coming from Yogi, it's just right.

There you have it. With this perspective, let's begin that direct journey.

DIRECT MARKETING HISTORY

Lester Wunderman, an advertising legend who is credited with being the father of direct marketing, the advertising guru behind the American Express Card, and the creator of the Columbia Record Club, first used the term "direct marketing" publicly in October of 1961. In a speech to the Hundred Million Club of New York, an organization of leaders in the direct mail business, Wunderman described direct marketing as a "new frontier."

Here are highlights from that speech:

We live in an age of convenience retailing—what is more convenient than to shop at home? Is there any more scientific method of merchandising than the scientific copy, price, and market testing available to the mail-order advertisers? Competition for shelf space at retail is becoming ever more fierce and costly—yet access to the home by mail grows more efficient each year. The din of advertising becomes louder and louder, and it costs more to make a consumer remember advertising he saw, heard, or read when he makes a buying decision. Isn't it logical to sell him at the point of his greatest conviction, when he has just absorbed the sales message? That's what a great mail-order ad or mailing piece does. For these reasons and many others, I am absolutely convinced that the future of our industry lies with . . . companies which must increasingly bring their selling and marketing influence closer to the consumer. I believe the next ten years will see a continuing decline of the mail-order business as it has been defined in the past. It will be replaced by Direct Marketing—a new and more efficient method of selling, based on scientific advertising principles . . . .

Wunderman had identified direct marketing and defined the role it would play in the larger world of general marketing and advertising. Though no one paid much attention to it at the time, Wunderman had set the future agenda of not only his agency but also the whole advertising and marketing industry. It is upon these principles that much of direct marketing is built and is operating today.

Even as far back as the 1930s, direct marketers found that one way to obtain a customer was to offer a premium to first-time buyers. This was one of the early attempts at direct marketing launched by the Book of the Month Club while on its way to direct marketing success.

THE NEED FOR DIRECT MARKETING

When you look at businesses today, two things come to mind: margins and growth. Without either, you are leading your company into decline or doom.

Those on the production or delivery side of the business equation participate in the margin discussion often. Cutting costs, eliminating jobs, efficient purchasing, etc., are often discussed. These same people don't always necessarily participate as eagerly in the growth discussion, but growth is the lifeblood of survival.

Margin management can only go so far. Growth is, theoretically, unlimited. That is why companies eventually turn to new products, new services, and new markets. What happens when new products and services are introduced? What happens when new markets are tapped? What happens when a company strategically kicks into growth mode? The answer? Marketing enters the picture and enters it in a big way.

In a 2001 survey by Pitney Bowes, it was determined that direct mail is the most effective customer relationship management tool to reach customers. It does the best job of providing consumers with information they want, when they want it, and in the way they want to receive it.

If you look at any of the books on direct marketing, even those published ten or more years ago, virtually all of them start out by saying, "Direct marketing has experienced one of the most rapid and radical changes in the past decade or even past few years." Even at the time of writing, this statement can be made.

THE SCOPE OF DIRECT MARKETING

As *Direct Marketing* magazine says, direct marketing is not a fancy term for mail order. It is an interactive system of marketing that uses one or more advertising media to effect a measurable response and/or transaction at any location, with this activity and related information stored on a database. Lots of key words in this description, and actually the basis of this whole book!

The same publication further states that direct marketing has the same broad function as traditional marketing but requires the use and application of a database.

The Dictionary of Marketing Terms, Third Edition (Barron's, 2000) defines direct marketing as:

> Selling via direct contact with the prospective customer. Direct marketing differs from general marketing in that the result of a promotion is measurable in terms of response. Direct marketing is also largely dependent upon the use of customer databases and lists.

Frequently associated with mail order, direct marketing also includes a variety of promotion media such as televised infomercials, door-to-door selling, newspaper inserts, telemarketing, take-one cards, and package inserts. Direct marketing is a more personal type of promotion than advertising. The direct marketer often selects the individuals who will receive the promotion and is the direct recipient of their response, if any. The response may be a purchase, an inquiry, or a referral that can be traced directly back to the individual. Through the use of lists and databases another essential of marketing, place, is brought to the individual consumer. Direct marketing is used by virtually every type of business and organization; however, the primary users are magazine publishers, catalog houses, political campaign organizations, and financial institutions. Testing to improve response is a key component.

It is this definition that will guide you through this volume of the Entrepreneur Success Series, *Ultimate Guide to Direct Marketing.*

Common forms of direct marketing are direct mail, telemarketing, direct sales, catalogs, and more recently, the whole arena of internet marketing, including web sites and e-mail marketing. Direct marketing is at the forefront of marketing not only because of the growth of business mentioned earlier but also because it has been proven to work. It carries all the information necessary for a buyer to decide to buy, and it generates sales. All are necessary for viability, survivability, performance, and growth.

Because of the "directness," direct marketing is almost like having a conversation with a prospect—communication that is personal in nature. People like personal communication and generally respond to it more than any other type of communication.

Direct marketers mostly market directly to their markets without involving any middlemen, stores, or brokers. They use direct-marketing vehicles in the form of mailers, postcards, catalogs, letters, and e-mail, all in an effort to market one-on-one with prospects.

Direct marketing is marketing activity that initiates, develops, and constitutes a relationship between you and your prospect or customer. It truly is a one-on-one situation. Today, it is more than just direct mail and telemarketing. Now there is a shift to include e-mail, point-of-sale in retail, web sites, loyalty programs, direct-response advertising, and the growth of wireless devices.

Direct marketing is more prevalent now than ever before. With the use of e-mail, the internet, web site marketing, and all the related technoloical advancements, marketing can now be more direct and more efficient.

Considering these developments, it's clear that direct marketing is the best way to acquire clients and maintain customer relationships, the key to all business growth.

The scope of all marketing continues to expand in all directions. New ideas, new applications, and new media continue to emerge on an ongoing basis. Direct marketing is no different. What was once a stand-alone discipline is now a significant part of a company's total marketing strategy.

In days of old, direct marketing was made up of mail order and catalogs. With consumer demand changing, business demands changing, technology changing, and our ability to target increasing, new direct marketing techniques are emerging over and beyond those of the mail-order days.

Simply put, direct marketing can get you customers and keep them buying from you. Along with getting the customer, your job as a direct marketer is to keep the customers you work so hard to get. Direct marketing also concentrates on how to sell more to customers, how to get them to buy more often, or how to get them to buy higher-priced, more profitable items from you. Planning which of these objectives fits your overall business plan is a good starting point. Here are other examples of direct marketing objectives:

- To get ten leads per week that are qualified, interested, and ready to buy
- To increase return visits to sporting events (more tickets sold)
- To sell higher-revenue products to those who have already bought from you
- To get more orders than in the previous period for a mail-order business.

SMALL-BUSINESS GROWTH AND DIRECT MARKETING

It is a well-known known fact that small businesses will play a major role in shaping the 21st century's economic landscape. Entrepreneurs will drive economic growth in this century. They account for half of the U.S. nonfarm private gross domestic products and employ half of the U.S. private work force. More important, over the past decade, small firms have provided 60 to 80 percent of the net new jobs in the economy. According to a U.S. Bureau of the Census working paper, almost all these net new jobs stem from start-up businesses in their first two years of operation.

There are over 15 million "small businesses" in the United States (defined by the SBA as under 500 employees), and these companies employ over 60 million people. This means that every other American worker owns or is employed by a small business. If viewed separately, small businesses in the United States would constitute the world's third-largest economy (behind the United States as a whole and Japan).

Said another way, small businesses represent more than 99 percent of all employers, and employ more than half the private work force. Small-business entrepreneurs create more than two out of every three new jobs and generate about 50 percent of the nation's gross domestic product.

The recently released annual report *Small Business Economic Indicators, 2003* found that the cautious atmosphere of the two previous years had given way to increased entrepreneurial risk-taking in 2003. Output expanded, the stock markets rose, the number of firms increased, proprietors' income grew, corporate profits rose, and bank lending standards were relaxed. These factors set the stage for expansion, the start of businesses, and subsequent hiring increases.

"Small business plays a key role in our economy," said Thomas M. Sullivan, chief counsel for The Advocacy Report. "Entrepreneurs launch new ideas and they propel our economy's evolution. This dynamic risk-taking results in 60 to 80 percent of the net new jobs, so when economic conditions are favorable for growth, job gains are not far behind. That is exactly what has happened." The report estimates that 572,900 employer firms were created and 554,800 terminated in 2003. This dynamic resulted in a net increase in employer firms of 18,100, or 0.3 percent, while the number of nonincorporated self-employed rose by 369,000, or 3.7 percent.

The outlook for future small-business expansion was positive at the end of 2003. Banks began relaxing lending standards in late 2003 for the first time since 1998, and the demand for small-business loans halted its decline. The National Federation of Independent Business index that gauges small firms' view of expansion over the next three months reached its highest level since January 2000. With good financials

▼ SMALL BUSINESS EFFECTS ON THE ECONOMY

With the count over 23 million, small businesses in the United States:

- create 75 percent of the new jobs.
- employ 51 percent of the country's private work force.
- represent more than 96 percent of all exporters of goods.
- represent more than 99 percent of all employers.
- generate a majority of the innovations that come from U.S. companies.
- account for more than 40 percent of the offline economy of the United States (*IDC*, January, 2003).

Source: U.S. Small Business Administration, April 2003

and an optimistic outlook, the stage was set at the end of 2003 for small-business expansion.

What do all these businesses have to do once they start up, once they are in business? They have to get customers. They have to let customers know about them, their products, and their services. They have to get the word out and communicate with customers over and over and over. They have to get orders and make sales. They have to market directly to their target audience. All this growth in small business points to a dire need for marketing these businesses—marketing for viability, survivability, growth, and expansion.

WHAT DIRECT MARKETING IS TODAY

With the growth of small businesses comes the concentration on viability, performance, and

▼ DIRECT MARKETING IS:

- Selling directly to customers; methods of marketing by which a company deals directly with its end customers, including mail order by catalog, direct mail, telephone sales, or advertising.

- Marketing direct to the consumer, and by direct mail or coupon advertising.

- Generally the easiest, fastest, and most economical way to reach a market niche.

- Sending a promotional message directly to consumers, rather than via a mass medium; includes methods such as direct mail and telemarketing.

- Marketing via a promotion delivered directly to the individual prospects and customers.

DIRECT-RESPONSE MARKETING

After September 11, 2001, businesses relied on their house accounts, their current book of business (at that time), to survive and continue. Prospecting was more difficult and more costly; however, businesses soon after realized that bringing in new customers is the key to survival, even before considering growth. The solution to that challenge clearly lies in the use of any and all direct marketing to make it happen.

Another related notion worth considering is direct-response marketing. Direct-response marketing and direct marketing can be used interchangeably. It still is marketing that requests prospects or customers to directly respond to the marketing by mail, by phone, online, by e-mail, or by some other form of communication. The response could be anything from requesting information or responding to a survey to actually placing an order for a product or service. Direct-response marketing is direct marketing.

INTERACTIVITY

Regardless of whether it's direct-response marketing or direct marketing, it takes two to tango. Interaction can only happen when two parties are involved. Call it interactive marketing. You can't interact without being direct (remember Webster's definition), nor can you interact without getting a response.

A critical goal here is to provide tools for the use of any business owner, professional, marketing manager, or entrepreneur. This book is full of practical advice, and you can use it *right now*.

The sale of products and/or services on the internet is very closely related to the concept of direct marketing and direct-response marketing. It is the goal here to translate many of the direct marketing principles into the realities of the online world. Most businesses require the dual

expansion. And with these comes the growth of marketing to accomplish each. Many small businesses concentrate on low- or no-cost marketing and the most cost-effective business growth ideas. Understanding cost-effective marketing that uses low- and no-cost methods with high return and results leads business owners to the use of direct-response marketing or direct marketing, the term most often used.

Companies in virtually every major U.S. industry use direct marketing. Half the total advertising expenditures in the United States today are made up of direct-response marketing. Why? Because it works. Direct marketing is targetable, measurable, affordable, and can be used successfully by any size business.

approach of online and offline marketing, using both in a direct fashion.

Interaction is the key. If you send out a brochure to a database of unsuspecting people, it truly is a one-way communication. If you send a letter announcing the availability of the brochure or other information to those who request it and you fulfill each request accordingly, you truly have created a two-way communication—an interaction and, if lucky (or by plan), the start of an ongoing relationship. The relationship continues because you have permission to continue via the request for the available information. You can't get any more direct than that. That's direct marketing.

THE FOUR KEY COMPONENTS OF DIRECT MARKETING

In the coming chapters, you will explore the interaction of many variables and the techniques that contribute to direct marketing.

There arc four components to all direct marketing whether online or off:

▼ DAVID OGILVY ON DIRECT MARKETING

David Ogilvy's agency, Ogilvy and Mather, was founded on two principles related to direct marketing: The function of advertising is to sell, and successful advertising for any product is based on information about its consumer. These were principles for direct marketing even before direct marketing was known as such. David Ogilvy was in many ways ahead of his time with his vision.

1. The Marketing Message
2. The Marketing Target
3. The Marketing Vehicle
4. Frequency and Timing

How the marketing message is crafted, the target the message is intended for, the vehicles to deliver all of this, the frequency and timing of the communication, and how they all relate (online and off) to the directness of this form of marketing will be reviewed in the ensuing chapters.

Another way to think of this for a particular direct marketing campaign is what are you going to say, to whom, in what way, and how often?

Many marketing pundits will tell you that it's easy to market if you know what you are marketing and to whom. Knowing what to market will be the basis of your message, and of course, who you market to is the marketing target. You obviously need a way to get that message to the target (marketing vehicle), and you must do it often enough to cause action (timing and frequency). Once you address these components, you are a full-fledged direct marketer.

These four components also are the basis of trouble-shooting your direct marketing campaign. If your response rates aren't high enough, maybe you are making the wrong offer or targeting people who aren't interested in purchasing your product. Maybe you aren't putting your message where your target market will see it, or you aren't doing it often enough. In analyzing this trouble-shooting process, you can see the importance of the four components mentioned above.

Upon completion of this book you will be well on your way to efficiently developing, designing, constructing, and implementing your own direct marketing program, as well as managing others you employ to carry out your campaigns.

DIRECT MARKETING AND TRADITIONAL MARKETING/ADVERTISING: *What's the Difference?*

By now you know that the term "direct marketing" is not synonymous with marketing. Although there are aspects of each that are subsets of the other, there are differences. Consider the following.

Awareness/Branding

Traditional marketing associated with advertising primarily seeks to create awareness for a business, product, service, organization, or brand. The goal is top-of-mind awareness so that when the time comes to purchase, the advertised brand, product, or service will come to mind and ultimately be purchased. The marketing in this case usually consists of memorable ads or commercials that make an impression on its intended target. Lasting impressions like the McDonald's "I'm lovin' it" campaign or "Fly the Friendly Skies" by United Airlines are the work of long, expensive, traditional advertising campaigns. These types of campaigns usually take a long time to become effective. It also takes a long time to determine their effectiveness. Stuffing image advertising and marketing into mailboxes is a campaign destined to lose money unless you can afford to do it often and for a very long time.

Measurability/Action Oriented

Direct marketing truly is sales-oriented marketing. That is why most, if not all, direct marketing has a "call to action," a directive offered to the prospect to do something toward placing an order, buying something, or responding in some way. There is an expectation that the prospect will respond directly back to the marketer. Direct marketing does not offer entertainment and is not an awareness activity but has a clear sales/results orientation associated with it.

The famed Time-Life Book commercials suggesting that operators were standing by are examples of this. Why else would operators stand by unless they were ready to talk to you and take your order, directly?

An infomercial for Suzanne Somer's ThighMaster™ is another example: a commercial or infomercial whose clear focus is getting you to call the toll-free number to order that product now, "as seen on TV."

Respective calls to action such as "Call this toll-free number," "Visit this web site," or "Visit this location for your free gift" are characteristic of high-impact, direct marketing advertising. It is the type of marketing that asks for your order and asks you to do it now.

Because of these direct-response requests and the shorter-term nature of this type of marketing, direct marketing is very conducive to being accurately measured. Direct marketers are not interested in how many people remember a particular ad or what their preference will be the next time they have a need for a particular product or service. Any retention, awareness, or recognition is considered a bonus and extra benefit to the direct marketing campaign. The emphasis of direct marketing is whether the recipient of the marketing responds to it or not. They either respond or they don't. It's a black-and-white situation. A response or lack of one is very conducive to accurate measurements. Direct marketing is a business of mathematics.

David Ogilvy did not believe that advertising/marketing should be guesswork. His firm, Ogilvy and Mather, researched what worked, how it worked, and whom it worked with. He shared its findings extensively through his speaking, writing, and professional relationships. It's amazing how many advertisers and marketers are still living with guesswork.

Targetability

Direct marketing is not mass advertising. Whereas traditional marketing is interested in appealing to as many viewers as possible, direct marketing is interested in a more focused, more interested group of prospects, which is usually, but not necessarily, smaller in number. These groups are very targeted and usually share a set of characteristics, demographics, and/or geographies.

Direct marketing tends to be very informative, giving the potential purchaser enough information to make a quick, informed buying decision. This can mean long sales letters instead of short catchy ads. In many cases, a direct mail ad, letter, or marketing piece is the only touch to a prospect. The marketer therefore has to tell as much of the sales story as possible in a single instance.

Creativity

True direct marketers don't care how "pretty" their ad or marketing looks. They are not as concerned about entertaining graphics as much as traditional marketers are. They subscribe to what David Ogilvy, in *Ogilvy on Advertising* (Vintage Books), said:

> *I do not regard advertising as entertainment or an art form, but as a medium of information. When I write an advertisement, I don't want you to tell me that you find it creative. I want you to find it so interesting that you buy the product.*

David Ogilvy was clearly thinking with a direct marketer's mind long before direct marketing became as popular as it is today.

The focus of direct marketing is on results, on sales, and on response; it's not a fancy graphic,

picture, or a commercial concentrating on peaking awareness and leaving a lasting impression.

Small vs. Large Entrepreneurial Orientation

It's often said that direct marketing levels the playing field for small companies vs. big companies. Just look at the pile of direct mail you receive at home every day. Can you really tell if a mailing came from a large corporation or a one-person entrepreneurial business? Sometimes you can, but most of the time it is impossible to differentiate. Because of this, small business can compete with big business on a level playing field of equal opportunity to market and sell directly.

With the growth of small businesses and entrepreneurial ventures comes the growth of direct marketing.

Look what Ron Popeil and Ronco did with direct marketing. Ron put "as seen on TV" on the marketing map. Over the last 40 years his products have pulled in via direct marketing more than $1 billion in sales. He changed the way we eat, drink, cook, and think about food. Known as "America's Inventor" and a true entrepreneur, Ron Popeil became wealthy from sales of the Veg-O-Matic, the Pocket Fisherman, and his latest, Showtime Rotisseries and BBQ, all by using direct marketing methods. He took a level playing field, played the game hard, and won—whether his competition was big or small.

Design

Talk to sophisticated advertising agencies, and they rave about their winning designs and staff of graphic designers. Talk to a direct marketer, and they couldn't care less about these. To a direct marketer, if the ad/marketing produces results, they don't care what the marketing vehicle looks like. Direct marketing, many times, will use more text than graphics in the design.

Claude Hopkins, the famed marketer, advertiser, and author of *My Life in Advertising* and *Scientific Advertising,* said to use pictures in ads only when they present a better selling argument than the same amount of space set in type.

The goal of direct marketing design, in contrast to traditional advertising, is to keep the prospect involved. The longer you can keep an interested prospect reading, the greater the response will be to the direct marketing message. That's why you see long copy used in direct marketing messages instead of just pretty pictures. The direct marketer must keep the prospect busy until the presentation and offer is so compelling that immediate action and response are taken.

Copy

It's clear that "copy is king" in direct marketing. Copy isn't king in a McDonald's "Lovin' It" commercial or a Revlon print magazine ad. Copy is king on a one-page, direct-response, sales-letter web site. Direct marketing is a selling medium. In a true selling medium, words are more effective than pictures. In direct marketing sales situations, the longer you can keep an interested prospect reading, the closer they get to a response or purchase. Direct marketing has often been described as being, copy intrusive, copy dominant, and copy pushy.

Every time you read marketing or advertising books, they tell you about the advertising clutter that exists today. This book is no different. They try to estimate how many messages you are bombarded with every day. They tell you of the challenge not only to break through with your marketing but also to stand out and be retained in the mind of your prospects. These points are all true and accurate, and they continue to challenge the general marketer.

For the direct marketer, the same challenge exists. The direct marketer, however, not only needs to break through the clutter with a message but also to break through with a specific offer. This is not the same challenge as communicating just words and images, and achieving retention of the messages. The focus is on how to communicate, again and again, an offer that is to be acted upon. Yes, you live in a world of interruptive messaging and marketing. The direct marketer interrupts to the point that their offer is responded to and action is taken.

It really is personal marketing as it tends to be one-on-one in nature. It is personal from the standpoint of developing a relationship. The direct marketer tries to find out as much as he or she can about the target market members, over and over. The gathered information is kept track of. This information is continually used to improve upon the marketing in place, ever aiming for a more refined target and better results.

Direct marketers want a direct response. The response may or may not be a direct sale. Direct marketers are most interested in getting a customer but not just any customer. They want profitable customers who buy over and over, more and more, with a high lifetime value. Their marketing achieves this with direct-response mechanisms and direct-marketing vehicles.

DEVELOPING THE DIRECT MARKETING MIND-SET

Mention the word marketing to most people, and immediately they think of sales or exotic advertising. Mention direct marketing, and most people are unsure as to the distinction or what it really is.

Direct marketing, a subset of all marketing, requires different thinking, different ideas, and different approaches. Having this "fixed mental attitude" is as important as having the right offer, the right marketing piece, and the right target for your marketing. A direct marketing mind-set is different than a general advertiser's or traditional marketer's mind-set:

- As a direct marketer, you know that your product or service is your identity. Fancy ads, entertaining commercials, and graphics-intensive marketing are not what you think about.

- As a direct marketer, you have the mind-set that you will market to interested prospects. This goes beyond permission or opt-in marketing. Interest is researched, defined, and ultimately targeted by the direct marketer. With this mind-set, you know that your best prospects are current customers, past customers, or prospects like them.

- As a direct marketer, you play the numbers game. This is an important component of the direct marketing mind-set because a large percentage of the marketing does not produce results. This is just like the baseball player hitting for a .333 batting average. By baseball standards, this is a very good hitting average, even though about two-thirds of the time the batter fails. The same goes for direct marketing. If the response rate is 2 percent, which isn't bad in the direct-mail world, 98 percent represents a "no response" rate. It takes a certain mind-set to accept this.

- With the emphasis on numbers, percentages, and data, as a direct marketer you will use the power of technology to organize and manage information. A database to a direct marketer is like gold. As a direct marketer, you would rather lock up your database or mailing list at night than protect your expensive wares and merchandise. As you talk like a direct marketer (with the proper mind-set), you will start saying things like compilation, segmenting, and sorting, as if databases are your whole life. Direct marketers are passionate about databases, and that's the mind-set you should work within.

- As a direct marketer, you have in your mind the three-step formula to marketing success: test, test, test! Armed with quantitative databases and playing the respective numbers game, measurement and testing are easily at hand. Testing one variable vs. a control will become a game with you. As a direct marketer, you're always trying to "beat" past performance, making changes to things like headlines, offers, and copy, to find the optimum marketing formula to meet your marketing objectives.

- As a direct marketer, you will also know that if, through all this testing, something is proven to be ineffective, you will fix it or scrap it and move on to the next campaign or idea.

- As a direct marketer, you will possess a mind-set that starts with a visualization of what words will be used in a message, not how pretty the pictures and graphics will be. Copy is king. You will hear this again throughout this book. That's what works in direct marketing, and it's the habit and mind-set you will have.

- As a direct marketer, you will have interactivity on your mind. Because response or an actual purchase is the primary objective, interacting with and involving the prospect is key. This has implication for offers, messages, and the related calls to action.

Even though you have a direct marketing mind-set, you are not in the "direct marketing business." Direct marketing is the process, the means through various media to market directly.

It is clear, then from these mind-sets that direct marketers know how to convert prospects to paying clients. They know how to fulfill responses quickly, and deliver sold goods and services. Direct marketers know how to collect and use the right data and information in the right way.

Five Steps for Thinking Like a Direct Marketer

Alan Rosenspan, president of Alan Rosenspan & Associates, a direct marketing creative services and consulting company in Newton, Massachusetts (www.alanrosenspan.com) and former Direct Marketer of the Year for New England, says that to be successful in the direct marketing business, you have to think like a direct marketer. This means keeping alert for opportunities to reach prospects, understanding how to recognize potential direct marketing opportunities, knowing what will appeal to people, developing and enhancing relationships, and taking advantage of market dynamics.

Mr. Rosenspan offers the following suggestions for how to think like a direct marketer:

1. One size does not fit all. Not all prospects are worth the same amount. Instead of creating a "one-size-fits-all" ad or direct marketing package, try to tailor your approach to the most valuable prospects, or the folks with the biggest problem, or the ones who will most likely become customers.

2. Innovation wins out. The person that said, "Why don't we put American Express applications in restaurants?" was thinking like a direct marketer. It's still responsible for a huge percentage of new card members. National Photos of Australia put their message on the motion sickness bags used by Quantas Airlines. It says, "Use

this strong bag to send your film in, and we'll have it back to you in seven days."

3. Your best prospect is still your current customer. As Polonius told Laertes, in *Hamlet*, "Those friends thou hast, and their adoption tried, Grapple them unto thy soul with hoops of steel. But do not dull thy palm with entertainment of each new-hatched, unfledged comrade." The direct marketing translation is: Bind your customers to you, and treat them better than prospects.

4. Stay a step ahead. Even though he lost to the chess playing computer Big Blue, Garry Kasparov has a lot to teach us about thinking a few steps ahead. If a prospect raises her hand, what do we do? If she doesn't buy, what do we do? If she does buy, what do we do?

For an AT&T campaign that was called "Speedy Delivery," telemarketers asked prospects to switch to AT&T. If they said "No," the telemarketer was required to ask "Why not?"

The "Why Nots" were grouped into three different buckets. They then received a direct-mail package targeted to their specific answer. For example, one letter said, "Thank you for spending time with us on the telephone the other day. You indicated that you thought you were saving money with your new long-distance carrier. We don't think that's true." The campaign regularly pulled a 50 percent response rate.

Even if someone buys your product, you must think ahead to solidifying your relationship, getting them to buy more, and getting them to refer you to others.

5. Think big, think everyone. Try to find a way to get everyone to respond. Try writing this into your letters: "Even if you don't need our product or service right now, here's why you should still take advantage of our offer." Or you could try, "If by some chance this package should not have been sent to you, may we ask that you please pass it along to someone in your company who you believe will benefit?"

By Example

Here are some examples of that mind-set.

The Bay State Gas Solution. Bay State Gas is the leading provider of clean natural gas in Massachusetts and most of New England. Their marketing focuses on getting people who use oil to switch to gas, and over 3000 of them do so every year.

In previous years, they would offer cash rebates of up to $500 to switch, as well as other incentives. These mailings would go to everyone who lived in the area served by Bay State Gas, and generally received a pretty ordinary response. Here is where thinking like a direct marketer comes into play.

First, they singled out those people who lived on a street where Bay State Gas already had a gas line. The reasoning was that switching to gas would be much simpler and much cheaper for these folks. Plus, they had neighbors who already enjoyed all the benefits of gas.

Bay State Gas had planned to send to this group a highly personalized postcard that said, "There's a gas line running right down (your street). And that means you can connect for free!" The plan called for a followed up direct-mail package with an outer envelope that read, "This is your street. This is our gas line. Now you (personalized with the name of the recipient) can make the connection for free."

Bay State Gas, though, was not comfortable in saying that all homes could connect for free, because there are some that are set so far back from the street that they couldn't easily be reached.

Thinking like direct marketers, they changed the outer envelope and the letter somewhat, but they couldn't say "Free Connection!" on the reply card as they originally wanted to. Here is what Bay State Gas considered as options:

1. They could still say "Free Connection!" and accept the fact that one out of every 100 people wouldn't qualify for one. If they complained, they could give it to them anyway. This didn't seem like the right thing to do, but it was tempting, according to Bay State Gas.

2. They could still say "Free Connection!" and put a big asterisk by the word free. They really didn't want to do that either because they felt that was a strong signal to the reader that "It's not really true." Plus, it directs them to stop reading and go down to the bottom of the page.

3. They could say "You may be able to connect for free," but that weakened the reply card pretty drastically.

Knowing that 99 out of 100 people would qualify for a free switch but that one wouldn't and that people like to feel special and enjoy having an advantage other people don't have, they proceeded forward with a direct-marketing solution. They changed the reply card to read "Do You Qualify for a Free Connection?" and invited people to find out. Even if they had no intention of switching to gas at the time, 99 out of 100 people responding would still receive the following letter:

Congratulations! Your home does qualify for a free connection, and that means you can be enjoying all the advantages of clean natural gas for much less than other people have to pay.

The Mazda Truck Strategy. Mazda was offering a tremendous financing deal on trucks for farmers—but there was a problem. Everyone they were talking to already had a truck. How could they know if and when those in their audience needed a new one?

They did know which farmers had bought trucks from them before and when they bought them. However, they wanted to expand their market to people who had bought trucks from other companies. At the time, this information wasn't available. Here is how Mazda Truck thought like direct marketers. They asked themselves the question, "How can we reach farmers who don't need a new truck just yet—but might need one six months from now?"

The answer was that they sent out a mailing offering the financing deal but also offering something else—a certificate that guaranteed the same terms for the next six months. "Think of it as an insurance policy for your old truck." The creative went on, "If it breaks down next week, or next month, you'll still be able to get this great deal. But you have to send for your certificate."

The response was phenomenal—and why not? All they were really doing was asking people who were worried about their truck breaking down to self-identify. And once they did, they marketed to this highly targeted group, every single month. "You have only two months left on your certificate." "If you choose to pay cash, your certificate is worth $500 off." And, of course, "We are extending your certificate for an additional six months—just in case."

Mazda Truck sold more trucks to more farmers than they ever did before. Mazda Truck was thinking like a direct marketer.

Bose. Most direct marketers will think direct mail as their only direct marketing mind-set. Today more marketers are moving to direct e-mail. The real underlying intention of a direct marketer's mind-set is always to be looking for ways to reach their target audience.

Bose thinks like a direct marketer—a lot. Just look at its ads. Look at where they show up. The print ads always suggest a visit to a web site because it knows more and more of its target market is becoming internet savvy. Bose takes this thinking and mind-set to another level when it places ads in the *New York Times* daily e-mail alert that subscribers and nonsubscribers opt in to. The ad shows up (in an html e-mail) right beside the headlines of the day. You can't buy front-page advertising in The *New York Times,* but you can buy front page advertising in *The New York Times* daily e-mail alert. In an e-mail, there is only one page, and with the ad prominently displayed at the top of the e-mail, it is essentially front page advertising! Bose is thinking like a direct marketer, reaching its target market in vehicles that its target market members see.

Look for innovative ways to reach your target audience. Visa offers a commission/fee for every credit card applicant approved who comes as a result of an Amazon affiliates page. Amazon customers are targets for Visa. Visa is using its direct marketing mind-set here to partner with Amazon.

DIRECT MARKETING IS AN INVESTMENT

Because direct marketing is so measurable and return on marketing dollars spent is a common (and appropriate) measurement, thinking of your direct marketing as a financial investment is an appropriate direct marketing mind-set. Obviously, a higher return on marketing dollars is an indicator of a successful direct marketing program. Successful direct marketing programs get repeated.

Thinking like a direct marketer also means thinking like an investment manager. If you have

> ▼ *"Advertising is an expense. But direct marketing is an investment."*

limited marketing funds—and who doesn't?—where can you use them for the greatest benefit of your company?

In his famous speech, "The Frontiers of Direct Marketing," Lester Wunderman quoted an article in *Financial World*. It read: "Want to torture your accountant? Tie him to a chair and tell him that advertising spending is an asset that produces a stream of revenues—just like a factory—and it should be put on the balance sheet and written off over time. Soon, he'll be begging for mercy."

The magazine is for investors. So what does it have to do with direct marketing? More than you might think. In many companies, there is more control over buying $100,000 worth of computer equipment than in spending $10 million in advertising.

Yes, direct marketing is an investment, but not only compared to general advertising. Direct marketing is an investment that you might want to compare with any other investment you make in your business. Determining your ROI (Return On Investment) will tell you the best place to put your marketing money.

LIFETIME CUSTOMER VALUE

Many people are coming to understand that the real value of a company is not in its products, its inventory, or its capital goods, but rather in its customer base. And the goal of business might be defined as increasing the value of your customer base.

A story about long-term value comes from Stanley Marcus's great book, *Minding the Store*:

In 1933, a woman came into Neiman Marcus to return an extremely expensive, handmade, lace-and-pearl-studded dress that she had ruined by washing.

Stanley refused to refund her money. "Of course, it's ruined," he said, "But don't you know better than to wash a $2,000 dress?" [By the way, a $2,000 dress then is probably a $25,000 dress now.]

Stanley's father, the founder of the store, called him over and said, "Give the lady back her money."

Stanley argued vehemently, but his father prevailed. "He just doesn't understand business," thought Stanley. So he gave the woman back her money.

Years later, in the course of writing this book, Marcus looked up the record of that woman, who had been a Neiman Marcus charge customer. He found that, over the years, she had spent a total of $750,000 in the store.

His father was right.

Measuring long-term value is a start, but it's only a start. Thinking like a direct marketer demands that you try to determine the long-term value of a customer.

Every business has customers with a higher long-term value than imagined. Thinking like a direct marketer will help you learn how to start tapping into it.

ALL CUSTOMERS ARE NOT CREATED EQUAL

When you think like a direct marketer, you realize that some of your customers are a lot more valuable to your business than others. And a small percentage of your customers may be responsible for a huge proportion of your sales and almost all your profits.

Suppose that 1 percent of your customers are responsible for 25 percent of your sales or profits. (Does the equation sound far-fetched? When American Airlines launched the first Frequent Flyer program, it was based on research that showed 3 percent of its customers were responsible for 67 percent of its business.)

So, when you decide to invest—in a database, in a communications program, in promotions, in loyalty programs, in direct marketing, or in almost anything else—it is important to invest in those customers who are the most valuable to your business.

Thinking like a direct marketer really involves dedicating yourself to your existing customers. Direct marketers know that 90 percent of all profits come after the first sale. In fact, many companies do not make any profit on their first sale at all—they regard it as a necessary expense in creating a profitable customer relationship. That's why it is often said that your best prospect is a current customer.

Using this information, and thinking like a direct marketer, leads you to the following conclusions:

▼

WHEN PEOPLE DON'T BUY

Direct marketing can profit you in both an up market and a down market. The fundamentals remain the same regardless of marketing conditions. The offer, messages, and other factors might change slightly to respond to conditions, but with no change to the fundamentals.

When markets turn down, marketing sometimes is viewed as an expense by the budgeters and gets cut. I'm not at all a fan of this and don't condone it, but it does happen. When marketing gets cut, it usually starts with an advertising budget cut and continues on down the marketing spectrum. Direct mail and other direct marketing are usually the last marketing expenses to get cut. The reason for this is the ever-present measurability characteristic of direct marketing. Low ROI items get cut in budget reviews. High ROI items remain. Items with an unknown ROI many times fall into the cut category. The measurability associated with direct marketing satisfies the budget makers and make it one of the last items cut.

In a down market, there are things that can still be done to give prospects a reason to respond to your marketing:

- Give prospects a reason to act now, not later.
- Focus on an offer of higher perceived value.
- Present those benefits that the prospect can't do without during tough economic times.
- Provide ROI in your offer/copy.
- Provide a valuable incentive—financing, credit, bonuses, gifts.
- Ask for referrals; others who might also be interested in the offer.
- If people aren't buying, at least continue to build relationships.
- Keep in touch but continue to offer and continue to see responses.

- *Customers already trust you.* They know you. They've already bought from you. When sending the same direct-mail package to prospects and customers, send it to customers first and explain that you're giving them advance notice or first crack at your offer.

- *Treat them exclusively.* Abraham Lincoln used to say, "Treat your friend so well that even your enemies will want to become your friends." In direct marketing, the corollary is "treat your customers so well that even your competitors will want to become your customers." It costs significantly less to retain a customer than to try to win one back.

- *Customer knowledge is gold.* The other side of their knowing you is that you know them. You should know what they buy, how often they buy, perhaps even why they buy. That will help you when you come up with new products or new offers. Your best source of market information is your existing customers. You can solicit their opinions; make sure they're 100 percent satisfied; ask them what other products and services they might need, and seek other market research information.

- *Repetitiveness and consistency is a process, not an event.*

Thinking like a direct marketer means you must think beyond single communication contacts with your customers and prospects, and that you should begin thinking of streams of communication.

The best chance to win people back is from a stream of highly targeted, very timely communications. Thinking like a direct marketer requires a different mind-set than thinking like a traditional marketer or advertiser.

DIRECT MARKETING AT WORK

Just pick up the latest issue of *Home and Away*, the bimonthly publication of AAA—Chicago Motor Club and you will see direct marketing hard at work.

Four pages into the magazine, you see a full-page ad from Bose. It seems like Bose advertises everywhere. It really doesn't. I notice it because I am in its target market and happen to read the publications it has identified that hit its target market. This particular ad is benefit-laden with offers for free shipping, a guarantee, and information. Bose offers a web site and a toll-free phone number as response mechanisms for its offers. This is direct marketing at its finest.

Two pages after Bose, Select Comfort Direct hits you with a double whammy. It is at this point of the publication that a business reply card is inserted between the pages. The card is simple with lots of white space and communicates several direct calls to action:

- Mail this card today.
- Call toll-free.
- Rush me a brochure.
- Send a free video or DVD.

Right under the reply card is a full-page, full-color ad for the same mattress product that is advertised on the BRC. Here, a few benefits are expounded upon, but the same direct reply options are also present. The toll-free number is also highlighted on a clip-out coupon to send in for the free video. It is explained that the video also gives details about a 30-night in-home trial.

On the following two pages, direct-response ads for two different products/companies appear. One is for a scooter wheelchair device, complete with a toll-free number and web site address. The offer is a free, over the phone, mobility consultation—no pressure, no obligation, as it is stated.

The other ad is a direct, in-your-face, full-page ad for official government-issued $5 gold coins. A huge headline and a picture of the nation's capitol grab the reader's attention. There is a call to action to call a toll-free number and to do it now… "They will not last long." Another sense of urgency is built into the ad: "Beginning today, telephone orders will be accepted on a first-come, first-served basis according to time and date of the order!"

The ad looks official, is attention-grabbing, tells the whole story, lays out the benefits, and instills a sense of urgency to buy now. This ad is direct!

Half-way into the publication is a two-thirds page full-color ad for the Talking Road Whiz. The offer is an AAA member special, with a full guarantee. There are testimonials and benefits galore. One outstanding aspect of this ad is that you can only respond by purchasing the item/product and can only do it via a toll-free number; no web site, no address, no coupon for more information—only a direct-sale offer.

MORE DIRECT MARKETING AT WORK

Turn on your radio, listen awhile, and chances are good that you will soon hear:

> *Hi. My name is David Oreck and I'd like you to take the Oreck challenge. Take my eight-pound Oreck vacuum cleaner for 15 days free . . .*

The sheer volume of direct advertising definitely pays off for Oreck. David Oreck runs millions of radio commercials a year and is at the top of the heap when it comes to direct marketing. Not only will you hear his message on the radio but you will also see him personally on infomercials, see his direct marketing abilities integrated into his web site and see his direct-response messages and ads in many, many publications, nationally, regionally, and locally.

There are a number of direct marketing principles at work here and a number of innovative ideas as well. All of Oreck's marketing efforts—print, broadcast, and direct mail—include a toll-free 800 number.

David Oreck is combining general advertising with direct marketing. He is blitzing the marketplace with messages that create awareness at the same time, unlike traditional advertising, he makes it possible to order on the spot.

Oreck's marketing reflects direct marketing fundamentals, or in his case, direct response fundamentals. Oreck himself says, "I believe that people used to respond to friendliness, and they still do. People used to respond to helpful information; they still do. Businessmen used to respond to facts that helped them solve a problem; they still do. People used to smile at general humor and warm up to the person who knew how and when to use it; they still do." All of these are fundamentals in successful direct marketing programs today, especially Oreck's.

David Oreck is surrounding the country while offering you an irresistible, no-risk product that you are able to order on the spot. Oreck's house list is over one million names.

Oreck's offer is powerful. Take the 15-day challenge. Let me send you my eight-pound Oreck XL. Vacuum your floor with your current machine and then go over what you just vacuumed with an Oreck. You will find dust in the bag—guaranteed or your money back. No questions asked.

David Oreck sums up what he does and his relationship with marketing, ". . . if you want to build a business, you need good marketing." The concepts, tips, techniques, and methods behind these examples will be discussed in subsequent sections and chapters.

THE DIRECT MARKETING PATHWAY

The right product to the right market, communication with the right message, making the right offer with a sales orientation, asking for the order, and fulfilling the order—all to the point of customer satisfaction.

DIRECT MARKETING ONLINE

Before diving headfirst into online direct marketing, I want to stress that the internet is a natural platform for direct marketing. With the advancements in technology and use, there are now more ways to track things like web site hits, e-mail openings, click-through of links, sales conversions, and the related "costs per _____."

The advancements in e-mail marketing have helped to enhance the effectiveness of direct marketing online. Businesses can now expose their marketing messages to those who are more targeted (through opt-in policies and procedures). Relationships extend beyond this, contributing to customer loyalty and repeat business, all fueled by online direct marketing.

Knowing how to approach direct marketing online and developing the methods and techniques to capitalize on this marketing revolution will be the objectives of the online and internet portions of this book.

DIRECT MARKETING COMPONENT DESCRIPTIONS

Communication—honesty, accuracy, promise

Customers—define targets precisely

Product—satisfy wants

Interested—choose customers who have bought before

Ordering—make it easy and clear

Fulfill—immediately and accurately

Guarantee—satisfaction; no strings

— CHAPTER 1 SUMMARY —

▶ Half the total advertising expenditures in the United States today is made up of direct-response marketing because it works.

▶ Direct marketing is targetable, measurable, and affordable, and can be used successfully by businesses of any size.

▶ Direct marketers are coming up with new ways to get their marketing messages in front of their target markets. They are only limited by their imagination.

▶ Direct mail is the most effective customer-relationship management tool to reach customers. It does the best job of providing consumers with information they want, when they want it, and in the way they want to receive it.

▶ Direct marketing has experienced rapid, radical changes in the past decade, and even the past few years.

▶ Direct marketing is not a fancy term for mail order. It is an interactive system of marketing that uses one or more advertising media to effect a measurable response and/or transaction at any location, with this activity and related information stored on a database.

▶ Direct marketing is at the forefront of marketing not only because of the growth of business but also because it has been proven to work. It carries all the information necessary for a buyer to decide to buy, and it generates sales. All are necessary for viability, survivability, performance, and growth.

▶ Simply put, direct marketing can get you customers and keep them buying from you. Aside from getting the customer, your job as a direct marketer is to keep the customers you work so hard to get.

▶ Direct marketing also concentrates on how to sell more to customers, how to get them to buy more often, and how to get them to buy higher-priced, more profitable items from you.

▶ Stuffing image advertising and marketing into recipients' mailboxes is a campaign destined to lose money unless you can afford to do it often and for a very long time.

▶ Direct marketing is interested in a more focused, more interested group of prospects. These groups are very targeted and usually share a set of characteristics, demographics, and/or geographies.

▶ The direct marketer needs to break through the clutter with a message and needs to break through with a specific offer.

▶ There are four components to all direct marketing, whether online or off:

1. The Marketing Message

2. The Marketing Target

3. The Marketing Vehicle

4. Frequency and Timing

▶ Direct marketing, a subset of all marketing, requires different thinking, different ideas, and different approaches.

▶ The advancements in e-mail marketing have helped to enhance the effectiveness of direct marketing online.

The Marketing Target

WHETHER YOU ARE DEVELOPING A direct mail campaign or troubleshooting one already in place, there are only four major direct marketing component categories to consider: What you say, how you say it, to whom you say it, and how many times you say it. Sounds pretty simple. It is, but each component takes careful attention, planning, and management.

IT'S ALL ABOUT THE LIST

Direct marketers are all in accord when they say, "It's all about the list." Some specialty retailers have experimented with e-mail marketing messages, different versions of direct marketing offers, premium offers, etc., only to find that it is always the same people who are always buying. Thank goodness these people are on their list. It supports this one main principle of direct marketing and direct mail, online or off: Establish and market to a good list.

The people to whom you want to present are the targets of your direct mail. Your overall target is the list or lists that you develop. The list is a compilation of the names, addresses, and other contact information of people or companies to whom you will market. The list IS your target market.

A mailing list is a grouping of names, addresses, and contact information of a collection of people or companies. Those on the list will generally have something in common:

- Demographics
- Geographics
- Already customers
- Belong to the same membership/association

Many direct mail professionals regard the list as the single most critical component in determining the success of a direct mail campaign. Pundits have asserted that having the right list is half of the direct mail campaign. Others have maintained that 40 to 60 percent of the success of a direct mail campaign depends on the list/target. Regardless of the precision of these percentages and comments, the list is a significant part of any direct marketing campaign.

FINDING THE RIGHT PEOPLE

No matter how attractive your marketing vehicle looks, how bold and attention-getting the headline, or how valuable and irresistible your offer is, if it doesn't reach the right people, direct marketing cannot do its job and will not be successful in meeting your marketing objectives.

The highest-quality mailing vehicle with the most compelling sales message sent over and over to the wrong target will always yield less than

THE REAL VALUABLES

Bob Hemmings, founder of Hemmings IV Direct and a member of the Direct Marketing Association's Hall of Fame, tells the story of his boss and mentor, Mr. May, a thriving jewelry store proprietor. Upon locking up his place of business one night, Mr. May wheeled his active customer list of 5,000 people into the vault, closed the door, and locked the vault. Hemmings was in awe. He was quick to point out to his superior that he failed to lock up the valuable jewels on display. Mr. May's reply was that the jewels were insured, would only represent a small loss if stolen, and could be replaced. His list could not be replaced and would cause him to go out of business if lost. His list of customers was his most valuable asset. Loyalty is not insurable.

a mediocre piece that communicates slightly, some of the time, to the right target/list.

Another way of looking at it is, you can change the copy, the offer, and other creative elements of your campaign and increase response, sometimes by 25 to 100 percent. Refined and tested lists, however, can increase response rates from 250 to 1,000 percent.

Not acknowledging the importance of your list is almost always a sure path to an ineffective mailing campaign.

Even a legitimate offer of the best discount offered to the wrong people will prove to be useless, or close to it. If, in your home mailbox, you receive a 99 percent discount on a cruise ship engine, O-ring seals for a space shuttle, or a laser-guided commercial table saw with conveyors, chances are you won't buy, even with the hefty discount. You may be interested and purchase these items, however, if you are the maintenance manager of a cruise ship line, flight director of NASA, or a commercial furniture builder. Mailed to the right people/target, a more modest discount of 3 percent may generate significant response and eventual sales.

Bob Hacker, a Charter Senior Fellow of the International Society for Strategic Marketing, Harvard Business School graduate, and direct marketing expert, points out that lists are not an inventory item. Too often, they are treated like an inventory item, not a key strategic component of the campaign. The first and perhaps most important thing to do is to research the available list universes and put together the best list targeting you can. Then, do your best job of defining the key emotional drivers within each segment. For example, a CEO may have very different concerns than a CIO or a CFO. You can't create your campaign until you know what makes these people tick.

Another good start to targeting and list development is really understanding who your ideal client is. Who benefits most from your products or services? The demographics, geographies, and characteristics that are the common denominators of this client definition will be the common denominators of others on your list. What are the commonalities of the top 20 percent of your current customers? This will add definition and specification to your list, whether you compile or purchase your set of names to market to.

Don't forget past customers when going through this exercise.

WHERE DO LISTS COME FROM?

No single list strategy will guarantee success. However, once you find one or parts of one that work, keep marketing to it until response dwindles. When this happens, move to a new list or add new names to it. The following represent different types of lists that may be used in your campaigns, and where they can be obtained.

House List

No, this is not a list of houses for sale in your neighborhood. Inhouse is a common term for those things you have on hand, internal to your business. Extending this concept to a list of names, the house list includes people you already know or have had contact with. Typically, this is a list of customers, a list of people who have inquired about your services, or who have sent in a response to you. The house list is an internal list compiled from information you already have.

One of the first logical sources for a list is your own collection of customers. There is no better prospect than a current customer. You will read this many times in this book, as it relates to many areas of direct marketing. Starting with this list and selling more to current clients is a good start

to any direct marketing campaign. If you are using other lists and ignoring your current customer list, you are missing a golden opportunity. Start using it or add it to your current campaigns.

This, of course, assumes that you keep track of who your customers are. Some businesses, believe it or not, don't have such a list. If this is you, start by establishing a list of your current customers and market to them. You will be glad you, did and your response will be higher within this group.

You don't build a house list on your first day in business. A house list is built over time and is as valuable to you as gold. Just ask Mr. Hemmings. It truly is one of your most valuable assets in business. Many times when businesses are bought and sold, it happens just for the customer list and all related information—the house list.

With your best prospect a current customer, your house list represents your best prospect list for selling more products or services to. It will far outpull or outperform a high-quality purchased or rented list. The people on a house list already know you, already trust you, and have confidence that you will deliver the value promised.

Your house list is essentially a list of names that you accumulate over time. The key is to keep the names and contact information in some type of database. Your house list grows as your business and sales grow.

Your house list can include names of people who have visited with you but not necessarily purchased from you. You can grow your house list simply by inviting people to be a part of it, by providing an incentive for being added. A simple request to join your mailing list will increase its size. You can offer an opportunity to enter a drawing for a prize and collect the names of the entrants. Asking, receiving, and recording names is a simple formula for developing your own inhouse list.

Compiled List

Because the word *compile* means to compose, collect, and edit, a compiled list is a volume of that composed, collected, and edited information. Somewhere, somehow, you need to find the information to compile. Usually, the data come from research that you have done. The names from this research usually have something in common. The commonality could be geography or some other demographic, characteristic, or preference.

Compiled lists, therefore, are lists of names that have been collected or accumulated from a number of sources and entered into a database program. The many sources that names and addresses may come from include:

- *Public records:* vehicle registrations, water and public utility bills, voter registration lists
- *Directories:* professional and public, on and offline
- *Phone books:* White and Yellow Pages

Compiled lists are best thought of as higher-volume lists of specific groups, e.g., all the pediatric doctors in the city of Chicago or all the mathematics professors at major universities. Compiled lists are lists compiled from directories, online and off, that have considerable demographic and other important information from database segmentations in them. The drawback is that they do lack the quality of being proven direct responders.

Take, for example, the phone book or any other directory of names and addresses. These lists typically draw fewer responses and are the least desirable of external lists primarily because of the inaccuracies and high turnover rates associated with

> ### ▼ SOURCES OF COMPILED LISTS
>
> - *Trade associations.* What trade associations do your prospects belong to? Do those associations offer their membership list for sale or rent? Many do. If you want to market to doctors, the American Medical Association list would be an appropriate target. This goes for other professional affiliation groups, clubs, and associations.
> - *Chambers of commerce.* Most cities and towns have a chamber of commerce made up of businesses, associations, and other organizations. If your target is business or nonprofit organizations, this is a good list to obtain. Many chambers of commerce offer these lists for sale to members and non-members.
> - *Alumni groups.* Colleges, universities, and other educational institutions offer an alumni list for sale or rent, especially if you are an alumnus/alumna of the institution. These lists are prime targets for educational and alumni-related products.
> - *Current and past customers.* This is actually your inhouse list.
> - *Survey groups.* Surveys can help build house lists.
> - *Guest book.* Online or off, those who visit you are interested prospects (or they wouldn't have visited you). Registering and compiling those names can provide another list appropriate for you to target and segment.

them. Standard Industry Classification (SIC) lists are another example of compiled lists.

Why then use compiled lists? Compiled lists are useful in direct marketing because of their targetability. They generally target a common characteristic like industry, profession, or business segment. This allows the marketer to target a larger market area. Sometimes a compiled list is all that is available for a set of list specifications. Sometimes, a response list might be limited in size. Supplementing a campaign with a compiled list will give you a large enough target group in which to achieve your established marketing and financial goals.

Response List

A response list is a list of people who have responded to an offer. This could be a response to ads (radio and TV), direct mail response, a catalog purchaser, a purchaser of mail-order products, magazine subscribers, free report responders, and infomercial customers. The best example of this is amazon.com. Amazon does a good job of compiling lists of prospects who have expressed interest in, purchased, or responded to certain types of products. The result of this is its e-mail communication to you that says, "People who have bought this book were also interested in these other books . . . ."

Another example is a list of people who have checked a box on an order form or survey that says, "Send me more information on your company's products or services" or "Yes! Send me my free newsletter."

The availability of these types of lists isn't as wide as some of the other lists described here. Their quality is also inferior, which is why most direct marketers resort to their house list or a compiled list.

Lists from Publications

These lists come from publications that have paying subscribers. They may or may not have telephone numbers, e-mail addresses, or other data points you may want. Known as magazine subscriber lists, they are good because they are generally very targeted to their audience, much like the magazine itself. With the abundance of magazines published today, chances are good that one or many are catering to the same target audience that you are. This makes their subscriber list prime for you to target and market to as well.

In this category are subscriber-based lists and catalog recipient lists. Usually magazine publishers and catalog companies have a list manager who manages their lists and also deals with those interested in renting lists. For example, if you are selling sporting goods, you could contact *Sports Illustrated* to rent its subscription list for your mailing campaign. If you are selling swimwear, you could contact Apple Vacations Travel to rent the list of its catalog recipients.

Any group membership, association, or publisher, no matter how large or small, is a good source for list rental. Many will be more than willing to rent their lists, so you can gain an instant market.

Hotline Lists

"Purchase recency" is associated with a greater propensity to purchase again. Hotline is a term used in the list business and direct marketing to signify the freshest, hottest, most recent members of a list. These lists contain information about people who have responded, purchased something, or were active on the list within the past 90 days. The best prospect is a current one. On a hotline list, the best prospect is a current or past customer (I told you that you would hear this often in this book!) who has purchased within the past 90 days. If they've responded once, they're likely to respond again. If they've responded recently, they're likely to respond again and soon. Add this to the fact that consumers tend to buy in cycles or spurts. Hitting them with your marketing message during this hot phase or hot cycle increases your chance of response. The quicker you can communicate to these people/prospects after they've responded to another offer, the better chance you have of a higher response. Fresh names also have probably not been marketed to as much by others. You can be one of the early marketers to approach hotline names.

Make sure you understand what "recent" means on a hotline list. If the names came from "recent purchasers" of an annual directory, they might be nine months old—nine months old, yet recent by annual-directory standards. Some marketers and fundraisers will only market to hotline lists.

Some list owners advertise a "hotter" hotline with updated lists every month or every week. Three months is considered the industry standard for being "hot."

Membership Lists

These are lists from the membership rosters of clubs, organizations, and associations. The benefit of membership lists is that there is a common interest that brings members together, making it easier to target the right type of prospect.

Associations, newsletter publishers, and other trade or charitable organizations have lists you may be interested in. They do not always make them available or even market them to direct marketers or list brokers. Sometimes the only way to get access to such a list is to contact organizations directly and arrange for list rental or purchase. If you ask your broker to research or track down these lists, be prepared to pay for the research and service time involved, unless the list owner pays a commission to the list broker.

▼ **UNKNOWN LIST SOURCE**

You may or may not know the source of a compiled list. This does not necessarily mean you should ignore or abandon the list. A compiled file may be the only list suited to the specifications of your particular mailing and offers a great opportunity for a test and an eventual campaign.

E-Mail Lists

E-mail lists may be obtained from many of the same sources as traditional direct marketing lists, provided that the list compiler collects the necessary data (e-mail address). There are other ways, too. Some are legitimate, ethical, and effective, and others are not. A lot of times you ask via e-mail messages or on a web site form. You can use the following qualifying questions to help obtain e-mails:

- Can we give you advance notice of private sales before opening to the public?
- Provide us your e-mail address so we can confirm your order.
- Your e-mail will allow us to contact you about updates and upgrades available.
- Please take a moment to fill out this survey.
- Send a blank e-mail for a special report to an auto-responder.
- Enter to win with your e-mail address.

Other Lists

There are other kinds of lists, but they generally fall into the categories described above. You will hear of subscription lists, membership lists, general prospect lists, and segmented lists. They are labeled as such based on their origin and the

▼
TRADE ASSOCIATION LIST SOURCES

Trade association membership lists are a good source of mailing lists. This includes your local chamber of commerce. These lists are good for local businesses and organizations and anyone else who wants to target a smaller area.

Trade association list sources include:

- State and regional associations directory, National Trade and Professional Associations of the U.S., www.columbiabooks.com.

- Related but different are trade show lists that list attendees and exhibitors, www.tradeshowweek.com

- *Tradeshow Week* magazine, (323) 965-2093

subsequent segmenting of the listed members. A more precise list will result in a higher response; therefore, list companies are continually segmenting, categorizing, and refining their list criteria to produce this precision.

Your "Golden 100 Prospect Wish List"

Even though I have gone to great lengths to tell you how to obtain lists, preferred sources, and the ins and outs about lists, you can still establish your own list ad hoc.

When you write a letter to someone you've not met, you do so for a particular reason and have, therefore, sought out that person's address. The same can be done for people you would like to have as prospects. Maybe there is someone in your market who fits your ideal client profile. Maybe there are leaders in your market who would pull others along if you did

business with them. Putting these kinds of prospects on your prospect list is almost as good as having a customer or past customer list—almost. A list of this type represents your cherry-picked, hand-selected prospect list. Call it your Golden 100 Prospect Wish List, your Grade A, or prime-cut prospect list. You can't buy a list this good or this targeted. Regardless of what you call it, know that it is a list of prime prospects you want to meet, do business with, or network with.

Don't forget to include large-volume purchasers here. Because you will be working with a small-count list, converting one or two of these ideal prospects to ideal customers will more than pay for your marketing efforts.

This list represents your own personal hotline list. Send them your best offer in sequence continually, and respond quickly to any responses. It's a campaign, not an event.

Business-to-Business and Consumer Lists

Business-to-business (B2B) lists reach individuals at a particular business. This is in contrast to business-to-consumer lists that target people at home. Today, with more and more people working at home, these lists can have crossover names and addresses. This sometimes makes it possible to target a home business with a consumer list. The rule of thumb is to target the place where the product or service will be used. Marketing coaches will not generally target their marketing to the consumer in the home. They will, however, target the lone entrepreneur, independent professional, or a marketing manager within a company. A company selling the latest "slicer and dicer Veg-O-Matic" will likely not target the marketing manager in a business. It will, however, target homeowners with children

> **▼ CAUTION**
>
> Consumer lists change at the rate of about 2 percent per month as people are born, relocate, die, or marry. (National Change of Address (NCOA) adjusts for all of these.)

living in a particular subdivision or community. Consumer vs. B2B is another important specification component when working with list vendors and brokers.

B2B COMPILED LISTS

The technology involved in sorting and segmenting B2B lists has improved dramatically. There are two main compilers with supply specialized lists that have been combined and refined through select after select, to come up

> **▼ LIST MANAGER SOURCES**
>
> • *Catalog Age* and *DIRECT* magazines, 203-358-9900
>
> • *Target Marketing* magazine, 215-238-5300
>
> • *Direct Marketing* magazine, 516-746-6700
>
> • *DM News*, 212-741-2095
>
> Catalog houses earn a stream of income from the sale of their lists. Your best bet is to call the catalog's business office and ask for their list manager. For a directory of catalogs, refer to:
>
> The Directory of Mail Order Catalogs, Grey House Publishing, www.greyhouse.com.

with the exact B2B list you want. Those two are Dun & Bradstreet (www.dunandbradstreet .com) and Info USA (www.infousa.com). Many local, regional, and state companies also offer compiled lists.

OTHER WAYS TO DEVELOP A LIST

• *Customer checks.* With luck, you have a record of all customers you do business with. Their contact information appears on an invoice, so it should exist within your system in one format or another. If, for example, you are a retail business that does not track customer information exactly, you can sometimes compile an appropriate database from checks used to pay for purchases. Name, address, and phone numbers are usually always available from checks. This is a good way to develop a list of those to communicate with in the future, either on an ongoing, keep-in-touch basis or a spot basis when communicating a special offer.

• *Hold a drawing or have a contest.* Enter-to-win information can be put into a database, the result being a list of interested prospects. Obviously, these people are not necessarily as interested as those who have already purchased or responded, but it's better than using a cold list.

• *Sign up to receive advance notice of sales or other information, including advance notice of special offers.* You see this type of list compilation mainly online; however, the same technique can work offline to develop names for a database/list. Having a sign-up form next to a cash register in a retail business, with a salesperson in a business-to-business situation, or other similarly located place of convenience can solicit interested prospects that eventually comprise a list to market to.

- *Those who respond to a special offer other than something offered via direct mail.* By now you know that accumulating names and contact information is very valuable when developing your direct marketing strategies and tactics. Sometimes, this involves inviting people to your place of business as the form of response to an offer. This is a good way to gather contact names for a database to market to later. This also assumes that you didn't start with a response list in the first place. It could be mass marketing that invited a prospect to respond to an offer and the name of the prospect was not known at the time of the offer. This can take the form of placing a classified ad in a leading newspaper or publication offering a free, how-to booklet aimed at your target market's interests. Only interested prospects will request it. Add all requesters to your database of prospects and your newly compiled list.

Lists come in all sizes, representing all types of people. Here are a few examples of lists that are available:

- Subscribers to do-it-yourself holiday decorations magazines
- Purchasers of model airplane kits
- Fashionable hunting-clothes buyers
- Collectors of wooden ship models
- Baseball uniform swappers
- Donors to Big Brothers, Big Sisters
- Buyers of antique chess sets
- Those involved in employer physical fitness programs
- Buyers of antique writing instruments
- Female-owned businesses

DIRECT-MAIL GENERATED LISTS

Direct-mail generated lists are lists of those who have responded to direct mail offers. When purchasing or renting a list of this type, you can find out from the list vendor what portion of the list is direct-mail generated. The whole list may be direct-mail generated, but some lists billed as such have only 90 to 95 percent of the names generated in this manner.

RENTING YOUR OWN COMPILED LISTS TO OTHER MARKETERS

As you get responses from those you make offers to, you can accumulate names to compile your own response list. This list is not only key in your future offers but can be made available for sale or rent to other direct marketers. This becomes an additional revenue stream for you the more you can rent or sell it.

▼
MORE LIST SOURCES

- Hugo Dunhill, (800) 223-6454
- American Business Lists, (800) 555-5335
- Edith Roman, (800) 223-2194

EXTERNAL LIST SOURCES

Aside from the internal lists of customers and past customers, there are external sources of lists. These external lists are either purchased or rented lists. They may be obtained directly from the company or organization whose list you want. Many magazine publishers, manufacturers, catalog companies, and other direct marketers have their own lists that they are willing to rent. If one of these organizations has prospects who may be interested in your products or services, it is worth contacting them directly for list rental.

WORKING WITH LIST BROKERS

Typically, if working with a company or sometimes even an association, you will work with a list manager. If you can't find the appropriate list manager within the company or organization, you can turn to a list broker.

A list broker is a person or company that researches a source for a list that matches your criteria and specifications and then obtains that list to sell to you. They also negotiate with list vendors and providers on your behalf. For this, a commission and/or fee is built into the rates charged to you, the marketer.

A list broker has many lists available or access to them, fitting many specifications. List brokers can also advise you on what type of list will work best for your direct marketing campaign.

The primary function of a list broker is to locate lists that include names and contact information conforming to a set of specifications provided by a direct marketer client. Their job entails recommending and testing various list components. It also includes looking for the freshest names and making sure they are among the first to have access to new lists. List brokers are continually negotiating between list owners and clients. This negotiation includes working out details of price, length of use, and any other use terms and conditions.

A good broker should

- be responsive to clients' needs.
- communicate availability and accessibility.
- communicate list use conditions.
- suggest ways to economize.
- handle general negotiations with list vendors.

- recommend the best lists for their clients' situation/campaigns.
- suggest any ideas on segmentations (although not the list broker's primary purpose).

A list broker is a representative of a company whose business is to secure mailing lists. These lists are obviously from outside your company.

Finding those willing to rent their lists and negotiating the conditions and price of the rental can be time consuming on your part. If this is the case, you can turn to a list broker. A list broker is someone in the business of buying and selling lists. The list business is a big business. You can find list brokers in any online or offline directory under Mailing Lists. Another source is the *Standard Rate and Data Source*, available at your local library.

List brokers have access to lots of information. They are best equipped to find the list that will help you accomplish your direct marketing objectives. They know response rates of typical lists. They understand demographics. They know what has worked in the past with particular companies that are similar to yours and what hasn't.

If your business is just starting out, you obviously don't have a large house list. This is also the time to consult a list broker for list rental.

Before approaching list vendors, you want to define your target as specifically as you can. This process includes defining your ideal client. The more specific, the better. You know that by now. Chances are good that a list broker can take your specifications and come up with a set of names, a list that conforms to them.

The *Standard Rate and Data Source* will show you different categories of lists. Using these categories and further refining them with your ideal client criteria and running them against the available names fitting those criteria will provide you with a list count. This will be the number of names that fit your specifications. From this count, you can then purchase or rent a specified quantity. Consulting more than one broker may provide slightly different counts but most will be close. You can then discuss the costs of purchasing or renting the list.

Lists are usually priced as cost per 1,000 names, or CPM. These range between $25 and $250 cpm.

Once people on a rented list respond to you, you can enter them into your own database as part of your own list.

List specifications and/or demographics are:

- Age group
- Level of income, individually or as a family
- Hobbies; special interests
- Community participation; group or association memberships
- Geographical area
- Buying habits
- Consumer or business

Qualifying a List Broker

Basically, all list companies and brokers are the same from the standpoint of access to mailing lists, pricing, and data available. In view of this, one primary criterion in choosing a list company/broker to work with is the presence of a specialist in the area you want to target or a specialist in working with related businesses. How well do they know your marketplace? You may prefer to work with resident experts whose areas of expertise dovetail with your needs. The following questions serve as the base of information you should consider before deciding on a list broker. Other, more complete questions and items are available in Figure 2.1, List Broker/List Vendor Checklist.

- Do they understand your specific market?
- Is the broker currently working with other marketers like you?
- Do they know/understand your competitors?
- Are they well-connected in the list management community?
- Does the broker know how the list was compiled, and is he or she willing to guarantee accuracy?

List Broker Advantage

There are advantages to renting or purchasing a list from a list broker. With many lists available to offer you, the broker can suggest alternative lists to test and use. Working directly with a list vendor or list owner presents a very biased situation as list owners are only interested in marketing their own list.

Even though list brokers are experts in what lists generally work and what ones don't, it is still up to you and imperative that you do the proper testing to truly determine the best list.

Qualifying a List

The best list for your purposes matches exactly the description of your target market. Usually there are lists that come close to your definition. Working together with a list vendor or list broker can help you to precisely identify your target market while at the same time develop list specifications. Using the Target Market Worksheet (Figure 2.6) is a good step in qualifying a list for your use.

Sources of List Brokers

- D & B Sales and Marketing Solutions, www.zapdata.com
- DMA's Statistical Fact Book, www.the-dma.org
- Federation of European Direct Marketing, www.fedma.org

| FIGURE 2.1 | List Broker/List Vendor Checklist |

❑ Review campaign and marketing objectives with vendor/broker.

❑ Allow enough time to obtain lists.

❑ Find out where list came from or the source used to acquire names.

❑ Get sample of marketing used to generate response names for lists.

❑ Obtain simple list description and specifications.

❑ Who has used the list successfully (type of company)?

❑ Ask to see a sample printout of the list (hard copy).

❑ Is the list in the order requested, e.g., zip code order?

❑ Are the titles and company types as requested?

❑ Are hotline names from this list available?

❑ Is the list broker an experienced marketer in your market/business?

❑ Double-check items specified:

__ Quantity

__ Title

__ Format

__ Order

❑ How well does the broker know your competition?

❑ What new lists might be available that are close to specifications?

❑ When was the last time the list was run through NCOA?

❑ Is there a seasonality factor associated with the list?

❑ Does the list include actual purchasers or just inquirers?

❑ What is the age of the list?

❑ When was the list last updated?

❑ When was the list last cleaned?

❑ Ask about the dates represented by the hotline list.

❑ How were the names generated?

❑ Telemarketing.

❑ Direct mail response.

❑ Catalog orders.

❑ Online response.

❑ How well does the list fit your target market description and ideal client profile?

❑ Determine list costs.

❑ Determine select and overlay costs.

❑ Are there any special inclusions or exclusions related to cost?

❑ Are there any deliverability guarantees?

❑ List format: How will it be delivered?

❑ What is the turnaround time for list delivery?

- Yahoo or Google or other search engine search for "list brokers"
- Hoovers Online, www.hoovers.com
- InfoUSA, www.infousa.com
- Yellow Pages
- Online directories
- Direct Mail Association
- Standard Rate and Data Services Direct, also known as the Direct Mail List Source or Direct Marketing List Source, www.srds.com

- www.mediafinder.com

THE STANDARD RATE AND DATA SERVICE (SRDS)

The Standard Rate and Data Service (SRDS) has references for all direct marketers. Its database of media rates and related information is the largest such database in the world, cataloging more than 100,000 U.S. and international media properties and direct marketing lists. SRDS verifies each listing up to 20 times per year, making more than 20,000 listing updates every month and earning the designation as the most comprehensive reference for all direct marketers.

SRDS is a reference. The service does not directly rent or sell direct marketing lists. It does, however, provide access to the largest and most current database of list rental/purchase information available. Because of this, SRDS is a reference for list brokers making recommendations to a direct marketer, a reference for a direct marketer looking to communicate with a precise target market, and a reference for list managers who want to generate interest in their own lists offered for list rental or purchase.

The database is accessed by subscribers through SRDS DirectNet®, an online service with the high-end functionality needed by brokers, and through SRDS Direct Marketing List Source®, which includes more basic online functionality and three print issues annually.

Complete list rental information is available, including list sources, select and overlay information, and costs and contacts for over 58,000 different lists (at the time of writing—and growing). These lists fall into more than 223 different SRDS market classifications. Also included in the directory are list compilers (those who market their own lists), list brokers (those who market and sell other companies' lists for a commission), and list managers (those who maintain and prepare mailing lists for their own company or for direct marketers for a fee). Data is updated nightly.

The SRDS database features data from many lists representing many categories, including the following:

- Club membership lists
- Alumni lists
- Association membership lists
- Demographic lists
- Geographic lists
- Purchasing pattern lists
- Subscriber lists

Database Listing in SRDS

Figure 2.2 represents a sample business mailing list listing in the SRDS Direct Marketing List Source, December 2004. Figure 2.3 represents a similar listing for a consumer mailing list. (Reprinted with permission, SRDS, 1700 Higgins Road, Des Plaines, IL 60018, www.srds.com, SRDS Direct Marketing Solutions, December 2004.)

Notice all the available information:

- The organization represented
- Number of list members
- Description of the list/source
- The order the list comes in (i.e., zip code, carrier route, alphabetical, etc.)
- Rental/purchase rates
- Method of addressing and media available (labels, tapes, discs, e-mail)
- Delivery schedule
- Minimum order
- Guaranteed delivery percentage
- Hotline list quantity available
- List segments
- Number in each list segment
- Net name arrangement
- Restrictions
- Payment terms

LIST USAGE FUNDAMENTALS

You already know that the biggest fundamental for all of direct marketing is list-related: Over 50 percent of the success of a campaign depends on the quality of the list. Aside from the fundamental, there are a few other list fundamentals to consider:

FIGURE 2.2 Sample Business Mailing List from the SRDS Direct Marketing List Source

SRDS - 98.006 | Record Number: 437012 September 23, 2004; 18:19; 347

45 Business Executives

AMERICAN DEMOGRAPHICS—cont

	Total Number	Price per/M
Sales volume:		
1,000,000,000+	1,838	+10.00
500,000,000-999,999,999	484	"
100,000,000-499,999,999	1,863	"
10,000,000-99,999,999	4,022	"
500,000-9,999,999	1,002	"
1-499,999	5,141	"

(*) Reuse or mailing w/phone follow-up 5.00/M off base rate.
Minimum order 5,000.

4A. OTHER SELECTIONS
SCF, Zip, state, 10.00/M extra; key coding, 3.00/M extra; run charges, 10.00/M extra; SIC, 15.00/M extra.

5. COMMISSION, CREDIT POLICY
20% commission to brokers. Cancel charges: Orders cancelled prior to merge are subject to a 50.00 flat cancellation fee plus any applicable production charges. Orders cancelled after merge-purge are payable in full.

6. METHOD OF ADDRESSING
Cheshire labels, 4-up; pressure sensitive labels, 10.00/M extra; diskette, 35.00 fee; e-mail, 75.00 fee; FTP, 50.00 fee.

8. RESTRICTIONS
Sample mailing piece required.

11. MAINTENANCE
Updated quarterly.

AMERICAN DEMOGRAPHICS EMAIL

Data Verified: Jul 14, 2004.

Location ID: 13 ICLS 45 **Mid 760921-000**

1. PERSONNEL
List Manager — Statlistics Management Group, 11 Lake Avenue Ext., Danbury, CT 06811. Phone 203-778-8700. Fax 203-778-4839.
URL: http://www.statlistics.com
E-mail: j.papalia@statlistics.com

2. SUMMARY DESCRIPTION
Email addresses of subscribers to a publication that defines and discusses consumer markets on terms of demographics, lifestyles, media preferences, and purchasing behavior.

3. LIST SOURCE
Controlled circ.

4. SELECTIONS WITH COUNTS
Updated: Jul 14, 2004.

	Total Number	Price per/M
Email addresses	3,091	*255.00
Primary business:		
Advertising agency	181	+10.00
Marketing service	116	"
Market research	104	"
Consumer/business product manufacturing	207	"
Financial services/insurance	187	"
Print media	138	"
Retailer/wholesaler	131	"
Non profit organization	150	"
Education	272	"
Personal/business services	448	"
Other	604	"
Job title:		
President/CEO	649	+10.00
VP/other	316	"
Director/other	368	"
Employee size:		
1-4	770	+10.00
5-9	224	"
10-19	266	"
20-49	308	"
50-99	263	"
100-499	539	"
500-999	154	"
1,000+	183	"
Sales volume:		
500,000,000+	214	+10.00
100,000,000-499,999,999	207	"
10,000,000-99,999,999	473	"
5,000,000-9,999,999	142	"
2,500,000-4,999,999	136	"
1,000,000-2,499,999	200	"
500,000-999,999	159	"
1-499,999	782	"

(*) Plus deployment fee, 120.00/M: HTML, 50.00 flat. Tracking available upon request. Transmission 24 working hours after test approval. All transmissions must be completed through Statlistics. 1 test included each additional retest, 50.00 flat.
Minimum order 4,000.

4A. OTHER SELECTIONS
SCF, Zip, state, 10.00/M extra; deployment, 120.00/M extra; personalization, 10.00/M extra.

5. COMMISSION, CREDIT POLICY
20% commission to brokers. Cancel charges: Cancelled orders are subject to a 250.00 flat cancellation fee plus any applicable production charges.

6. METHOD OF ADDRESSING
E-mail, shipping, 75.00 fee.

8. RESTRICTIONS
Sample mailing piece required. All orders are approved on a reciprocal rental.

11. MAINTENANCE
Updated quarterly.

AMERICAN ENTREPRENEUR SERVICES NETWORK

Data Verified: Aug 9, 2004.

Location ID: 13 ICLS 45 **Mid 102699-000**

1. PERSONNEL
List Manager — Name-Finders Lists, Inc., 160 Sansome St., 4th Floor, San Francisco, CA 94104-3709. Phone 415-955-8595 Ext. 247. Fax 415-955-8581.
URL: http://www.namefinderslists.com
E-mail: bill@namefinders.com
Key Contact: Bill Badiner, Phone 415-955-8595 Ext. 247.
E-mail: bill@namefinders.com

2. SUMMARY DESCRIPTION
Corporate leaders who are members of an organization committed to meeting the needs of business in the U.S.; includes on-line access to discount phone services, corporate rates for hotels and car rentals, discounts for office equipment and computers, access to legal and accounting services and group insurance programs.
Average unit of sale 80.00.

3. LIST SOURCE
Internet/online/website registration online service subscribers.

4. SELECTIONS WITH COUNTS
Updated: Apr 26, 2004 Counts Thru: Apr 2004

	Total Number	Price per/M
Members	202,900	*95.00
With phones	202,874	120.00
Employee size:		
1-19	65,348	+10.00
20-99	54,670	"
100-499	82,882	"
Sales Volume:		
Under 900K	45,134	+10.00
$1M-$4.9M	63,033	"
$5M-$9.9M	12,606	"
$10M+	44,715	"
SIC Code Groups:		
Manufacturing	78,926	+10.00
Business & Professional	65,573	"
Wholesale	21,513	"
Retail	23,056	"
Construction	15,908	"

(*)Fundraising Rate 75.00/M.
Minimum order 5,000.

4A. OTHER SELECTIONS
State, SCF, Zip, gender, 5.00/M extra; SIC, 10.00/M extra; key coding, 2.50/M extra.

6. METHOD OF ADDRESSING
Cheshire labels, 4-up, 20.00/M extra; pressure sensitive labels, 10.00/M extra; mag tape, 9T 1600 BPI, 35.00 fee; diskette, 35.00 fee; e-mail, 75.00 fee.

8. RESTRICTIONS
Two sample mailing pieces required. One time use only. Signed list agreement required for approval.

11. MAINTENANCE
Updated quarterly.

THE AMERICAN EXECUTIVE NETWORK EMAIL LIST

Data Verified: Sep 15, 2004.

Location ID: 13 ICLS 45 **Mid 846795-000**

1. PERSONNEL
List Manager — Worldata, 3000 N. Military Trail, Boca Raton, FL 33431-6375. Phone 561-393-8200. Fax 561-368-8345.
URL: http://www.worldata.com
E-mail: mail@worldata.com

2. SUMMARY DESCRIPTION
Email addresses of U.S. business executives, managers and professionals in a broad assortment of occupations in all 50 states who subscribe to business magazines.

3. LIST SOURCE
Compiled multi-sourced.

4. SELECTIONS WITH COUNTS
Updated: Mar 15, 2004.

	Total Number	Price per/M
Total list	3,225,973	*275.00
Region:		
New England	91,000	275.00
Mid Atlantic	712,239	"
South Eastern	546,778	"
Mid Western	747,352	"
South Central	404,643	"
Mountain Region	97,490	"
South Western	102,836	"
Pacific	401,471	"
North Western	102,594	"

(*)(Transmission fee, 75.00/M. Suppression files:Less < 100 names 75.00 flat greater > 100 names 1/M with a 150.00 flat min. Charges are epr order.
Minimum order 5,000.

4A. OTHER SELECTIONS
HTML image hosting, 25.00/M extra; flash email hosting, 50.00/M extra; 3rd party email merge/purge (each), 10.00/M extra; personalization of transmission, 5.00/M extra; greater than 2 tests/changes (each), 10.00 fee; greater than 3tracked URLs (each), 50.00 fee; geo, job title, # employees, $ volume.

5. COMMISSION, CREDIT POLICY
Cancel charges: If order is cancelled within 48 hours and job hass not been executed (regardless if copy/creative has been received) 250.00 cancellation charge. If prior to execution date, mailers/brokers are entitled to one revision of mail date without penalty. 100 applies to additional revisions.

8. RESTRICTIONS
If reserved mail date passes without execution of order, full charges including transmission apply. Once executed regardless of mail date, full charges inicuding transmission apply. Once order has been tested, and order is cancelled 500.00 charge applies. Order tested and copy needs to be changed. Full charges including transmission apply. Reselecting corresponding data on previously selected order 500.00 flat. Requested creative alterations (i.e. resize images) 500.00 flat.

11. MAINTENANCE
Updated monthly.

AMERICAN EXECUTIVES ETHNIC DATABASE

Data Verified: Aug 10, 2004.

Location ID: 13 ICLS 45 **Mid 845206-000**

1. PERSONNEL
List Manager — Chessie Lists, Inc., 13321 New Hampshire Ave., Ste. 202, Silver Spring, MD 20904. Phone 301-680-3633. Fax 301-680-3635.
URL: http://www.chessielists.com
E-mail: info@chessielists.com

2. SUMMARY DESCRIPTION
Business executives by their ethnic heritage.

3. LIST SOURCE
Compiled telephone numbers.

4. SELECTIONS WITH COUNTS
Updated: Aug 10, 2004 Counts Thru: Nov 2003

	Total Number	Price per/M
Total file	17,643,667	70.00
Job title:		
Owner	4,582,925	+10.00
Senior management	4,984,012	"
Officer	23,732	"
Vice President	1,229,072	"
Director	1,335,658	"
Manager	3,266,130	"
Other ethnic:		
Administrative executives	1,998,425	+10.00
Agriculture & forestry	653,609	"
Amusement & recreation services	265,583	"
Automotive	342,275	"
Automotive repair	371,536	"
Business services	1,290,933	"
Construction	1,290,265	"
Corporate executives	9,867,745	"
Eating & drinking establishments	571,742	"
Education	388,776	"
Engineering & accounting services	980,979	"
Finance executives	380,635	"
Finance, insurance & real estate	841,503	"
Food	289,270	"
Government	376,464	"
Health services	1,341,896	"
Home furniture	557,026	"
Hotel & motel, resorts & camps	218,845	"
HR & benefits executives	512,832	"
Insurance agents & brokers	648,711	"
IT/MIS executives	405,534	"
Legal services	355,243	"
Manufacturing	1,831,935	"
Mfg. operations & production	391,712	"
Membership organization	691,338	"
Organizations, clubs & social services	25,043	"
Personal, business & recreation	480,695	"
Personal services	517,500	"
Purchasing executives	519,999	"
Real estate	102,176	"
Repair services	247,839	"
Retailer	1,241,028	"
Sales & marketing executives	1,095,070	"
Social services	421,692	"
Transportation & communicaiton	813,556	"
Wholesale	1,173,098	"
Job function:		
Executive	9,357,664	+10.00
Administration	1,936,770	"
Systems/data processing	227,830	"
Finance/accounting	470,183	"
Personnel/benefits/HR	229,898	"
Purchasing	210,056	"
Mfg/ops/production	268,213	"
Sales/marketing	792,128	"
sales volume:		
0-250.00	10,500,388	+10.00
251M-500M	1,806,117	"
501M-1.9M	2,348,603	"
2MM-4.9MM	1,059,475	"
5MM-9.9MM	557,528	"
10MM-14.9MM	272,795	"
15MM-19.9MM	162,980	"
20MM-30.9MM	221,015	"
31MM-49.9MM	179,617	"
50MM-99.9MM	199,746	"
100MM-499.9MM	238,513	"
500MM and up	96,890	"
Legal status:		
Proprietorship	4,228,732	+10.00
Partnership	968,278	"
Corporation	9,211,885	"
Import/export:		
Both import & export	55,161	+10.00
Export	103,119	"
Import	94,402	"
Ethnicity (also available by country of origin):		
Indian	114,242	+10.00
Arabic	808,069	"
North African	62,885	"
Northern Europe	2,682,589	"
Asian	461,944	"
Central Europe	9,568,694	"
Eastern Europe	569,933	"
South African	85,493	"
Company size:		
0-6	11,342,869	+10.00
7-10	1,762,810	"
11-15	813,413	"
16-20	502,402	"
21-25	347,434	"
26-30	278,256	"
31-49	502,352	"
50-100	764,563	"
101-250	559,528	"
251 and up	770,040	"

Minimum order 5,000.

4A. OTHER SELECTIONS
Age, company size, employees location, ethnicity, gender, geo, import/export, job function, job title, legal status, max per site, minority owned, phones, public/private, $ volume, SIC, small business, SMSA, subsidiary, 10.00/M extra.

5. COMMISSION, CREDIT POLICY
20% commission to brokers. Cancel charges: Orders cancelled after mail date will require payment in full. All cancelled orders are subject to a 50.00 flat charge plus applicable running and shipping/material charges. 10% commission to agencies.

6. METHOD OF ADDRESSING
Cheshire labels, 4-up; pressure sensitive labels, 10.00/M extra; mag tape, 30.00 fee; diskette, 30.00 fee; e-mail, 40.00 fee.

7. DELIVERY SCHEDULE
Delivery from 3 to 5 working days.

AMERICAN LIST COUNCIL/B2B OPT-IN E-MAIL ADDRESSES

Data Verified: Jan 8, 2004.

Location ID: 13 ICLS 45 **Mid 758833-000**

1. PERSONNEL
List Manager — American List Counsel, Inc. (formerly Max-Direct), 400 Columbus Ave. East Lobby, 2nd Fl, Valhalla, NY 10595. Phone 914-741-0500. Fax 914-741-1171.
Key Contact: David Honig, Phone 212-620-1711.
E-mail: dhonig@maxworldwide.com

2. SUMMARY DESCRIPTION
Professionals that have indicated their interest in offers and promotions relating to business products and services.
65% male, 35% female.

3. LIST SOURCE
Internet/online/website registration.

4. SELECTIONS WITH COUNTS
Updated: Jun 24, 2002.

	Total Number	Price per/M
Total list	275,000	200.00

Minimum order 20,000.

4A. OTHER SELECTIONS
Age, gender, 10.00/M extra; state, 6.00/M extra.

5. COMMISSION, CREDIT POLICY
20% commission to brokers. Payment due 30 days after mail date. Cancel charges: 50.00 cancellation fee, 8.00/M run charges, selections in full, mag tape and shipping. Prepayment required for new customers.

6. METHOD OF ADDRESSING
E-mail, 55.00 fee; diskette, 100.00 fee.

7. DELIVERY SCHEDULE
Delivery fee, 25.00/M extra.

8. RESTRICTIONS
Reciprocal terms required.

11. MAINTENANCE
Updated monthly.

AMERICAN MANAGEMENT ASSOCIATION - APPROVING MANAGERS

Data Verified: Sep 21, 2004.

Location ID: 13 ICLS 45 **Mid 108032-000**
Member: D.M.A.

1. PERSONNEL
List Manager — Direct Media Business List Management, P.O. Box 4565, 200 Pemberwick Rd., Greenwich, CT 06830. Phone 203-532-1000. Fax 203-531-1452.
URL: http://www.directmedia.com
Key Contact: Mike Mayhew, Phone 203-532-2418.

2. SUMMARY DESCRIPTION
Executives, supervisors and middle managers who have given their approval for one or more of their staff to attend a seminar on building business skills.
58% male, 32% female.

3. LIST SOURCE
Association/memberships.

4. SELECTIONS WITH COUNTS
Updated: Sep 15, 2004 Counts Thru: Jul 2004

	Total Number	Price per/M
Approving managers (24 months)	36,440	*115.00
12 months	19,725	"

(*) Consumer rate, 75.00/M; fundraiser rate, 70.00/M.
Net name arrangement (minimum 50,000), 85% plus 8.00/M running charge.
Minimum order 5,000.

4A. OTHER SELECTIONS
Zip+4, 3.50/M extra; SIC, state, SCF, Zip, gender, employee size, max per company, 6.00/M extra; recency, job function, title, 11.00/M extra; key coding, 2.50/M extra; industry, 11.00/M extra; individual name, business address.

5. COMMISSION, CREDIT POLICY
Cancel charges: Orders cancelled after mail date require payment in full. All cancelled orders are subject to a 75.00 charge plus applicable running and shipping charges.

6. METHOD OF ADDRESSING
Cheshire labels, 4-up; pressure sensitive labels, 6.00/M extra; diskette, plus run charge 5.00/M, 50.00 fee; e-mail, set up, 50.00 fee, cartridge (IBM 3480), 25.00 fee; Zip tape, 8.00 fee.

8. RESTRICTIONS
Sample mailing piece required.

11. MAINTENANCE
Updated monthly.

AMERICAN MANAGEMENT ASSOCIATION - INQUIRIES

Data Verified: Sep 21, 2004.

Location ID: 13 ICLS 45 **Mid 049954-000**
Member: D.M.A.

1. PERSONNEL
List Manager — Direct Media Business List Management, P.O. Box 4565, 200 Pemberwick Rd., Greenwich, CT 06830. Phone 203-532-1000. Fax 203-531-1452.
URL: http://www.directmedia.com
Key Contact: Mike Mayhew, Phone 203-532-2418.

2. SUMMARY DESCRIPTION
Business managers at business address who have responded by mail to membership solicitation.
46% male, 42% female.

3. LIST SOURCE
100% internet/online/website registration, direct mail.

4. SELECTIONS WITH COUNTS
Updated: Sep 7, 2004 Counts Thru: Jul 2004

	Total Number	Price per/M
12 month inquiries	19,705	*75.00
24 month inquiries	37,005	65.00

(*) Consumer rate, 60.00/M.
Net name arrangement (minimum 50,000), 85% plus 5.00/M running charges.
Minimum order 5,000.

4A. OTHER SELECTIONS
State, SCF, Zip, gender, employee size, max per company, 6.00/M extra; Zip+4, 3.50/M extra; key coding, 2.50/M extra; recency, SIC, title only, 11.00/M extra; individual name.

5. COMMISSION, CREDIT POLICY
20% commission to brokers. Cancel charges: Orders cancelled after mail date require payment in full. All cancelled orders are subject to a 75.00 charge plus applicable running and shipping charges.

6. METHOD OF ADDRESSING
Cheshire labels, 4-up; pressure sensitive labels, 6.00/M extra; diskette, plus run charge, 5.00/M, 50.00 fee; IBM cartridge - 3480, 25.00 fee; e-mail, set up, 50.00 fee.

8. RESTRICTIONS
Sample mailing piece required.

11. MAINTENANCE
Updated monthly.

346 Domestic Business Lists October, 2004

FIGURE 2.3 — Sample Consumer Mailing List from the SRDS Direct Marketing List Source

- *Are you wondering how often to use a particular list?* If a list garners response, keep using it. You are the only person who will tire of your own marketing. It is naïve to think that every prospect will remember everything you ever sent to them. The more often they see your marketing, however, the better the chance that they will respond. Resending the same marketing piece within 30 to 60 days to the same list will often produce 75 to 90 percent of the original response. Here again, testing the optimum frequency will help determine all timing factors. In terms of testing, concentrate on longer-term response rates vs. short-term hits.

- *If you rent or buy a list that also has been purchased or rented by someone else, find out what their experience was.* Preferably, do this before your transaction with the list supplier, in case you find poor results that are list-based. A list that performed well for companies selling similar products will generally perform as well for your product.

- *Test for optimum frequency.* Testing is a common thread in all that is discussed here. It's easy to say that once a month is an optimum marketing frequency, but this will differ according to offer, vehicle, and target. Testing other variables enough times with enough test prospects is also an important fundamental.

- *If it works, keep doing it.* Marketers are always on the hunt for new prospects, but if an old list works and produces the response you want, continue to use it. Don't overlook what has been proven.

- *If seasonality is involved, market well in advance of the season.* An important aspect of your direct marketing planning is being mindful that the season will soon be upon you. Lack of planning springs the season on you before you have time to react to the right "timing window in advance of the season."

- *Use all the tools at your disposal to sort, segment, and manage your list.* This is a function of your database and your database management system. Be creative in your segments and sorts. Test each accordingly. The objective is to achieve a high response efficiently. This sometimes might mean more mailings to a smaller, segmented list, driving up ROI.

List rental agreements are generally for one-time use. There are special pricing provisions that allow for multiple mailings. List companies, list managers, and vendors all include in their rented lists some names and addresses that come back directly to the list vendor. This is done to monitor the usage of the list and allows list owners to monitor and record list activity. Usually a list purchaser or renter cannot detect which names are decoy names and which are legitimate.

Some list usage agreements point this out directly in the list usage agreement and further advise that you should not try to find the decoy names:

> It is agreed that each use of this list is monitored by decoy names and that any violation of these usage restrictions will result in additional billings, suspension of rental and purchase privileges and/or litigation. It is further agreed that the list user will not employ any method to detect decoy names and therefore eliminate them from list usage.

Technically, usage also applies to telemarketing follow-up. Calling to follow up on the mailing constitutes one more use of the list and may be prohibited, depending on your agreement with the list vendor/broker.

COMMON TERMS

Here are common terms and list-related items:

- *Usage.* This will describe who else has used or purchased the list.
- *General description.* This will describe what the list consists of without too many details or segments. Sometimes, there are further descriptions related to the respondents' profile. Beware of subjective terms like "seniors" or "highly compensated." If you can get further qualification of these, you will be better able to assess the potential success of your list.
- *List source.* In many cases, if you are requesting a "mailing" list, you will get names of those who have responded to direct mail offers. The list source in this situation is described as "direct mail," which tells you very little. You don't know what the target of the original mailing was, what was sent, or at what point during the course of mailings it was sent. Some list vendors will be glad to supply you with more detail about the "mailing" that generated the names on the list, but you have to request it.
- *Last update/next update.* Assess the day you actually will use the list by comparing it to the most recent update or the next update. You may be able to offer to wait for the freshest list available, determined by these dates.

PURCHASE OR RENT?

Many lists have an option of purchasing the list for endless use or renting the list for one-time use. There are pros and cons to each. Here are the primary ones to consider before making your list decision:

- You don't own a rented list.

- You didn't produce it.
- You can't use it over and over without paying over and over.
- You are dependent on a third party's external sources for the accuracy of the information within the list.
- Information is limited unless you purchase more add-on components to the list. Additional information may not be available.

Multiple Use/Purchase

A purchase agreement allows you to do whatever you like with the data other than sell it. Many multiple-use agreements are also purchase agreements. "Multiple use" means that the list can be used by the client many times. In most instances, this means you can use the list as often as you wish, ad infinitum. Some suppliers add a rider to multiple use, e.g., multiple use for a period of up to one year or multiple use for up to X number of uses. Lists sold for multiple use with these riders are often described as being sold on multiple use rental. Most telemarketing lists are available for multiple use; some are available for multiple use because policing a list for single use for telemarketing is difficult to achieve. For inclusion in a database, data must be bought on a multiple use or outright purchase basis. Multiple use or outright purchase is the most expensive option for buying a list.

Single Use/Rental

Rental means that you have no rights to the data you have purchased. Generally, the term applies to buying the data for use over a stated time period and may include single or multiple use during the period of the agreement. Single-use agreements are almost exclusively rental agreements.

"Single use" means that the list can be used once only by you. Normally, this is a usage applicable to mailing lists; however, with care, it can be used for telemarketing lists.

In many instances of single-use list sales, for security reasons the supplier will not allow the list to go directly to the client. The list is only released to a third-party agency on the condition that the client never gets to see the original data (sometimes called a "site unseen" list). Other suppliers are more trusting of their clients and will provide a single-use list directly to you. The major benefit to you of single use is cost. It is the cheapest way of using a list. The major drawback is that you only get to keep the responses to the mailing or telephone campaign; you can't keep or reuse the original data. The conditions around single usage can get hazy when it comes to telemarketing. At what point is a record classified as having been used? When the researcher gets a questionnaire completed? Or is a record used as soon as the first dialing has been made, irrespective of the outcome (what if the result is the engaged tone)? As you see, the situation is open to interpretation. Most single-use lists bought on magnetic media require that the tape/disc is returned within a specified time period. The supplier often charges a refundable deposit on the tape/disc be encourage this. Sometimes, you are contractually obliged to return the tape within a specified time frame or risk incurring a penalty. This is a technique designed to limit the abuse of data under the single-use agreement.

Note that no list supplier will allow you to resell or sell his list without first making some special arrangement with the list owner. Such agreements are rare.

Things to Know Before Renting a Mailing List

The difference between an effective or ineffective list could be the list broker; however, a broker by any other name is still a middleman. If you are an entrepreneurial company and can't find a list broker specializing in what you want, you may have to undertake some of the list research yourself, independent of the broker. Here are some of the things you need to know about buying or renting lists, researching list sources, or working with list brokers:

- Trade publications, newsletter publishers, and membership organizations have lists. They also do a pretty good job of updating and cleaning lists as their base changes. These organizations will communicate information related to their own list management and availability.
- Nothing is as comprehensive a source in the list business as the SRDS *Direct Marketing List Source*. This directory describes every list available in the commercial marketplace and is a great place to start your list research. This research will provide you information for further discussion with your own list broker.
- List owners use fake names and addresses in a list to track your usage. Make sure you know whether you are purchasing or renting the list and what the terms of usage are.
- Lists with contact names cost more than lists that only have generic titles, e.g., Director of Marketing, Technical Director, and Human Resources Manager.
- A very inexpensive list is a red flag, warning of possible poor quality or outdated names.
- Some of your purchased list names will be undeliverable. This factor should be considered when negotiating with your list vendor.

Customers should be targeted according to their needs and wants, their interests, how and where they buy, their financial means, and general family and community status.

This translates into characteristics/demographics that define your target market and eventually become the basis for your list specifications. The overall objective, of course, is to formulate a set of specifications that define those most interested in purchasing your product or responding to your offer. These objectives and resulting specifications should be shared with your list vendor or list broker.

LIST QUALITY

With the quality of a list being of paramount importance to a campaign, the following information is best discussed with your list supplier to ensure your objectives of highest quality or best use when developing your own target list:

- Dig deep to find out where the names on your list come from. Did they result from an actual purchase of a product or service? If so, what type of product, and how similar was that product or service to yours?
- Did the names result from a response requesting more information; a visit to a web site?
- Did some of the names come from uninterested prospects who just wanted the free offer?
- Who else has purchased and used the list? Was a portion of the list used for a test, or was the full list used in an entire campaign?
- Was the list generated from mail responses? If so, this is a strong indicator that these prospects will buy from a mail offer again.

If your list broker or list vendor says that much of this information is unavailable, it means they have not dug deep enough to ensure the quality of the list. If this is the case, you may want to consider changing to a broker who has this quality assurance information.

Once you find a list that works, stick with it. Your list broker can inform you of updates to it. If the first list pulled in responses, chances are good that new, updated names from the same place and of the same type will pull a similar response.

Precision is a key advantage of direct mail; in this illustration, it is the precise selection of a list along with precise definition of segmentation criteria. Still, many small businesses and organizations forgo this precision. They purchase a list and blast-mail to it before any study, manipulation, sorts, or modifications. Sorting and segmenting will optimize, economize, and produce better results.

Many list purchasers purchase lists that can't be corrected, sorted, or segmented. Know if this option is available before your list purchase is made. Realizing all that can be done, as in the

HOW TO ENSURE THAT YOUR MAILING LISTS HIT YOUR TARGET

State this directly on your marketing vehicle:

"If this mailing is of no interest to you, please forward it to the most appropriate person in your company who could benefit."

OR

"Please forward this to others in your company or organization who might be interested."

This one also works:

"We realize the timing of this mailing might not be right for you. You can still take advantage of our offer. Check here (on a BRC) if you want a reminder in three months and send it back to us."

above illustration, can mean much more to your company's bottom line.

LIST TESTING

With the list being the most important component in your campaign, it is wise to test, regardless of how similar the lists appear to be. Sometimes one list will outpull another with no explainable or obvious reason. This further substantiates the need for adequate testing.

When looking at all possible test variables in a direct marketing campaign, the list is primary. The determination of which lists you choose to use, until tested, is based on the assumptions of your target-market definition and your personal prejudices. Until one list is compared to another, you don't know how true your assumptions are related to campaign response.

Once you have received adequate feedback from your list, you can then decide to add it to your database (positive feedback and response) or put it aside for further testing or deletion (negative feedback with lack of response).

FIGURE 2.4 **List Use Conditions Template** (reprinted from www.megalist.co.uk with permission)

The following template may be used for your mailing list use policy by filling in the appropriate blanks for your company or business:

(Your company or organization name) **Mail List Usage Policy**

(Your company or organization name)'s names and addresses are proprietary and are protected by copyright.

(Your company or organization name) is the sole owner of the names and addresses and rents its mailing list electronically or in the form of labels for one-time use for each approved request. Agreement and approval for such a request must be in writing. Labels may be provided for a fee to organizations, publishers and businesses wishing to promote products and services to our list. Those on the list have agreed to this and are considered opt-in names for this one-time purpose. (Your company or organization name) requires preapproval of all items to be mailed and is the sole judge of the suitability of materials for mailing to its list members. (Your company or organization name) reserves the right to deny requests where the purpose or use may not be considered in the best interests of (your company or organization name)'s list members.

Nonprofit institutions wishing to rent the mailing list for educational purposes may purchase mailing labels at a reduced fee. (Your company or organization name) may require verification of an organization's nonprofit status.

(Your company or organization name) will not be bound by conditions printed or appearing on order blanks or copy instructions that conflict with provisions of its rate card.

CONTINUED

| FIGURE 2.4 | List Use Conditions Template (reprinted from www.megalist.co.uk with permission) |

Rental of (your company or organization name)'s mailing lists to vendors and outside entities does not constitute an endorsement or guarantee of the product or service being marketed. Unless expressly agreed to by (your company or organization name) in writing, any representation by the buyer(s) and/or his client(s) or agent(s), whether overt or implied, of (your company or organization name) endorsement or guarantee of a product or service is prohibited.

(Your company or organization name) specifically prohibits use of its membership names and addresses for the following purposes:

- Copying and entering names and addresses from the provided labels into a client's computer database for any purpose. This applies to duplication and/or storage in any form and by any means, electronic, mechanical, photocopying, recording, or otherwise. Violations are subject to prosecution under federal copyright laws.

- Announcements of openings or positions at companies/institutions.

- Membership recruitment mailings or related promotions for external organizations.

- Announcements of educational programs, equipment, or other products and services not related in some way to the field of _____ (your company's field or area of concentration).

- Use of member names and addresses for on-site visits to members' homes/offices for any reason.

In addition:

(Your company or organization name) shall not act as a broker, through providing its membership mailing labels, for any product or service not manufactured or provided directly by the purchaser of the mailing labels.

Use of the list is for one time only and limited exclusively to the specific offer or service as described in the mailing sample submitted in conjunction with the order form.

Payment is due upon receipt, and is past due 30 days after billing date. A client with three or more unpaid invoices shall be cause for disqualification from use of our mailing list. Reinstatement requires the payment of all but the last outstanding invoice.

The use of the (your company or organization name) names and addresses in any of the ways prohibited above shall be cause for, at a minimum, permanent disqualification of the buyer(s) and/or his client(s) or agent(s) from use of the (your company or organization name) mailing list. Violation of this policy as set forth above may also be grounds for legal action.

LIST COSTS

Most lists will have a base rental cost per thousand names. Selects or segments of the base list then have an up-charge associated with them, e.g., +$5/M to break a nationwide list down to a statewide list. Adding other selects also adds more charges. All totaled, the cost to refine a list as precisely as you can will pay off in terms of response from truly interested prospects. Although these costs are estimates and vary from vendor to vendor, they will be close. Watch out for surcharges, fees, and add-ons. Understand as much about pricing as possible before exchanging money with your vendor/broker.

Consumer lists are priced on a per-name basis or per-household basis. These represent individual "records." Basic consumer lists range from $95 to $140 per 1,000 names or records. Some high-demand lists can push the upper end of this range to $180 per 1,000 names. These costs are for a one-time use of the list. Some list vendors will then charge 1.25 to 1.5 times this pricing for a two-time usage of the list or 1.5 to 2.0 times this pricing for unlimited uses or purchase of the list.

LIST MAINTENANCE

Your list should not be treated as an inventory item or an event. Whether you purchase one or compile it yourself with your own data, the list is one of the most important assets you will own. Treat it the same as you would the purchase of a major piece of equipment and with the same care you would show when hiring a key person in your business.

WHY SOME LISTS DON'T MEET EXPECTATIONS

- *List fatigue.* This is especially true for catalogers in specialized markets that market to a relatively smaller target over and over. Sometimes taking a break from a list that has been used a lot, then starting it up again, will revive list success. New products and services and reintroductions help here, too.
- *Timing.* Earlier in this book I discussed trouble-shooting your direct marketing campaigns by looking at the four fundamentals that this whole book is based on: the target, the message, the vehicle, and timing and frequency. When a list no longer meets the direct marketer's requirements, you have to look closely at timing. Are you marketing at the right time in the right season or in time enough before a season hits? Of course, you know by now or will by the time you finish reading this book that testing is the answer to this question.
- *List cost vs. response.* You might be getting frequent responses to your list, and these might turn into sales. If you feel the revenue from this is good but that the whole direct marketing campaign to generate these sales is not profitable, you then must evaluate the cost of the lists. You certainly have to evaluate cost against list quality to approach optimum cost. This optimum cost measured with your response revenue or response then determines the optimum profitability of the list. Again, testing is an

> ### LIST COST TERM
> Net Name Arrangement. Paying the list owner only for the names you use after you have deleted undesirable and duplicate names.

important component here that will confirm that all other campaign components are under control.

- *Available names.* If your specifications are too narrow and too tight, you limit the number of available names. This leads to list fatigue much sooner strictly because of the limited number of potential buyers/responders on your list.
- *Not specifying correctly.* Your best prospect is a current customer, past customer, or one who resembles these two groups. Specifying your future lists as closely as possible to current or past customers will yield satisfactory results. Straying from this, which happens when a marketer tries to shape a future prospect or wishes for a particular type of prospect/client, can make a list ineffective. Proven results are a good basis for future results.
- *Customers change/customer demands change.* If you have a list of VCR and VCR tape buyers and you want to sell more VCR tapes, logically you would use this list and have good response. At the time of writing, the trend in video entertainment is completely away from VCRs and VCR tapes and toward DVDs. Selling your same VCR products to the same VCR/VCR tape buyers that you once had success with will not work today. Consumer lists change at the rate of about two percent a month. People move, die, get married, change careers, and are born. In the business-to-business world, companies don't change, but the people at them do. Employee turnover can be as high as one percent a week. This makes a business-to-business list outdated in fewer than two years. Customers change, customers' demands change, and the conditions that shape their demands change on an ongoing

basis—and at some point, away from the product you once sold.

All the above conditions are perfect test situations. Don't be afraid to pull out old lists to retry or retest them. Times change.

DATABASES

In the *Silver Anniversary Edition* of *DM News*, in a review of catalogs, the importance of database marketing is reviewed.

Before the 1980s, few companies, including catalogers, divided their data into different segments to target and market to. One of the early database marketers was J.C. Whitney, an auto parts and accessories catalog owned by the Riverside Company.

Whitney targets many niche markets of jeep and motorcycle enthusiasts, including Jeep, Honda Gold Wing Motorcycles, and Volkswagen. It has corresponding catalog titles for each, as well as an overall general, all-inclusive catalog.

Without the associated database marketing and the ability to target these niche/segments, it would be at the mercy of a large general catalog with less efficient targeting. These niched catalogs, as a result of database marketing and segmentation, allowed Whitney to penetrate those niche markets much more efficiently and increase market share.

This certainly got away from the strategy of mailing a general catalog to everybody, hoping that they'd find what they were looking for or at least find something of interest. This also was the beginning of the age of the specialty catalog—all a result of database management and marketing.

Databases are so important in direct marketing that some have used the term database marketing synonymously with direct marketing.

Databases make it possible for direct marketing to be targeted to those prospects you want targeted. Whether assimilating data from a current customer list or finding prospects like them in certain geographic areas, it is all possible with a database of information.

In direct marketing, a database is a program (or series of programs) that processes and sorts information used to target prospects. A database is a collection of data of specific groups, a comprehensive collection of interrelated data that can be manipulated and segmented by the many variables the data represent. This data consist of simple contact information, along with demographic and purchasing-pattern information. This allows for the segmentation necessary to precisely market to a particular target. Knowing the precise specification of a target allows the direct marketer to craft the most appropriate message/offer with the optimum frequency to generate the necessary response, all with the help of databases.

Building a database can be as simple as entering a name and purchasing information about a customer who purchases from you. The more information/data obtained and entered, the more segmentation and targeting you can do with your marketing.

The compilation and organization of databases can be done by you but are often left to professional database management companies. These service organizations might perform tasks as simple as eliminating duplicate names, sorting according to zip codes, or eliminating those names and addresses you have already mailed to.

Database Objectives

- Identify a common profile and characteristics of your best customers.
- Establish ongoing relationships that provide high lifetime value.

- Improve profitability by lowering cost of sales and cost of marketing while increasing response and return on marketing dollars.
- Provide more and more data to make related marketing, product, service development, and strategic decisions.
- Track the trends that point to the highest potential new business opportunities.
- Improve efficiencies through the accumulation and organization of information.

What a Database Can Do for You

The whole purpose of database marketing is based on the 80/20 rule applied to customers. Eighty percent of business will come from 20 percent of your customers. Selling more to existing customers and finding these 20 percent is a goal of database marketing. Finding customers and prospects like these 20 percent is also a goal.

- A database can create a customer with a high lifetime value through ongoing relationship management, not just a sale.
- Database marketing is the truest customer focus.
- A database encourages targeted communication, approaching one-on-one intimacy.
- A database helps direct marketers to get in the heads of their customers and know what they want and what is important to them.
- Customer behavior can be predicted.
- A database gives you the opportunity to match your products and services with those who want and need them.
- A database of prospects can be sorted to find those who fit the profile of your existing customers.
- Personalization can be done effectively through the use of a database.

- A continual supply of new information about customers and prospects can be maintained through the use of a database.
- Most of all, the proper database aids in the measurement of the direct responses and results, allowing for campaign refinement along the way.

Other Uses of Database Marketing

- Notify customers of specials or items relating to their past purchases
- Periodic reminders—pet checkups, oil changes, birthdays, renewals, etc.
- Birthday and anniversary greetings
- Surveys
- Event marketing invitation list
- New product/service announcements to customers first
- Loyalty programs; frequent buyers
- General marketing communication/keep-in-touch programs
- Request referrals
- Offering of a special report, article, or press release
- Communication of a success story

Typical Information Contained in a Database

- Customer identification, which might be an account number or customer number
- Name
- Address
- Zip + 4
- Title
- Source of response (order, inquiry, referral)
- Telephone numbers (voice, fax, cell)
- Purchase information (items, amounts, frequency)
- Demographic data

- If a business, relevant business information:
  - Number of employees
  - Industry—SIC
  - Company sales or some other measurement of size

All this information is in a dynamic state of flux. Consider customers moving, getting married (name change), adding family members, and changing jobs (demographics). An ongoing database maintenance program will ensure optimum database (direct) marketing.

GETTING INFORMATION FROM CUSTOMERS

Why do you think companies you buy from ask you to fill out, in great detail, a warranty card upon each purchase? They do it to get information from you. Usually the information requested is more than just name, address, phone, e-mail, and date of purchase. Several questions (as many as they can get away with, without totally annoying you) are usually asked. You will see questions on the warranty card such as: Where did you buy your product? Why did you buy? Who will actually be the one using it? Where did you hear of the selling company?

Companies then compile all this data and use it in a number of ways (sorting and segmenting with their database program):

- Future advertising and marketing decisions are made based on the analysis of information.
- Companies make strategic and product-offering decisions based on all you tell them.
- Follow-up programs are put in place to sell you more product, more often.
- Your information is used for other list compilations, which may be sold or rented to other list users.

RECENCY, FREQUENCY, MONETARY VALUE MODEL (RFM)

For several decades now, direct marketers have studied the use of models created from their databases. Over time, database models have been created that *directly link the future value of a customer with the customer's behavior*. These models have been proven to predict accurately in interactive TV marketing, catalog marketing, online marketing, and other direct marketing.

The most powerful and simplest to implement of these models is called RFM—the Recency, Frequency, Monetary Value model. RFM is a behavior-based model that analyzes how recently customers have purchased, how frequently they purchase, and how much they purchase to make predictions based on this behavior.

The RFM model states three findings:

1. The more *recently* someone has done something, the more likely they are to repeat it.
2. The more *frequently* someone has done something, the more likely they are to repeat it.
3. The more *monetary value* someone has realized by doing something (purchasing), the more likely they are to continue to purchase.

Customers who have purchased or responded to you more recently and more frequently, or who have created higher monetary values are much more likely to respond to your marketing than those who have responded less recently and less frequently, and who have realized less monetary value.

Using your database to create an RFM model, you can predict the future value of customers and their likelihood of responding to your marketing and your offers. It is all based on the finding that a buyer who has purchased most recently is the one most likely to buy again. It is also based

on patterns like the one that suggests that a two-time buyer is at least twice as likely to buy again as a one-time buyer. Armed with this kind of information, you can craft your campaigns for the highest return on your direct marketing investment. None of this can be done without a database and the appropriate information/data for the database.

SEGMENTATION EXAMPLE

The more information you have on your list members, the better. A database allows you to divide, segment, recombine, and focus your list in a virtually unlimited number of ways. Possibilities for segmentation of your list depend on the amount of information you collect on all those listed.

When the proper information is entered into the database, sorting it according to your marketing objective, target, and specifications becomes easier. Here is an example of different ways a list or database can be sorted. This example is for a communications company:

- Internet connection customers who also have telephone connection
- Internet connection customers who also have satellite dish TV connection
- Internet connection customers only
- Satellite dish TV customers only
- Telephone connection customers only

The most logical collection of information includes anything and everything about a customer's purchase. That is what allows the communications company to segment as in the above example. It enables an office supply store to target marketing to their existing customers. Office supply stores maintain a list of customers according to the type of supplies they purchase. Tailored coupons and special promotions are then mailed, in a very targeted fashion, to those

▼ LIST UNDELIVERABILITY

Sometimes, not all mail is delivered to the entire list. Undeliverable mail is mail not delivered by the postal service because of an incorrect or insufficient address. One of three things happens in this situation. The mail is discarded (happens way more than you think), the mail is forwarded, or the mail is returned to the sender.

A high undeliverable percentage does not always mean a low response. A highly deliverable list does not always mean a high response. There are many other variables at work. That's why direct marketers measure the quality of their list (after sufficient testing) by response, not deliverability. Expect all lists to have some undeliverable percentage. Discuss undeliverable expectations and provisions for undeliverable mail with your list vendor/list broker upon purchase of the list.

The United States Postal Service, www.usps.gov, has identified the following reasons for undeliverable mail.

The first line of the address:

- Address unknown to carrier
- Addressee temporarily away
- Addressee's name misspelled
- Addressee's street address errors
- Missing address line or street name
- No such or incorrect number
- Missing house number/P.O. Box

The last line of the address:

- Incorrect or missing zip code.

Other reasons for undeliverability:

- Change of address on file
- Forward order expired
- Moved, left no address/box closed, left no order
- No such or incorrect apartment, suite, etc.
- Missing or incorrect street directional or suffix
- No such rural route number/rural route box
- Rural route address changed to city-type address
- Incorrect or missing city and/or state
- Address vacant
- No label/illegible label
- No mail receptacle

in that database. Buyers of toner and ink cartridges receive coupons and offers related to toner and ink cartridges. Pocket and file folder customers receive coupons for pocket and file folders, and so on.

Sometimes, if you've been recording frequency of purchase, you can alert your customers to a special offer right before they're likely to buy again or just as they are about to run out of a particular item.

Amazon.com has taken this a step further online. Based on the types of books or music purchased, periodic e-mail messages are sent announcing a new title or new music CD, consistent with each individual consumer's interest. How do they know what the consumer's interests are? Amazon keeps track of every detail of every purchase and stores the information in a large database. They are able to tell how much each consumer spends, how much they buy, how often they buy, and where they spent the most money. This represents a gold mine of information for Amazon and for their selling efforts. Is this approaching a Big Brother environment as George Orwell described in *1984*? Not really. It approaches the best application of database marketing.

A database does more than sort customers to target. It allows you to understand habits, characteristics, and other information about your customers. Finding prospects with similar habits and characteristics improves your chances of a satisfactory response rate in your marketing.

Databases also help you to predict future trends. This might be seasonal volume purchasing or the purchase of a particular item. Knowing this will enable you to plan for the proper service and fulfillment to support trend buying.

Knowing who is buying from you, when they buy, and why they buy is invaluable information.

You can sell more to current customers, and this increase is compounded as you use your database information to target and focus.

LIST PLANNING/LIST SELECTION

By selecting the right lists and then pruning them down using various segmentation criteria, you can target those prospects with the highest likelihood of response—which leads to the highest likelihood of purchase. Being selective, as the following example shows, will increase response rates while reducing mailing and printing costs, making the marketing more efficient, more targeted, and more direct.

A marketer starts with a universal list of one million names. From that, the list is reduced to 750,000 names with a geographic segmentation. Because the marketer in this case has defined her ideal client, she uses the criteria to compare to the 750,000 names. Because some of the names don't match her ideal client criteria, the segmented list quickly narrows by 200,000, down to 550,000.

In this example, the marketer had information about who on the list had made purchases within the past zero to two years and the past two to five years. Eliminating those who had purchased within the past two to five years reduced the list by another 200,000, down to 350,000.

Other factors such as brand loyalty and creditworthiness eliminated another 100,000 names, leaving 250,000 refined, targeted, prime prospects to mail to. The results in this case were that 6 percent responded directly to the offer, with 1 percent calling a toll-free number or visiting a web site.

This clearly shows the benefits of using database information and segmentation techniques to effectively achieve direct marketing objectives.

TARGETING YOUR DIRECT MARKETING

The whole purpose of defining your target market is to find people who have a need for your product or service or a want. "Everybody" is not a target market.

People with common characteristics, habits, desires, and activities that stand out from a total group represent a market. If these common characteristics, habits, desires, and activities are shared by people who will buy your product or services, then they represent a target market.

Targeting involves determining who buys what, why they buy it, and where they buy it. Identifying these markers is essential to your marketing and using your resources in the most efficient way possible.

Target Market Considerations

People with common characteristics, habits, desires, and activities that are from those of a total group represent a target market. Here are the primary points to consider for each of these components.

Characteristics. Characteristics are also sometimes defined as the demographics of a market. Age, income, occupation, and ethnicity are demographic characteristics that can describe a market. Usually characteristics are measurable statistics. They are the questions the U.S. census taker asks.

Habits. Habits or lifestyles describe what your target market likes. Do they like less filling or more taste, or do they like vivid colors and loud music? Habits are sometimes referred to as psychographics and relate to values, beliefs, and lifestyles.

Desires. Desires represent the demands or expectations a target market has. Do they go first class in everything they buy, or are they always looking for something on sale? Do they value delivery and availability or price and quality? What do they really want?

Activity. Activity describes the typical practices of those in a target market. Do they buy books once a week and only drink socially at a dinner party? Do they always take a spring-break vacation to the South or shop at particular food store weekly? Do they do their own taxes and financial planning, or do they seek the help of a paid professional?

Geography. One more distinguishing factor about a target market is geography, the location of those who purchase from you. Geography is where your prospects do business and where you will sell to. Are you global? Do you have a territory? Can you only serve a particular county, state, or region?

Once the target market is defined, you are ready to take aim with your marketing message.

Target Audience Specifications

It is a fact that the more precise your target is, the greater the number of responses your campaign/mailing will generate. Precisely targeting your market means defining the characteristics, demographics, and geography of your target market.

Target market specification example:

Married homeowners, with two or more children, whose income is over $75,000/year in a particular zip code area.

Taking this list specification to a list broker will result in a "count"—the number of prospects on a list available for rent or purchase by you, the marketer. Negotiate accordingly for multiple uses of a rented list. It will take more than one contact to a prospect to generate a satisfactory response.

DIRECT MARKETING TARGET CHECKLISTS

Now that you know everything you need to know about your direct mail target and related lists, the question remains as to how you will use all the information gained. Use the handy checklist in Figure 2.5 to help implement the targeting and list portion of your direct marketing campaign. The checklist will take you right up to the point of campaign execution.

Target Market Worksheet

The purpose of the worksheet in Figure 2.6 is not only to define your target market but also to pin down and refine as precisely as possible whom you will target with your marketing. In direct marketing, precision wins out.

Having the answers to all these components and questions will provide you with the information to drill down and refine your target market with the greatest of precision. The more complete your answers and thoughts are, the more precise your target market will be. The more precise your target definition is, the higher response rate you can expect from your marketing campaigns.

FIGURE 2.5 **Target List Checklist**

- ❏ Decide on a tentative target market.
- ❏ Define the target market as precisely as possible.
- ❏ Find catalogs, magazines, and reports that serve your target market.
- ❏ Locate the publication's list manager.
- ❏ Inquire into purchasing or renting a list.
- ❏ Investigate usage conditions.

- ❏ If no list is directly available, contact a list broker.
- ❏ Define list specifications with a list broker.
- ❏ Obtain a count of list members fitting this specification.
- ❏ Run costs on the count, selects, and overlays.
- ❏ Establish total campaign costs using this cost component, and take to the next step of campaign implementation.

FIGURE 2.6 **Target Market Worksheet**

What do I sell? _____

_____

What are the three top benefits that I offer? _____

_____

CONTINUED

FIGURE 2.6   Target Market Worksheet

What am I really selling? _____
_____

Who typically buys this product or service? _____
_____

For a business-to-business

What industries are likely prospects for my products or services? _____

Identify primary SIC codes of targeted businesses? _____

What are the secondary related SIC codes of targeted businesses? _____

What size are the companies? _____

Sales dollars _____

Number of employees _____

Location/geography _____

Years in business _____

Who in the company buys the products or services? _____

    C-level officers _____

    Purchasing manager _____

    Department head/supervisor _____

    Actual user _____

What are some trade associations that the businesses might belong to? _____

Identify publications of the trade. _____

Is the business:

    Conservative or flashy? _____

    Prominent or well-known? _____

    Established or start-up? _____

    Community-oriented or national in scope? _____

For consumers

Identify the age group that the product or service is designed for. _____

Who uses the product/service? _____

What are the income levels of consumers? _____

What is the geographic location? _____

CONTINUED

FIGURE 2.6	Target Market Worksheet

Where is the product/service purchased? _____

Are customers married? Single? _____

Do they have any children? _____

What is their education level? _____

Do they own or rent? _____

What publications do they read? _____

— CHAPTER 2 SUMMARY —

▶ The people who you want to see your message are the targets of your direct mail.

▶ Your target market is your list (or lists) that you develop.

▶ Your list is a compilation of the names, addresses, and other contact information of people or companies to whom you will market.

▶ No matter how attractive your marketing vehicle looks, how bold and attention-getting the headline, or how valuable and irresistible your offer, if it doesn't reach the right people, direct marketing cannot do its job and will not be successful in meeting your marketing objectives.

▶ No single list strategy will guarantee success. But once you find one or parts of one that work, keep marketing to it until response dwindles. When this happens, move on to a new list, or add new names to it.

▶ People whose common characteristics, habits, desires, and activities stand out from an overall group constitute a market. If these commonalities are shared by people who are likely to buy your product or services, then these individuals comprise your target market.

▶ Aside from the internal lists of customers and past customers, there are external sources of lists. These external lists may be purchased or rented, and can be obtained directly from the company or organization whose list you want.

▶ The best list for your purposes is one that matches exactly the description of your target market. Usually there are lists that come close to your definition. Working together with a list vendor or list broker can help you precisely identify your target market while at the same time developing list specification.

▶ Because the list is the most important component in your campaign, it is wise to test, regardless of how similar the lists appear to be.

▶ Database marketing is based on the fact that 80 percent of business will come from 20 percent of your customers. Selling more to existing customers while also finding these 20 percent is a goal of database marketing. Finding customers and prospects similar to these 20 percent is also a goal.

▶ RFM is a behavior-based model that analyzes how recently a customer has purchased, how frequently he or she has purchased, and how much has been purchased. Predictions are then based on this behavior.

▶ By selecting the right lists and then pruning them down using various segmentation criteria, you can target those prospects with the highest likelihood of response—which will lead to the highest likelihood of purchase.

The Marketing Vehicle

ONE OF THE FOUR PRIMARY COMPONENTS of direct marketing is the marketing vehicle. Essentially, this is the component that defines how you will reach your targeted prospect. Direct marketing is not just direct mail, and even in today's electronic world, it is not just direct e-mail. Both are primary strategies but certainly not the only ones. There are many different media and formats to consider when developing a direct marketing campaign:

- *Direct mail.* This is the obvious vehicle, and the one that most people think is synonymous with direct marketing. Simply stated, direct mail is printed matter prepared for soliciting business or contributions and mailed directly to individuals. Direct mail is considered one of the most cost-effective ways to market, so there will be considerable emphasis on it here.
- *Direct e-mail.* This is almost the same as direct mail except in electronic form; electronic messages prepared for soliciting business or contributions are e-mailed directly to individuals. Direct e-mail is a format for e-mail-based campaigns in which stand-alone marketing messages are sent to a targeted list of recipients. This medium is very cost effective and considered to be direct marketing without printing or stamps.
- *Catalogs.* Dictionaries define a catalog as a complete enumeration of items arranged systematically with descriptive details, or a pamphlet or book that contains such a list. To take this further, the items are usually products, and the products are usually similar in one fashion or another. The good news about catalogs is your ability to market (directly) many items with one vehicle.
- *Telemarketing.* If direct marketing is marketing that directly asks for an order or a response, then telemarketing clearly falls into this category. Nothing fancy here. Telemarketing is the marketing of goods by telephone. There

must be a reason you are bombarded by telemarketing calls during dinner or other times throughout your day. The reason is that this form of direct marketing works, and it works in a profitable way for those businesses and organizations using it. It's still part of the direct-marketing numbers game and is a viable direct marketing strategy.

- *TV and radio.* The best examples of TV direct marketing are the many infomercials you have been exposed to. Just think of Suzanne Somer's ThighMaster or George Foreman's grill. Radio infomercials and radio-response advertising also carry a direct aspect. It's direct marketing if you are soliciting a response or purchase and not worrying about building a brand or awareness. More on this in the following pages.
- *Other direct marketing vehicles.* Those mentioned above make up 95 percent of all direct marketing. There are still other marketing vehicles that solicit a direct-response. Postcard decks, Sunday supplements in newspapers (inserts), take-one brochures, or fliers at the point of purchase and more.

These are just the most common ones. The simple definition of a direct marketing vehicle is that it is targeted for the purpose of soliciting a response. The different types of direct marketing are only limited by a marketer's imagination.

DIRECT MAIL

Direct mail is a means of direct communication that involves sending a marketing message directly to a targeted list of prospects, most times using the U.S. Postal Service (USPS) to distribute the message.

Using the USPS means that your message ends up in your prospect's mail piles, not in the mass communication environment that may or may not hit your target, like traditional advertising.

Direct mail is historically the cornerstone of direct marketing. Even with the internet and alternative forms of direct marketing, direct mail continues to be the workhorse.

It must be a workhorse. Just look at the mail that individuals and companies receive every day. According to the USPS, Americans spend in excess of $528 billion in response to direct mail marketing. The Direct Marketing Association's *2001 Statistical Fact Book* tells us that over 25 percent of the U.S. population orders merchandise or services by mail. This number is staggering and represents a business opportunity for any business venturing into direct mail marketing.

Direct Mail Statistics

Despite some major distractions for direct marketers in 2003, United States spending on direct mail rose to $48.6 billion, up 5.6 percent compared to $46 billion in 2002. Spending for 2004, was forecasted to exceed $51 billion. Some $29.2 billion was spent marketing to consumers and another $19.5 billion to businesses, according to the Direct Marketing Association. These trends are forecasted to continue through 2005. Of the 19 promotion tactics listed in the 2004 *Industry Trends Report*, marketers said they spent the most on direct mail (41.7 percent of total spending).

Sales generated by direct mail totaled $689.3 billion in 2003 compared to $634.4 billion in 2002. B-to-C sales reached $423.8 and B-to-B totaled $265.5, the DMA found.

A study published by the Graphic Arts Marketing Information Service (GAMIS) in mid-2004, a special-interest group of the Printing Industries of America and Graphic Arts

FIGURE 3.1   U.S. Marketing Media Expenditures in 2004

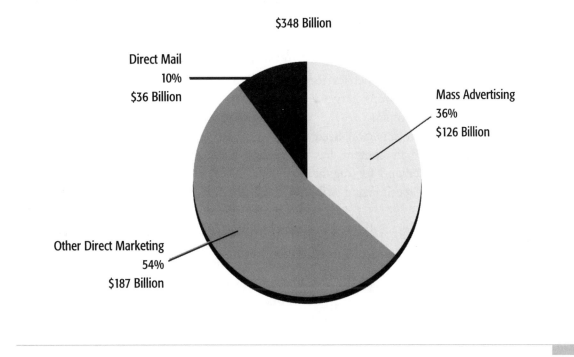

$348 Billion

Direct Mail
10%
$36 Billion

Mass Advertising
36%
$126 Billion

Other Direct Marketing
54%
$187 Billion

Technical Foundation, provided an in-depth look at the future of direct mail. This new GAMIS study completed by Kubas Consultants, Toronto, Canada, provided market size estimates, industry trends and demand forecasts through 2010, as well as insights into advertisers' attitudes and use of direct mail.

According to Kubas, direct mail will represent about $36 billion, slightly less than the DMA study, or 10 percent of all U.S. media and marketing expenditures in 2004. (See Figure 3.1.) Direct mail expenditures will continue to experience above-average growth, projected at 5.6 percent per year in real terms between 2004 and 2007. In Canada, 2004 direct mail expenditures are projected to be $1.8 billion in Canadian dollars, or $1.4 billion in U.S. dollars, based on an exchange rate of 0.74 Canadian per U.S. dollar.

Canadian real annual expenditure growth rates are forecast to be 3.3 percent through 2007.

Research from the Direct Marketing Association indicates that sales effectiveness of direct mail per-dollar-of-expenditure continues to grow, and continues to outperform direct marketing overall, measured the same way. The GAMIS study supports DMA's findings and reveals that, over the past five years, direct mail volumes and expenditures have continued to grow despite the internet, despite online marketing, and even despite a weakening in consumer response rates. One explanation for this is that direct mail's sales effectiveness and return on investment have continued to strengthen.

The study noted that advertisers strongly focus on improving returns on their marketing dollars invested. Direct mail is known to deliver an attractive Return On Marketing Dollars (ROMD), and offers a mechanism by which to measure results. The research study also revealed two other areas of emphasis among direct marketers:

- Targeting has been improved through database management and related metrics to reach specific individuals, groups, targets, segments, and types of customers.
- Emphasis on delivering more personalized and customized direct mail content has increased. As a result, demand for digital printing and variable data imaging will increase.

Advertisers will increasingly look to commercial printers to handle most elements of direct mail production and processing, from preparation and printing all the way to complex one-to-one, targeted direct mail campaigns, including distribution and delivery.

Direct mail gets read. In a 2003 survey published in *Advertising Age* citing Lightspeed Research, it was reported that direct marketing does the best job of providing a high return on marketing dollars, with a five-to-one margin over media ads.

Survey respondents said this is what does the best job for them in terms of ROI:

- Direct marketing: 59 percent
- Media: 11 percent
- Coupons: 10 percent
- Sales promotion: 8 percent
- Event marketing: 3 percent
- Public relations: 3 percent
- Other: 6 percent

Finally, although U.S. postal issues are a concern at the time of writing, the general consensus is that industry efforts will be successful in bringing about reform and reducing the threat of huge postage increases.

The bottom line to all this research is that despite do-not-call lists, Can-Spam restrictions, and other reforms, direct mail still remains popular with marketers and consumers alike.

It is because of this popularity that some have described direct mail as one of the most lucrative marketing techniques known to the business world. Aside from that, it has been the springboard for many other supporting businesses and professionals: copywriters, list brokers, list and database managers, graphic designers, mail processing houses, etc., creating a whole industry and a subsegment of marketing.

Direct mail comes to us in all shapes, sizes, and colors. It arrives in the form of fliers, postcards, letters, and catalogs. Some of it is creatively disguised as overnight mail, awards, and winning sweepstakes entries. It must be a workhorse, or we wouldn't still be coming home every day to the junk vs. love mail sorting ritual that everyone goes through. And these companies that keep mailing to us are making money—further indication that direct mail is a workhorse in all marketing. Direct mail continues to be used by marketers because the cost is relatively low compared to other marketing choices, such as advertising. Adding a direct mail component to your marketing will, if done right, add to your bottom line.

Mail Order History

There are records of regular mail runs between New York and Boston that date back to the 1600s. There are stories and records of Ben Franklin's mail involvement in the 1700s. This development included the establishment of postage rates, postal routes, and home delivery. This new communication and distribution system soon caught on for not only correspondence but also for the purchase and delivery of goods.

Although this purchasing and delivery of goods started during the colonial and Revolutionary War periods, the first true mail-order houses were established 100 years later in the late 1800s. At that time, the opportunity to sell and deliver to American farmers in remote areas was recognized. It was difficult for farmers to find high-quality merchandise at prices they could afford. Local merchants and retailers could not fill this bill. Their offerings were limited and expensive.

Aaron Montgomery Ward recognized this opportunity. He went straight to the largest farm organization at the time, the National Grange, to supply the much-wanted and much-needed goods. In 1872 he formed the first mail-order house.

Based in Chicago, Ward sold goods ordered by catalog to farmers all over the Midwest. Soon after, Richard W. Sears and A. C. Roebuck joined in on the existing opportunity.

Farmers liked the large selection of goods that local merchants could not offer. These same farmers also liked the convenience factor of mail order—much the same benefit that drives mail order today. Orders could be placed in mailboxes and goods could be delivered by mail carriers days later.

Fast-forward to the 20th century. Mail order has grown in popularity. Mail order, or shopping by mail, saves time and enables people to avoid crowded shopping centers. Toll-free numbers and credit card acceptance have fueled this popularity.

It is these roots that grew into face-to-face selling of merchandise via the establishment and growth of retail stores. These roots further spread to direct marketing today. The same selling techniques, now applied to direct marketing, are used to sell information, technology products, services, memberships, and just about anything bought and sold in person.

It is these "interest" and "convenience" factors that drive those who buy through mail order to continue doing so. Retailers and marketers try not to miss an opportunity to notify these "interested" customers about new products, using mail to communicate with them. These premises form the foundation of direct marketing through the mail on a continuous basis.

Junk Mail

When you hear the term "junk mail," what do you think of? Junk mail has joined the lexicon of generic associations like, Coke®, Kleenex®, and Xerox®.

Most people associate junk mail with the pile of mail they receive every day. You typically find junk mail, bills, magazines, catalogs, letters, and other items of interest in your mailbox. Wait! Mentioned in that list was "items of interest." If there is interest in a particular mail piece is it in fact junk mail? What if you are interested, but others aren't? Is it junk mail to them, but not to you? What if others receive items of interest to them that you are not interested in? Is this now junk mail to you and not to them?

The formal definition of junk mail according to *Webster's Dictionary* is "third-class mail, consisting of advertising and often addressed to resident or occupant."

While this formal definition can apply to junk mail, it is not all-inclusive.

What if third-class mail consisting of advertising and often addressed to resident or occupant is of interest to the recipient, catches his attention, or prompts a purchase or response? Is this, then, still junk mail? It conforms to *Webster's* definition.

Along with from the generic connotations, junk mail is also mail that is of no interest to the recipient. It is mail that did not hit its intended target.

Clearly, we all have different definitions of what is junk and what is not. To prevent your mail from being considered "junk", you must send it (as much as possible) to those who you know will be interested in what you have to say. In order to do this, you must understand your prospect in all facets and segment your target into those interested in your offer.

Furthermore, to stay out of the junk-mail category, the mailing piece must prompt action. If the piece is interesting and action is postponed, the probability of the recipient later picking up that piece to act upon it is very slim. Chances are it will end up in a pile somewhere, covered up with other mail or papers, mixed in with junk mail, and eventually discarded into the recycling bin or trash. Prompt, immediate action would have prevented this.

What Direct Mail Can Do for You

In today's constantly cluttered marketing environment, direct mail still offers one of the best ways to reach your target market and interact with them, almost on a one-on-one basis.

Direct mail is a one-on-one conversation between you and the person receiving it. This conversation is usually designed to be a selling conversation. You control the message, and you control who gets the message. No other marketing medium is as targeted. Keep this one-on-one conversation in mind when "talking" to your prospect or designing the direct-mail message and identifying the marketing vehicle.

Because this is a conversation with a sales orientation, direct mail is really taking the place of a sales representative. Direct mail becomes your in absentia in sales force. You don't have to worry about what your salesperson might say or do in front of your prospect. You don't have to worry about how you will

really be represented. You control the representation because you control the direct mail. You control this "salesperson."

Direct mail reaches your prospect when you cannot. Maybe all your prospects don't see your ads, don't drive by your signs or place of business, and haven't heard your on hold-message. The viewing of ads, the drive-bys, and visits are usually controlled by your prospects.

On the other hand, keeping in touch via direct mail and putting your message in front of your prospect is under your control and may be done at whatever frequency you wish. This, coupled with targeting, makes direct mail precise.

Successful direct mail relies on four things:

1. The list—the target; your market
2. The offer—the incentive; the deal
3. The vehicle—the attention-getter; the physical format
4. The placement—the incentive; timing and frequency

Direct Mail Advantages—The Benefits

There are reasons why so many goods and services are sold via direct mail. There are reasons why both small and large businesses use direct mail. There are reasons that direct mail is so popular with so many. Take a look at the advantages.

Targetability. You choose with whom you want to communicate in direct mail. You choose who you want on your list and who you want to zero in on with your message and offer. Unlike advertising, direct mail is sent only to those you target. You try to target those most likely to respond.

A hairdresser is not going to send out information on styling to those who are bald. A lawn-mowing company is not going to entice apartment dwellers to sample its latest and greatest lawn mower. Snow-blowing equipment companies don't have Florida residents on their direct mail target list. A local pizza delivery company won't have residents from two states away on its targeted mailing list. You get to pick the demographics, geographies, and other important characteristics of those receiving your mail.

When purchasing a list from a list broker or list company, these choices are spelled out in your specifications. The more precisely you can narrow the characteristics of your target, the more successful your mailing campaign will be. No other form of marketing is as targeted as direct mail.

Measurability. Measurement often poses as a challenge to direct marketers. How many people really hear your radio commercial? How many people purchase your product or service as a result of those radio commercials? Measuring these outcomes is difficult at times for most marketers.

Measuring other forms of mass marketing is equally challenging.

Measurement is critical in managing your bottom line. Direct mail is very measurable. You generally know how many pieces you mail out and what each piece costs to develop and deliver. You generally can track how many responses you got from particular offers or messages presented in your direct mail. An analysis and quick calculation of pieces sent and responses received show you the return on your direct mail investment. This is much more measurable than marketing that is more "mass" in nature. This measurability allows you to make the proper decisions regarding your marketing. Should you do more, should you change your target, or should you revise your message and offer? Without measurement, these questions go unanswered and your marketing could wander aimlessly while costing you money.

Once you find a campaign, a vehicle, a message, or an offer that works (as a result of this measuring), then repeat it. On the other hand, if your measurements determine that something isn't working, fix it or get rid of it, and move on to a new campaign.

Carrying out these measurements also keeps you accountable to your own marketing. Accountability is a good marketing habit to develop.

Reliability. Direct mail is considered reliable. The post office rate of successful delivery is very high, especially when compared to e-mail and mass marketing vehicles that may or may not reach their intended targets. There are many things that can be done to ensure that delivered direct mail is read and acted upon, increasing its reliability

Effective marketing. Direct mail is effective. Because of the repetitive nature of a consistent direct mail program, and the reliability discussed earlier, you are likely to make enough impressions on your prospects to cause them to take some kind of desired action or respond in the fashion that you wish. This action many times is a direct purchase. Obtaining more money from those purchases than what you spent on a direct mail program makes it profitable. This is done more in direct mail than most other forms of marketing, making it one of the most effective vehicles. Add to this the targetability and other advantages discussed here that other forms of marketing can't claim, and you have effective marketing.

Personalization. Direct mail can be personalized. You can't do that with a radio ad. Nor can you, personalize a newspaper or magazine ad. Personalization is a definite plus.

Take the case of direct mail letters. The more specific you are in addressing the envelope, the more likely it'll get opened. Rather than addressing your envelope to "Occupant," "Resident," or "Dear Friends," use actual names. Take this beyond the envelope and use it in the body of letters as well. Also include things like company information, family information, and other personal references. The more *personalized* your envelope, letter, and marketing are, the better chance you have of getting your pieces opened, read, and acted upon.

Personalized reply cards and letters will ALWAYS outpull nonpersonalized mailings. But you have to be sure to use personalization that does not appear to be a mass communication. Don't overdo the personalization. This looks like very sales-oriented hype, and screams *advertising* immediately.

The real goal of personalization is to gain your customer's or prospect's attention. Attention leads to response and eventually increased sales. You want to gain this attention because your average prospect and customer is barraged with thousands of marketing messages each day.

Specifically addressing your prospects will do this. Instead of receiving a generic direct mail piece, using the recipient's own name makes it obvious that your message is for him alone, increasing response. You aren't nearly as likely to discard something if *your name is on it* and the offer is *for you.*

Personalization can be as simple as using the recipient's name in the salutation to as sophisticated as changing blocks of text according to the individual's past purchasing patterns. Higher levels of personalization do add to the cost of the mailing, so you'll want to consider this when projecting potential return on your marketing dollars.

Levels the playing field. When receiving direct mail, you many times don't know if the mail came from a large company or a small one. If it addresses your wants and needs and makes you interested enough to take some type of action, it doesn't matter the size of the company. But if you are a small company, you don't want to get pushed around by the big guys.

You don't need a direct mail department, mail processing center, or even a mailroom to build your business with direct mail. One-person businesses and professionals get business all the time through direct mail campaigns that fit their budgets. Small retail operations, start-up businesses, and nonprofit organizations gain as well through the use of direct mail. In these cases, the size of the business or organization does not matter. Small organizations can compete with large ones in the direct-mail arena. The playing field is clearly level when using direct mail.

Sells when you can't be there. Direct selling to prospects done on a repetitive basis is most effective. Being in front of your prospect can become expensive and time-consuming. It represents another touch to a prospect and contributes the repetitiveness that is needed to make a sale or extend a relationship. It communicates your messages, makes your offers, and allows for response, all without you being there. Direct mail sells for you when you can't be there.

Easy to test. The three ways to make sure your campaign will be effective are to test, test, and test again. This form of marketing lends itself testing better than almost any other. Sending small test lots to target markets and changing one variable at a time, with the ensuing measurement, proves which test variables are most effective. These may include headline, the format of the mailing, the day it was sent out, the frequency of the mailings, colors, and messages. The list of test variables is quite extensive. When you find something that tests positive and is over and above the control lot, stick with it until you find another vehicle that beats the control. Direct mail is very conducive to ongoing tests.

Low profile (when needed) marketing. Broadcast a mass-media commercial on television and the whole broadcast area has the opportunity to see you and your message. This includes your competition. While it's not as big an advantage, you still have that opportunity to market without being in plain view of your competition. Direct mail allows that. You pick the list. It's not mass media, and chances are slim that your competitor will see your marketing vehicle.

Pass around/shelf life. Direct mail is a physical entity that your prospect receives. There is still a good number of marketing recipients who want to hold something tangible in their hands. Sometimes direct mail is set aside to refer to another day by the recipient or to pass along to an associate. This is especially true with catalogs. The more people who pass around your mailing or save it for later, the more effective your total campaign will be. You can't do this with a radio commercial or a billboard.

What Direct Mail Is Not

Not all marketing is direct marketing. One example is a newsletter. Many newsletters sent out by businesses are filled with personnel information, customer profiles, photos, event information, and employee recognition. One editor describes content of the company newsletter as, "babies, bowling and birthdays." While there is nothing wrong with babies, bowling, and birthdays, there is nothing direct about them from a marketing point of view. Many companies continue to send these kinds of newsletters and say

they are doing direct marketing. I'm sure their response to these is nil.

There is a PR and awareness component to this, but unless a newsletter or any other form of marketing is providing an offer and a response mechanism for that offer, it is not direct marketing. Yes, it will contribute to top-of-mind awareness, but that isn't the primary purpose of direct marketing. The goal here is to make the newsletter work harder and act as a direct marketing piece. This can be done by including a special-offer coupon or an offer of information for a new product or service. That's the essence of direct marketing. Absent those components, your marketing or mailings are not considered direct marketing.

Direct Mail Disadvantages

Response rates. It's hard to imagine something that that fails 98 percent of the time or even 99 percent as being still successful. But 1 to 2 percent response rates translate into success. More and more of this 98 percent is thrown away unopened as consumers and get more savvy about what is being sent to them or as they are bombarded with so many other marketing messages. A lot of times, people will only open mail from known people, companies, or organizations they already have a relationship with. This makes direct mail much more effective with current customers than in gaining new customers.

If your average sale is not enough to recoup your expenses at this response rate or to make money, direct mail at a 99 percent failure rate is not for you. Identifying your break-even points and expected response rates will determine if this choice of marketing is right for you.

Junk mail perception. Direct mail can be seen as junk mail. Whether right or wrong, the perception of direct mail as junk mail is real for most recipients. Junk mail is covered more extensively in this book, but for now let's say it is mail that does not reach, interest, or motivate prospects. Our culture has responded to this with do-not-call lists, spam filters, and all the related privacy policies.

Up-to-date list information. Although lists are bought and sold every day, there is still an issue with getting up-to-date information from list vendors and brokers. This especially is true as more and more consumers try to get their names removed from lists. The lag time from the removal request to the point of delivery for a purchased list can be relatively long. This turnover contributes to outdated lists, which results in ineffective mailings and inefficient marketing.

Costs. There are still those who view direct mail as an expense rather than an investment. If you get $1,000 in returns and your cost is less than $1,000, your campaign or mailing is profitable. Taking into consideration the lifetime value of a client, your campaign or mailing is even more profitable. There still are cost components to manage as you try to increase your profits. Paper, printing, and postage costs are all on the rise. Database management, list, and fulfillment costs are all on the rise. Cost increases require the marketer to manage campaigns closer, and test more to determine optimum conditions. These can be viewed as disadvantages. Done right and managed close to the belt, direct mail can still be a very viable marketing option for you.

DIRECT MAIL FORMATS

Selecting the right format for your direct mail program isn't as easy as it may seem. You have to look at your budget and who you are trying to reach. Some target audiences prefer one format over another. Some formats are highly effective while at the same time very expensive to produce. The other expense consideration related to format is postage. Generally, the formats of your direct mail will fall into one of four categories:

1. Letters
2. Postcards
3. Self-mailers
4. Dimensional mailing

There are then an infinite number of variations related to size, shape, color, etc., within these general categories.

Finding the right basic mailing format that consistently outperforms others should be a subject of testing. You are probably beginning to recognize the importance of the testing component in a direct mail campaign. That component is as important in designing format as much as determining the right headline or the right offer.

These formats will be reviewed in detail before we get to establishing your direct-mail marketing objectives and the planning of your campaign.

Letters

One of the most popular direct marketing vehicles is the letter. The direct mail letter is the most personal form of commercial writing.

Letters date from before the 1500s when goose quills were dipped into homemade dyes (ink) and applied to crude papyrus or parchment-like paper and then folded and sealed with embroidery silk. Such letters were used to warn Britain of the impending Spanish Armada in 1588 and were mentioned by Shakespeare in *King Lear* when Cordelia, the king's daughter, reacted emotionally while reading one. Letters soon assumed the importance that they have today, as a most personal and effective form of communication, second only to conversation.

Letters are used extensively in direct marketing: sales letters, collection letters, announcement letters, follow-up letters, etc. Their use is popular because of their ease of production, their communication potential, and their power to generate a response.

Find your targets, write, and send them a letter, and you are using one of the simplest forms of direct marketing—simple yet extremely effective.

A letter with the right message to the right target will get a response. People love to receive and read stories, stories about personal experiences and human interest. Stories get read, not just skimmed. Letters that get read get responded to.

In direct marketing, the letter is often the central focus of the communication. It could be by itself in an envelope, as part of a direct mail package, or printed within the body of a brochure.

The letter is popular because it is personal and direct. It truly is one-on-one communication. When you are writing a letter, you are truly addressing just one person. Your copy should reflect this, even though it might go to many. Whenever possible, personalization to this one person should be included to reinforce the intimacy. Group salutations should be avoided. Dear Homeowner is OK; less personal but still one-on-one. To All Illinois Homeowners is not effective; it addresses a group. This immediately loses the one-on-one aspect of a letter. Direct mail recipients are discriminate. They like to feel exclusive, as if they are the only one you're talking/writing to. This technique gets more results than writing to groups.

Types of letters. In direct marketing, thousands of types of letters are used in many different kinds of campaigns. Here are a few:

- Sales letter/solicitation letter
- Fundraising letter
- Collection letter
- Announcement letter
- Thank-you letter
- Customer service follow-up letter

The goal of direct-mail letters. In direct marketing, the letter is your sales representative. It is doing the selling job for you. It's your salesperson in absentia. Because of this, you need to be direct, comprehensive, clear, and persuasive. Many times this "salesperson" is the only contact you will have with prospects until they buy your product or service or respond to you.

The goal of letters used as direct marketing vehicles is to get a response. In order to do this, letter copy has to be just right. We will save copy techniques for the section on direct-marketing messages, but some basics are covered here. You will note some similarity to other marketing vehicle fundamentals.

A typical direct mail letter should:

- Grab the attention of the recipient. This is where your primary focus should be. It is important to make your best point first.
- Lead your reader into the body of the copy. Take advantage of the fact that you just caught your reader's attention.
- Clearly communicate what's in it for them, the reader—how he or she will benefit. The keyword here is "clearly." Tell the reader exactly what he or she will get. Be as specific as possible.
- Overcome objections to why he or she should respond now. The first objection to avoid is sounding too much like a pitch or advertisement. Readers will be skeptical and come up with every objection imaginable. Think of as many possible objections as

you can and head them off before they arise. Testimonials, case studies, and endorsements help in this regard.

- Motivate the reader to take action to respond right away. This is what tells you whether your letter had done its job or not. Once the letter is tossed aside or discarded, you miss the opportunity for response. So provide a logical reason for acting now. Tell the reader exactly what you want him or her to do. Don't leave anything to the imagination or risk his or her lack of initiative.

Postcards

A postcard is a single sheet of stiff, heavyweight paper (card stock as it is known in trade circles) with marketing messages, graphics, and related information printed on one or both sides. A postcard can include a mailing address, return address, and a place for postage if it is to be mailed. It can be just about any size, but size does influence postage rates. The post office has guidelines as to acceptable shapes; however, they are introducing new programs that accommodate just about any shape.

Postcards are usually about 8½" by 5½" (half of a standard 8½" by 11" print sheet size) or smaller. Many things influence the response rate in direct mail. The format may or may not, depending on many other factors and variables. This is further support for testing the format as another variable in your campaign testing as you search for optimum response.

When the prospect is already familiar with the marketer's product and minimal information is given to respond to, postcard marketing enjoys good success.

Through recent terrorist activities, we learned that not even our mail is 100 percent safe. When the first terrorist event hit the mail, many companies got very concerned about direct mail programs and how to get their messages to their target markets. Envelopes are of particular concern. Before this problem arose (and even more so now), postcard marketing had proven to be very effective. You will soon learn that the use of postcards in a marketing program or direct mail campaign can be carried out quicker, better, and cheaper than many other direct mail approaches. Doing things quicker, better, and cheaper is sometimes the key to business survival. It is also the key to good business management and can make the difference between survival mode and success. All businesses love to succeed. All businesses think they know what to do, but when it comes to marketing, there is sometimes a lack of interest, a lack of direction, or a lack of a turnkey tool that allows business managers to create high-powered marketing, efficiently. Postcard marketing addresses this and all of the above.

Marketing with postcards is quick, easy, and, you will find, less expensive than many of the traditional advertising, promotional, and marketing vehicles used today.

History of Postcards

The first postcards can be traced back to the late 1800s. The first copyright on a private postcard was issued to John P. Charlton of Philadelphia as early as 1861, and later transferred to his fellow townsman, H. L. Lipman. The early cards were decorated with a border pattern. The first government-issued postcards showed up around 1873. Plain postcards were in use well before that. They were issued by the post offices of various countries with the country's stamp imprinted on them. These early cards were referred to as "Postals." Postcards requiring affixed postage were offered in Austria in 1869. By 1870, picture postcards were being published throughout Europe. Lagging behind Europe were the first American postcards that appeared shortly after that. It is interesting to note that writing on the address side of any postcard was not allowed by law until 1907.

Postcard Advantages

- Targetability
- Stand out in the mail pile
- Can be produced and fulfilled quicker
- Easily tracked
- Less expensive than a direct-mail letter package
- Can generate a response in 90 seconds or fewer.
- Lower postage costs

Postcards are considered the fastest, easiest, most reliable way to dramatically increase your revenue and customer response.

But wait—there's even more good news about postcards. You can't "delete" a postcard. A spam filter will not toss out a postcard. A postcard will not get lost in cyberspace. A postcard does not require an accurate e-mail address. Postcards don't carry electronic viruses.

Next to e-mail, postcards are the most cost-effective marketing vehicles to generate customer response.

Alex Mandossian, managing director of Heritage House Publications and author of *Marketing with Postcards*, says that today the quickest and easiest way marketers can win new customers and influence more referrals is to revert back to the traditional prospecting methods of the "physical world." Postcard marketing is a tested grassroots strategy that does this.

Alex goes on to say that a postcard can generate a direct response in 90 seconds or less:

- Prospect glances at the front, attention-getting postcard side (three seconds).
- Prospect turns over to read return address, (five seconds).
- Prospect reads headline (seven seconds).
- Prospect reads body copy (45 to 60 seconds).
- Prospect takes action if message works (15 seconds).

This can't happen if you add an envelope, envelope-opening, and letter-unfolding to the process. It usually takes the full 90 seconds just to do this.

This can't happen if you have a boring e-mail subject line that is suspect and subject to a delete button.

Postcard Marketing Benefits

Postcards have many benefits. These benefits will ensure success and profitability to your direct marketing campaign. Once again, some of these benefits are directly related to the direct marketing aspect of postcards; others are not.

- Postcards make for quick communication—there's not usually a lot to read.
- They're easy to send and easy for the recipient as no envelope is required.
- Postcards are less expensive than other marketing pieces as they are economical to produce and less expensive to send.
- Recipients are used to receiving them and report liking them.
- They can be produced in large quantities with the mailing scheduled accordingly.
- Postcards have a higher readership level on both sides.
- They get prospect attention, the sine qua non of a successful campaign.
- Postcards can start relationships.
- Top-of mind awareness is enhanced.
- They can be made graphically attractive.

Uses for Postcards

Postcards are ideal for direct marketing, but they can be used for other types of marketing as well. Let's look at a few other ideas. Some are direct-marketing-related and others are more traditional in nature.

- *Lead generators.* Get people to contact you by offering something for free: information, gift, booklet, sample, consultation, etc.; then collect their contact data for follow-up later.
- *Response mechanism.* Much like internet auto-responders, send a series of postcards outlining different features and benefits of your products and services with irresistible offers to respond to.
- *Consistent message.* Timing is everything in marketing. Mailing postcards on a consistent basis, usually on the same day of the month, takes the guesswork out of when your prospect will be touched by you. Consistency is key.
- *Reduced prices/free offer/discounts.* Entice customers and prospects with a two-for-one offer or percent off or even something free, all with simple postcard messages. Use simple graphics and short sentences for the most impact. This is good use of this vehicle in a direct marketing sense.
- *Up-sell.* Create value opportunities for those who are already customers. Your best prospect is a current customer. Offer something as a "thank you for being a preferred customer," or some value for the purchase of your higher-margin products and services. Postcards communicate this efficiently.
- *Introduction.* Introduce you, yourself company, and your products or services to those who are new to the area, the business, the organization, or simply new to your market. The introduction can be made quickly, while taking advantage of your speed to market.
- *Reminders to reorder.* Customers like to be "taken care of." Letting customers know it's time to reorder something is a great service. "Did you know that you are about to run out of (your product here)? According to our records, it's time to reorder." You will be surprised at how this simple technique can generate business.
- *Invitation to return.* Sometimes we lose customers. This happens for a variety of reasons. It's OK to communicate via postcards, telling former customers that you want them back. Better yet, start before you lose them with a friendly , "We haven't seen you in a while."
- *Web site reminder.* In the world of internet marketing, traditional postcards are used extensively. Sometimes it is just a matter of communicating a web site, "Visit us at www.1-800-inkwell.com," or communicating the look of the home page of a particular site. Use of traditional marketing is widespread in the marketing of online businesses.

▼ POSTCARD DEVELOPMENT TIP

Think of a postcard as an index card (or vice versa). Now write down a headline, benefit points, and any other marketing message on the index card. This is the start of postcard development. From this rough-draft start, you can then give it to a graphic designer for layout, formatting, and preparation for printing.

These are just a few ideas. As you can see, postcard marketing can be the basis of a company's total marketing program or just one more part of a multifaceted program.

The Self Mailer

A self-mailer is anything mailed by itself without an envelope, package, or some other outside component. It can be a simple piece of paper or card stock 8.5" by 11" or smaller folded and usually sealed shut with an adhesive tab.

This format is best suited to product or service marketing where the "personal touch" of a letter in an envelope is not usually necessary for adequate response. A self-mailer can be very efficient with the right market and the right message.

A self-mailer is cheaper than a letter in an envelope. And like all other direct marketing, testing will determine its feasibility and inclusion in a campaign.

Something in an Envelope

There are dozens of sizes and shapes of envelopes to consider when creating a new direct mail package. You can even have them made a custom size. The standard-size envelopes commonly used by direct marketers are:

- Number-10 business envelope (9.5" by 4.125")
- Booklet envelope (6" by 9")
- Catalog envelope (9" by 12")

The most common size is the standard number-10 business envelope, or a standard business envelope. A number-10 envelope may or may not have a window or windows that show some of the contents, including a send-to address. Contents will vary with the type of offer being made, the type of company being marketed, and the target audience being mailed to. Once again, postage rates are affected by size

and weight, so consider this when choosing an envelope.

Number-10 envelopes are standard in the business world. Because of this, many marketers use this size for their campaigns. Recipients are used to receiving this size and may not label a number-10 envelope as "advertising" mail as quickly as other obvious vehicles. The large-size envelopes, like the 6" by 9" booklet or the 9" by 12" catalog, many times will scream "advertising" to the recipient and be discarded unopened.

The 6" by 9" booklet format is great for sending out large, colorful brochures and booklets that are 8.5" by 5.5" in size.

The 9" by 12" catalog format is used often but does have an increased cost associated with it. Notice an 8.5" by 11" document will comfortably fit within the 9" by 12" envelope. One advantage of a larger-size envelope is the display potential for showing product graphics and photos printed right on the envelope or showing through a window.

Selecting common-sized envelopes such as those described here might save you money, but might also get mixed in with everyone else's direct marketing messages and not stand out in the mail pile. Marketers sometimes use custom-sized and designed (and costlier) envelopes to gain immediate attention and prompt opening. Proper campaign testing will determine the feasibility of using a custom envelope with a premium price and justifying its increased cost.

CHOOSING A FORMAT

Choosing the format of your mailing is part of the creative process. It's crucial because it influences how the art, copy, and graphics will come into play and be used. You need to know exactly what vehicle you want to use, because it affects how much space is available to get your message across.

In choosing a format, you want to ask yourself if you are marketing something that needs minimal information communicated or is a fast read. If so, a postcard might be your choice. You might need the personal touch of a letter in an envelope or want something larger to show and tell more about your products and services. All of this needs to be considered when choosing a format (see Figure 3.2), especially if you employ outside help (graphic designers, art directors, agencies, etc.) to craft your campaign.

Oftentimes, the decision of which format to use is driven by your budget and/or purpose. Format considerations need to be determined first before a single word of copy is written or graphics are designed. Format does have a direct impact on the look and feel of the final piece.

| FIGURE 3.2 | Direct Mail Format Worksheet |

What is your mailing objective? _____

What is your target audience used to reading? _____

What do they like to read? _____

What do they want to receive from you? _____

What would interest them? _____

Is it a consumer or business mailing? _____

Will it reach a family member, businessperson, or gatekeeper? _____

What product or service are you marketing? _____

Are you raising funds or communicating information about an event? _____

Do you have a particular identity to communicate in these efforts and campaigns? _____

_____

What competitive influences are present? _____

Is your competition mailing out something similar? _____

What other marketing will the mailing have to compete with to get a share of your recipient's mind? _____

_____

What is your budget? _____

What can you financially and mentally afford to do properly? _____

FIGURE 3.3   **The Most Common Formats**

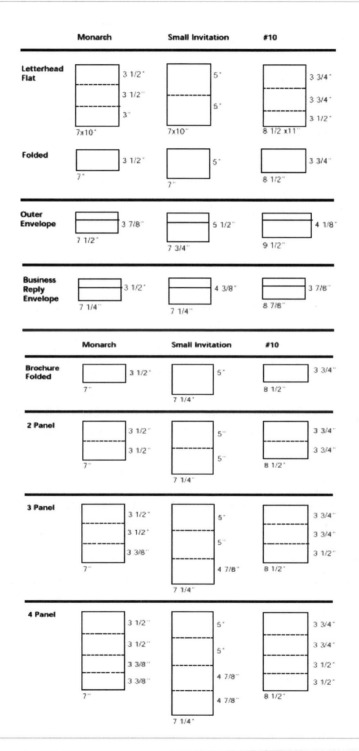

▼ WHAT GETS READ THE MOST

According to a 2001 survey by Vertis Direct Marketing, direct mail recipients are most likely to read mailings from fundraisers. Fifty-five percent of their respondents said they read fundraising mail followed by entertainment mail at 50 percent, subscription-related mail at 42 percent, book and music club mailings at 38 percent, financial information at 36 percent, and automotive mailings at 35 percent.

DIMENSIONAL MAIL

Related to lumpy mail, dimensional mailings are 3-D in nature and not flat. Dimensional mail consists of packages, boxes, tubes, and other three-dimensional packaging. Lumpy mail is usually just a lumpy envelope. Dimensional mail grabs attention quickly and almost always gets opened.

Dimensional-package mailings make a significant impact on response rates. Dimensional mailings stir up curiosity in a recipient. Just think of the times that you received an unexpected package in the mail or via an overnight service. Curiosity and excitement lead to increased responses. A 1993 study at Baylor University found that by using dimensional mailers, response rates go up (when compared to direct mail alone).

The Baylor study tested three groups. Each group member received a different direct-mail vehicle. Group I received an envelope with a sales letter, sales collateral, and a postage-paid business reply card for responding. Group II received an envelope with exactly the same contents as the Group I envelope but also included a promotional product. Group III received the same contents as the other two groups delivered in a box with a die-cut slot to show the address, instead of an envelope. Here are the response rates:

Group I: Sales literature only   1.9 percent

Group II: Sales literature and promotional product   2.1 percent

Group III: Sales literature and promotional product packaged in a box   3.3 percent

These response rates show that the dimensional mail had more than a 50 percent greater pull-power than a plain envelope, with product, and 75 percent more response than just a sales letter with accompanying information.

Now after all is said and done, you still have to revert back to evaluating your return on marketing investment. Dimensional mail unit costs are relatively high. Not only are you paying for more complex packaging (compared to an envelope), but you are paying for the premium in the box and the increased postage to deliver the heavier piece. Despite these apparent drawbacks,, dimensional mailings are still great vehicles for marketing to smaller target markets.

Dimensional mail works well in getting past gatekeepers, as they rarely fall into the junk-mail category. Anything can be put in a box or an expanded package.

When something resembling a package arrives, it looks special and gets special, nonmail attention. Unique packaging stands out, allowing for communication of messages to intended targets.

Dimensional mailings encourage and almost force interactivity. A dimensional mailing can also seem like a gift, envoking an emotional response as well.

Osprey

Osprey, a North Carolina-based company that delivers technology solutions to manufacturers and distributors, wanted to make a strong initial impression on prospects. They worked with Tivoli Partners to create a dimensional mailing campaign.

Their target consisted of just 200 high-level information technology managers and company presidents. Playing off of the client company's name, Tivoli Partners developed the campaign around the "Osprey" theme (see Figure 3.4).

The Osprey is a bird with the ability to see through murky waters; what a great positioning statement! The package consisted of an actual leather-and-brass spyglass with the Osprey logo emblazoned on it. Inside the package was a note that said, "Look closely. Is your business where you want it to be . . ."? The note went on to explain how Osprey could help the business get to where it wanted to be by providing the appropriate technology solutions.

The spyglass sent the message that Osprey could provide the insight necessary for the business to grow. The spyglass was enclosed in a box, complete with bird feathers and straw material. The subliminal message hoped for by Tivoli and Osprey was that the bird had left a gift behind to aid in their vision.

The boxes, marked Extremely Urgent, were delivered via priority mail directly to the recipients.

| FIGURE 3.4 | **Osprey Direct Marketing Package** |

Used with permission, Tivoli Partners, www.tivolipartners.com; Osprey www.osprey us.com.

The offering range for Osprey solutions was between $20,000 and $200,000. Just one sale would more than cover the cost of this mailing and show a high return on the investment of marketing dollars.

The results: Over 30 percent of the prospects booked an appointment with Osprey.

Note: This campaign was an ECHO award finalist, given by the Direct Marketing Association. The ECHO award is the "Oscar" of direct marketing and a much sought-after industry honor recognizing strategy, creativity, and results in the direct marketing industry.

Lumpy Mail at Work

One thing that most, if not all, people open in their mail piles is overnight and priority mail. Also frequently opened is mail that looks like it was urgently delivered, even if it wasn't. Add to this a lumpy package and the open-rate increases significantly. Mark Victor Hansen, coauthor of the *Chicken Soup for the Soul* series of books and many others did just this. A mailing that marketed one of Mark's famous Mega Book University seminars for potential and current authors was recently done in this fashion. The outside envelope had bold red, black, and yellow colors with a full-size picture of an eagle, like you see on many government and post office-related printed pieces. Across the front of the envelope the following was printed in big, bold, can't-miss letters:

Rush Priority Express

Rush to Addressee

Extremely Important

At first glance, the package looked just like something you would get from FedEx, UPS, or USPS. In actuality, there was nothing express, rushed, or prioritized about this mailing other than the sender's personal preferences.

The reverse side said, "Express Document Enclosed," and bore a code number, a rush priority-looking stamp and other official-looking printing. I received this in the mail. I immediately opened the envelope, thinking it was urgent and important. I also wanted to see what made it lumpy, the natural response of most recipients.

I pulled out the sales letter that was part of the package. There in bold letters was this banner headline:

"How to Get All the Customers, Sales, and Revenue You Can Handle . . . Delivered on a Silver Platter"

For any entrepreneur, author, or businessperson, this would certainly grab their attention, create interest, and cause them to continue reading and checking out the lumpy-mail package.

Not wanting to wait any longer after reading the catch headline, I needed to find out what the lump was. It turned out to be a small silver platter! It wasn't plastic or gimmicky. It was a miniature 6- to 7-inch silver, oblong, ornate platter. If nothing else, one could use it for serving small appetizers or desserts.

Not only was the silver platter the common theme throughout, it also served as a hook. It inspired me to read the entire package and remember it. I'm sure the response rate was very high for all the reasons mentioned and for the high-quality product associated with a marketing icon.

CATALOG MARKETING

In 1981, Bill Gates said, "A 640K hard drive ought to be enough for anybody."

In 1899, Charles Duell, commissioner of the U.S. Patent Office proclaimed, "Everything that can be invented has been invented."

In 1943, Thomas Watson, chairman of IBM, predicted, "I think there is a world market for maybe five computers."

In 1876, an internal memo from Western Union concluded, "The telephone has too many shortcomings to be seriously considered as a means of communication. The device is of no value to us."

And finally, it was once predicted, "The popularity of the internet will reduce the amount of printed direct mail, especially catalogs."

Tell this last quote to the area mail carrier in October, when the load is backbreaking, and he or she will put it in the same category as the first four.

The Start of the Catalog Age

Almost anything can be sold through a catalog. That's what Aaron Montgomery Ward thought in 1872, when he worked out the arrangement with the National Grange—America's largest farming organization—to offer 163 items of merchandise under the title "The Original Wholesale Grange Supply House."

That's what a train station agent in Minnesota, Richard Warren Sears, was thinking when he did something in 1886 that changed the world.

One day a shipment of watches arrived at a train depot for a local jeweler who refused to accept them for one reason or another. They sat on the loading dock for a time, until the enterprising Sears noticed them, made a deal for them, and used his telegraph to tell other agents along the train line about them. Offering the watches at a very good price, he was able to sell the watches quickly and efficiently, thereby effectively becoming the world's first long-distance direct marketer.

This venture proved so successful that within the year, Sears quit the railroad business, bought and sold more watches, and started the R. W. Sears Watch Company in Minneapolis, Minnesota. He eventually moved the company to Chicago and hired watchmaker Alvah C. Roebuck.

In 1892, Sears changed the company name to the now famous, Sears, Roebuck and Company, and began to sell mail-order merchandise other than watches.

Sears used a catalog to sell his merchandise. He wrote the catalog himself, and it quickly expanded in size. He offered excellent prices, credit policies, and guarantees. By 1894, the catalog had grown to five hundred pages of short and simple product descriptions, along with detailed and compelling graphics.

Little did he know at the time that he was to set the direct marketing world on fire. His dreams, aspirations, and initial ideas continue to flourish into the 21st century.

Catalogs Today . . . the Age Continues

If you have any doubt about this, just look at your own daily mail pile and take a look at what is there. You see the monthly or quarterly Victoria's Secret catalog. You see the latest gadgets from Sharper Image. You gaze at the delectable fruit sold by Harry and David. You see the latest casual fashions from Lands' End and you see how many more computer models are available and the ensuing price wars in the latest Dell computer catalog. So much for Thomas Watson's prediction in 1943. So much for the prediction of the internet replacing catalogs. The opposite has happened. Retailers have made catalogs a very important part of their direct marketing mix and have in turn used them to support online sales.

Catalogers are using their print marketing to drive consumers to their web sites. Catalog recipients grab their stack of mail, peruse their catalogs of choice, and head right to their laptop or desktop computer to place their orders.

A catalog can be not only the heart of a company's marketing but the heart of its whole business. Antropologie, a Philadelphia retail store and catalog marketer, does not advertise. It spends its entire ad budget on catalog design and circulation. Eighty percent of its online purchases are driven by its print catalogs.

From a direct marketing point of view, catalogs generate direct sales, or in the case of readers jumping on the internet to place orders, they generate leads. Both catalogs and now web sites are direct marketing vehicles that sell related multiple products; they're quite different than most other direct marketing.

The Catalog Entrepreneur

Just the mere mention of the word catalog and many people immediately think of that classic Sears and Roebuck catalog. We grew up with it, our parents grew up with it, and their parents experienced its evolution as well. It is ingrained in our culture. Today, its mention brings forth images of glossy photos, swimsuit supermodels, and specialized niche products. While this is a large part of what is seen by the masses, catalogs are much more than this, and much less. Catalogs are used by many small businesses as much as other direct marketing vehicles. All you need are a few products, a targeted audience, and a professional-looking catalog online or off, and you will get business. It's not always large layouts and the expenses that go with it. They are used by the entrepreneurial masses daily.

Successful Catalogs

A great catalog is obviously one that sells a lot of products and services for your company while making a profit. Just like all other direct marketing, a successful catalog must reach the right audience with the right message, establish brand and product differentiation while grabbing attention, clearly present the product, make offers, communicate benefits, motivate the buyer to take action, and finally, end up with an order.

Who Uses a Catalog?

A targeted audience is really the start of any direct marketing, and that certainly is true when considering using a catalog. Today's catalog market is made up of many, many specialized niche product catalogs. In order to succeed, and by definition to be niched, the products have to be sold to a very tightly defined target audience. This also usually means that the products aren't always available from common mass-merchandise outlets. If this is you, then chances are good that selling your products in a catalog will be a successful venture.

If your target market is also beyond your local geographic area or beyond your local place of business, a catalog will work. Using them as direct mail pieces, you can reach an audience as close or as far away as your postal service will deliver. Catalogs are ideal direct marketing pieces that also can take advantage of selling cycles and seasons. If you are a landscaper or garden/flower seed company, for instance, you can time the delivery of your catalogs to coincide with the spring planting season. If your products are conducive to gift-giving, you can time the catalog to land in your target market's mailbox right before the holiday gift-buying season. You can do this with other direct mail vehicles, but nothing can show your products, offer a wide range of your products, and realize orders as well as a catalog.

What Products Can Be Sold in a Catalog?

If you had asked this question of Richard Sears in 1886, he would have answered, "Watches." But

20 years later, he would have answered, "Anything anyone will buy." This was his approach as he served outlying farms and those in rural areas who couldn't travel to concentrated shopping areas. This served the groups of people who weren't close to shopping. Today, this approach is not as practical. We are all surrounded by malls, stores of all types, and specialty outlets. Today's successful catalogs serve very targeted audiences with niched products geared to particular needs and wants. Everything from fruit to electronic gadgetry to stylish lingerie is now sold effectively with this direct marketing vehicle of choice.

Producing a Catalog

To put out the latest Victoria's Secret catalog or a display of Sharper Image's new gadgets is very costly from a photography, copy, and production standpoint. For entrepreneurs and the small-business operation, the production of a catalog does not have to be as expensive or elaborate as the former. With today's digital photography technology, many businesses take their own photos. Digital photography fits right in and is very cost-effective. There are many opportunities to hire interns, students, and freelancers to write copy, draw illustrations, and even format and lay out catalogs. Catalog copy can be as simple as short, simple descriptions of what you are photographing. Laying all of these components in today's consumer-friendly print layout programs and working with local printers will make your production of a catalog very feasible and cost-effective. Sure, there can be a lot more to this (that makes the catalog industry the powerhouse that it is), but not every business that can use a catalog can afford to be as elaborate as today's big-name catalogs that are in the public eye.

Distributing a Catalog

Most, but not all, catalogs are distributed through the USPS. Once that is determined, the distribution of your catalog becomes just like any other direct mail campaign that you undertake, with few differences. You already know what your are mailing so that part can be checked off on your checklist. You now have to determine who you will send your catalog to. Who is your target market and what list will you send to? Just as in all other direct mail campaigns, send it to your own house list, your own current customers. Even if this group has access to your products through other means, still send them your catalog. It is a direct-response mechanism, and you could generate immediate sales. You can also purchase or rent a list, as discussed in Chapter 2, "The Marketing Target." Work with your local mail house or the USPS office to determine mailing format and postage costs. This will be a major factor in determining the size and frequency of your campaign.

Obtaining Sales

Because a catalog is a direct marketing vehicle, your goal is to obtain sales. You will have an order form in your catalog that directs readers to a web site. Both of these mechanisms will allow you to take full advantage of a recipient's interest once she browses through your catalog. Once again, the same rules apply to catalogs as to all other direct marketing. Make it easy for a customer/prospect to purchase. The photos and descriptions will serve as your offers. Make them as compelling as possible. Include other direct marketing components like bonuses, free shipping where applicable, and guarantees.

Catalog Benefits

Even with shoppers migrating to the internet, catalog marketing and selling are still strong.

Catalogs help businesses to expand, either with new products or geographically. A catalog is another form of direct mail. It is a presentation of your products on many sheets of paper instead of a single direct mail piece. It is direct mail that offers convenience and variety, two major selling benefits, to your target audience. Catalogs represent that category of direct mail that is generally "accepted" by the consumer. This acceptance is due to its many benefits:

- *Convenience.* Shopping in your pajamas is one way to realize the convenience of catalog shopping. They truly are stores on paper that never close.
- *Variety.* Right in your own home is a whole store's inventory for you to review. Usually the catalog you shop from is made up of only those categories of products you are interested in.
- *Complete descriptions.* Chances are that the picture of the product and the short description is more information than you might get from a retail sales person.
- *Comfort and confidence.* More and more people have purchased by catalogs in the past, establishing the right confidence level for future purchases. Where trust is suspect, strong guarantees overcome.
- *Fulfillment and shipping.* Thanks to today's more efficient distribution systems, the old days of mail order's "four- to six-week delivery" are gone. Shipments today are received in a matter of days.
- *Specialty/niche markets.* You will probably only shop from catalogs that carry products you are interested in. Today, specialty-products catalogs are more abundant, allowing you a more focused shopping experience.

Catalog Considerations

In order to be successful with catalog marketing, you need to take the following factors in to serious consideration:

Graphics/photos. Creative graphics and photos must first grab the attention of your reader, then describe the product, motivate or make it easy for a customer to reach a purchase decision, and make it easy to order. A picture or visual has a microsecond to do all of that. The customer has to see it and want it in the blink of an eye, or at least go through the purchase decision process that fast.

The human eye sees photos first on a catalog page, then sub-photos or headlines, then the copy. The first part of the copy that's noticed is the price and then any body copy. Once a customer starts reading body copy, you have her ready to purchase or at least consider your product as an option.

Photo creation represents 10 to 20 percent of your total catalog costs. This includes hiring the photographer and photographing the actual products. Don't scrimp in this area. This is what your customer sees first; it's what makes the greatest impression and what they base purchase decisions on.

As a final note, the human eye continues around the page in a counterclockwise motion starting at the top-right hand corner of the catalog. This has major implications for photo placement and the related copy. The eye also moves "down" from any attention-getter. These are rule of thumb, but rules that have been studied over and over by the pundits.

Catalog products and performance measurements. Much goes into product selection for catalogs. In fact, those companies that market only by catalogs, whose catalog is the crux of their business, spend much time analyzing many product factors. Catalogers analyze product sales per square inch of catalog, sales per catalog page, and the usual statistics of highest-volume-product, and highest sales product.

Successful catalogers will concentrate and build on their most successful products. Not all products can sell as well as others. By understanding what customers are responding to, losing or underperforming products can be eliminated or upgraded while giving target audiences more of what they want.

It sounds like a lot of detailed analyses, but looking at each page and each product and its respective performance is of great benefit to the catalog merchant and those who make product and creative decisions.

Sometimes, in addition to product volumes, these analyses will turn up layout opportunities or challenges on a particular page. Patterns, sections of the catalog that perform well, and the effects of photos, graphics, and copy are also explored. It's almost like a volume of "direct marketing tests."

Once the metrics are understood, standards can be established, along with ensuing sales goals.

▼ A CATALOG EXAMPLE

A 24-page catalog is mailing 100,000 pieces for a seasonal issues. Cost per catalog mailed is $.30. Total costs therefore are $30,000. A good rule of thumb is that 20 to 30 percent of a catalog's sales go into the catalog cost. Based on our example, the total sales goal, assuming a 20 percent cost number is $150,000.

Using the same numbers, this works out to an estimated sales goal per page of about $6,521 (for purposes of calculations the front cover is not included in this calculation.) This number can be used to monitor the catalog's performance on an ongoing basis and to make comparisons from year to year.

From these numbers, barometers, and subsequent performance, you can assess your products, placement, layout, and overall catalog performance and related profitability.

The profit contribution of each item and page are usually emphasized more than units sold and absolute sales dollars. This information is very helpful to product buyers and creative staff, if a large company, or to the entrepreneur and his/her partners or team, if a small company.

- Size, postage, and shipping cost considerations
- Creative—the right copy and descriptions, including headlines, categories, and headings

Understanding customers' aesthetic expectations is what this first element is all about. One suggestion that is often made for new or redesigned catalogs is to examine other existing catalogs and select those whose covers, layouts, and other design elements are most in line with your expectations. It might be a business catalog or a retail or consumer catalog. By identifying creative elements you think will work with your target customers, you have an excellent starting place.

Main Considerations after Concept

Once you have decided your overall catalog concept, there is a lot left to do! Here are the key things you will need to do now:

Product Decisions and Specifications

- Actual product review or review of spec sheets if product is not available
- Product specification review
- Product benefit review
- Product justification for target market and catalog inclusion

Catalog Creative

- Number of pages
- Size
- Artwork/colors
- Order form/calls to action
- Bindings
- Inserts
- Cover
- Layout
- Postioning of products/sections
- Production review and timing
- Direct mail processing and timing
- Expected sales goals

Catalog Design

- Cover thumbnail sketch, rendering, and proof
- Page layout thumbnail sketch, rendering, and proof (each page)
- Company identity information
- Borders, headlines, sidebars, captions
- Illustrations
- Photos
- Typefaces
- Coverage

Obviously, I have mentioned page art and page layout in this list. This means that these activities must take place for all pages. Much goes into each page, with product selection, layout, art, etc. In addition, page layout proofs must be reviewed along with all inclusions and covers. A mock-up or "dummy" catalog is produced before moving into final production.

Copy

In the old days, most mail order catalogs did one thing only and that was to sell products. Think back to Richard Sears and his one sheet offering watches and jewelry. No one cared about his company identity or mission. He just wanted to sell something. These days, with more and more competition in the catalog world and more and more marketing clutter, companies are starting to use catalog design to do more than sell. Catalog companies are building in design that give their prospects and customers a real feeling for the business represented. Harry and David, Starbucks, and others come to mind.

Consistent with design parameters (total number of words, headlines, captions, sidebars, etc.), product and catalog copy must be developed. This also includes product numbers, SKU identification, pricing information, and page numbers. This information is also proofed and approved before final production.

As you can see, there is a lot to the creative process for a catalog. Figure 3.5 helps to make sure you have covered all the bases. There are associated costs with all of this that have to be managed, monitored, and negotiated. It is a major marketing investment and should be measured. Done right, you will find this to be a highly effective product direct marketing vehicle.

DIRECT RESPONSE ADVERTISEMENTS

The local newspaper still remains an integral part of practically everyone's daily life. It still is a preferred vehicle for small businesses and

FIGURE 3.5	Catalog Checklist

❑ Ease of ordering. Ordering from a web site or a toll-free number is standard.

❑ Order fulfillment

❑ Target your market. Catalog targeting interested prospects

❑ Organize information

❑ Copy

❑ Merchandising program

❑ Marketing

❑ Catalog distribution

❑ Cover

   ___ Front cover design

   ___ Back cover design

❑ Size/pages/format

   ___ Inside page design

❑ Trends

❑ Costs

❑ List/target

❑ Response

❑ Objectives

❑ Audience

❑ Products/prices/fulfillment

❑ Groupings/content

❑ Catalog production

❑ Design/layout

❑ Mailing

entrepreneurs to advertise in, whether with paid advertising or PR. Newspapers have sections that further segment targeted readers, allowing for the direct marketer to also target. Sections such as sports, business, lifestyle, and home are common today. Newspapers remain one of the best direct marketing media. Inserts, supplements, and ads offer perfect places for direct marketing. To see how perfect, analyze how well they reach your demographic and chosen target market.

Because of this, direct-response ads are common in newspapers. Here are a few key pieces of information to consider about using direct response ads:

- Advertising for leads, prospects, or inquiries will generally require less space than advertising for orders.
- Color can increase responses but needs about a 20 percent increase in response

dollars to justify the increased printing expense.

- The closer to the front of a publication you can advertise, the more visible your ad will be and the more response you will generate.
- Right-hand ads pull better than left-hand ads. This is because of the way the human eye travels and how the human mind works.
- Insert cards pull better than ads.

Following are some examples of successful direct response advertising campaigns.

Gevalia Kaffe

In a local suburban Chicago newspaper, Gevalia placed a full-page, direct-response ad. It was a classic direct-response ad, representative of direct marketing at its finest. Here are the components that made it a classic. Calling it a classic does not imply an older age of the ad, for the ad was placed in early 2005. It is deemed a classic because it has all the essential direct marketing components in the form of a direct-response ad.

Headline. The main headline—

Much to Savor. Nothing to Join.

—is OK up at the top quarter of the whole newspaper page. The phrase, "nothing to join," is an attempt to immediately take away the objection of having recurring shipments with recurring payments. What connotes "joining" is turned completely around by this headline, thus averting an immediate objection. The word savor plays on the senses and is benefit-oriented.

Sub-headline. The sub-headline is really a bold, first sentence of the first paragraph:

Delight in the exquisite taste of Gevalia Kaffe and all this can be yours for only $16.95, with no commitment.

Like other parts of Gevalia marketing, this direct marketing component serves a number of different purposes. The first word is benefit-oriented, "delight." The "all this" is referring to the large photo of an upscale coffeemaker next to two packs of Gevalia Kaffe. This serves as an incentive. Finally, the end of this sentence, "no commitment," is another attempt to overcome any immediate objections, just in case the reader still might be thinking of that word "join," in the headline. This whole opening statement is very powerful.

The bottom of the ad consists of a larger order form. The choices are worded as such:

Choose two flavors that delight you most.

This, once again, subliminally once again plants that word "delight" into the reader's mind.

The bottom left contains the rest of the essential direct marketing components:

- A guarantee statement.
- Reserved deliveries. Notice the use of the word "reserved," which implies that the customer is part of an exclusive group, an effective direct marketing technique.
- Convenient billing. A definite benefit and one they know prospects like and will respond to.
- No commitment. Again, for the third time in the ad, an attempt to overcome the objection associated with "joining" something.

Within the order form of approximately 8" by 8", there were six calls to action:

1. Choose the two that delight you most.
2. Choose one from each column (regular/decaf, whole bean/ground).
3. Call 1-800-GEVALIA.
4. Visit www.gevalia.com.
5. Complete and mail to Gevalia Kaffe.
6. Choose your coffeemaker color.

Gevalia's direct-response ads show up in many types of direct marketing vehicles, especially national publications. When someone sees the "nationally offered" product in their own hometown newspaper, they have a higher likelihood of responding. Gevalia is reaching their market in many ways.

Special author's note: After reviewing many ads in researching this book I was persuaded by the Gevalia ad to the point of actually making a purchase from them. I saw them "everywhere," and their direct marketing appealed to me as part of their target market. My response was a purchase, exactly what direct marketing is supposed to do.

Barix Clinics

Barix Clinics used a direct marketing newspaper ad that solicited a response that was not an actual purchase. The call to action for their direct response ads was to "register for our free seminar." There was more benefit-oriented text and a testimonial in addition to the call to action.

Here are more direct marketing components that were well-crafted:

Headline. The headline was a grabber:

> *My New Year's Resolution*
> *Was to Lose 150 lbs.*
> *I did it with Barix Clinics.*

The Barix Clinic ad had benefit points that were action oriented:

- Discover why it is important . . .
- Meet the dedicated, board-certified surgeons . . .
- Talk with a patient counselor . . .
- Learn about our unique facilities . . .
- Hear how Barix offers the most comprehensive program . . .

The ad is about one-half of a tabloid-size newspaper page and reads very cleanly; another example of an effective direct response ad.

J.G. Banks

J.G. Banks, a training institute for real estate investing, also uses a full-page newspaper ad with a response objective of attending a workshop. Its ad has a lot of attention-getters. Just reading the bold headlines would give the reader enough information to respond. J.G. Banks must know how readers scan these types of ads. If they want to read more, there is more there for the interested prospect. If the prospect is in scanning mode, the ad still does its job. Here are some of its attention-getting techniques:

- New (in a starburst)
- Free two-hour workshop
- Top five reasons

- Free admission
- Bonus
- Discover

J.G. Banks is so intent on its offer and mode of response (workshop attendance) that nowhere in the ad does it offer a web site address or phone number to call. The only way to respond is to show up at one of their free workshops. The admittance coupon states that reservations are not required and gives the address of the workshop. You can bet that those who do show up are interested prospects. J.G. Banks probably has a high closing percentage with this approach.

Joint Flex Pain Relieving Cream

Joint Flex Pain Relieving Cream is another classic direct-response ad because of the effective use of headlines. You can understand everything about the offer just by scanning the headlines. The headlines offer benefits, ask "pain" questions, challenge the reader, and take out all risk. The prospect is led to the lower right corner of the ad, where all the different ways to respond are clearly enumerated. Certainly, featuring the product in the middle of an ad like this, surrounded by headlines and information about the appropriate response mechanisms, is effective.

FC&A Publishing

FC&A Publishing, a medical publishing company offering self-help health, consumer advice, and craft books, uses bulleted information to the max! In a full-page newspaper ad, three medical books are being sold:

1. *Unleash the Inner Healing Power of Foods*
2. *Fitness for Seniors*
3. *Natural Cures and Gentle Medicines that Work Better than Dangerous Drugs or Risky Surgery*

Each book sells for $9.99, and the response desired by the marketer is a direct purchase.

The full-page ad is split in half vertically and one of the vertical halves is split in half again, making three sections. Each section covers a separate book. Each section also has an attention grabbing headline:

The Closest Thing to a Fountain of Youth

What Never to Drink if You're Taking High Blood Pressure Medicine

Grape Juice is an Artery-Clearing Wonder!

Each headline is followed by one or two small paragraphs, followed by several bulleted points of information. The larger of the three sections contains over 80 bulleted points. People would rather read bulleted points of information than half a newspaper's worth of straight text. This is yet another ad playing on reader habits and the psychology of a prospect.

DIRECT TELEMARKETING

Mention telemarketing, and many think about the phone calls at dinnertime offering the lowest in long-distance telephone rates Or maybe your mealtime buzz has to do with credit card processing.

First, there is way more to telemarketing than this, as you are about to discover. Secondly, there has to be a reason these calls continue, at dinnertime or any other time of day.

I'll comment on the second point first. The reason these calls continue is because they work and produce results. Direct marketing of any type, including telemarketing, is a numbers game. Call 100 people and get a purchase, commitment for a trial, donation, or some other form of response from two of those called and you have a 2 percent response rate. By direct

marketing standards, this is acceptable, justified, and a satisfying return on the telemarketing investment.

Consistent with the direct-marketing definition, telemarketing entails calling a prospect or customer for the purposes of generating a response. The response can be an order (the ultimate goal of any direct marketing) or as you have learned, another type of response.

Telemarketing can take many forms with many marketing objectives. Here are some of them:

- Selling a product
- Confirming contact information for a prospect or client
- Soliciting a donation for a fundraiser
- Renewing a subscription
- Generating or qualifying a lead
- Surveys/market research
- Up-sell, cross-sell
- Political campaign work
- Bill collections
- Thank-you calls
- Reminder calls
- Follow-up calls after a sale
- Keep-in-touch calls
- Support and follow-up for other marketing

While this is not exhaustive, you can see many similarities to other direct-marketing objectives.

Outbound Telemarketing

When you think about it, telemarketing is fundamentally a very good direct marketing vehicle. It is response-oriented. Phone calls are not necessarily made to build a brand or to create awareness. It is a quick (usually) vehicle to generate a response while on a call. True, most times the response is a "no," but so is the response for most other direct-marketing vehicles. The numbers make it work. Remember, with a 2 percent response rate, you get a 98 percent rejection rate. If Babe Ruth achieved a major league batting average of .333, which is good, he failed .667 of the time.

With marketing made up of so very many things, effective marketing requires many touches to customers and prospects, whether with the same marketing vehicle over and over or different vehicles frequently. This plus the fact that making a face-to-face direct sales call is significantly more costly makes outbound telemarketing a logical vehicle to add to your direct marketing mix.

This sounds familiar. Just as in other direct marketing, the success of an outbound telemarketing program depends upon the list of names to call. The target audience needs to be precisely defined in order for the campaign to succeed. The other direct marketing success factors—the offer and the message—apply here as well. As in direct sales, the person doing the selling (or in this case, the calling) is also a factor that can determine the success of such a program. The success of the telemarketer is usually related to the "script," or message. Once again, you see the fundamentals of direct marketing at work here: the vehicle (telemarketing), the message (script), the target (list), and frequency.

The script. Making a phone call is still a very personal touch. The touch still incorporates the personality of the person making the call; however, every caller is different, and this produccs different results. To help improve the caller's message and to standardize as much as possible, outbound telemarketing companies/marketers develop scripts for callers to follow.

The telemarketing script has a quick introduction, with a probing question that gingerly attempts to develop instant rapport. Most of the time (just look at the numbers) an immediate objection is raised by the prospect. You've been there; you know what I'm talking about. The script then serves to supply answers or more questions in response to all the potential objections. Research shows that the caller has 20 more seconds to create interest or make a sale after the initial objection is expressed. This applies to each objection, even as the caller overcomes each one with the script.

Like the message in a direct-response ad or direct mail campaign, testing needs to be done to determine the best pitch/script.

The numbers. It was stressed earlier that there is a reason why outbound telemarketing calls are made, even in light of the possibility of an unwanted interruption. The numbers work. Direct marketing is a numbers game.

The cost of outbound calling is on the length of message delivered and the amount of time the caller is on the phone with a particular prospect. This determines the number of calls that can be made in a finite period of time.

Generally speaking, you will know your cost per minute or per hour of phone time. You will know how many calls are made in a particular time frame, yielding a cost per phone-call number. Calculating the number of responses will give you a cost per response. If the response is a purchase, you can then arrive at a cost per purchase and eventually a return-on-sales number.

Response rates. On average, response rates in the world of telemarketing vary between 5 percent and 15 percent. Remember the definition of response in your calculation; it's not always a purchase, depending on how your direct marketing was set up. A 5 percent response rate means you made 20 phone calls for every response. When looking at the time and expense involved compared to face-to-face selling or even other direct marketing, you can quickly see why telemarketing continues to be vital, despite its lack of popularity with prospects and its regulation by legislators.

Response rates have to be reconciled with the size of your orders taken, if using telemarketing to sell. If you are selling a high-priced/high-margin item, a response rate of less than 5 percent might be justifiable and totally satisfactory. Don't forget about the lifetime value of a client when evaluating the numbers and return on marketing dollars.

Using telemarketing to support other marketing. Telemarketing can be one more marketing touch to a prospect, and in view of how many times it takes to get a prospect into purchase-readiness mode, it can support all other marketing. Here are a some helpful of the complements:

- Announcing beforehand that a letter or direct mail package will be arriving
- Calling to see if a letter or package was received
- Making sure requested information was received
- Making an appointment to follow up on another response
- Inviting prospects to an open house, demo, seminar, or workshop
- Follow up on product/service use or experience
- Reminder calls to buy before a particular deadline
- Calls to make private and special offers, or to alert prospects to a special sale
- Renewal or upgrade calls to existing customers

Timing this right after a mailing, an ad, or other marketing effort that can be scheduled can increase response rates by at least 10 to 20 percent.

Inbound Telemarketing

We've been discussing the outbound variety of telemarketing: calls made from the marketer to the prospect. The corollary to outbound telemarketing is inbound telemarketing: calls from a prospect or customer to a marketing company for purposes of placing an order or requesting information, (in response to other direct marketing, like a catalog). The Time/Life Books TV ad which says that "operators are standing by" is an example of inbound telemarketing at work. This is what is commonly known as a call center within a company.

The following telesales tips are contributed by Art Sobczak of www.businessbyphone.com. He also suggests that the use of the phone in sales and marketing is a process, not an event. It is direct because a response is always requested, thus complying with our definition of direct marketing.

The telemarketing process and each individual call has many parts. There are opportunities along the way to improve the process. The goal of these tips is to get more responses, and more business, and to avoid much of the rejection that is common with this vehicle. This list of tips can be viewed as another checklist in your marketing planning and management.

Telemarketing Overview
Pre-Call Planning

- Have a primary objective for every telemarketing call, expressed as, "What do I want this person to DO as a result of my call, and what do I want to do?"

- Prepare questions for your telesales call using your call objective. Ask yourself, "How can I persuade them to take this action as a result of asking questions, as opposed to talking?" Remember, people believe more of their own ideas than yours.
- Also have a secondary objective for each telephone sales call . . . something you'll strive to accomplish, at minimum, every time. Pick something you'll have a reasonably good chance to succeed with, such as, "Getting their agreement that they will accept my literature and place it in their Backup Vendor file." This way, you can enjoy success on every call you place, and that does wonders for your attitude.

Before Reaching the Decision Maker

- Treat the screener as you would the customer—this person determines whether or not you'll even have a chance to speak with the buyer.
- Gather as much information as you can from whomever you are able prior to speaking with your prospect; busy decision makers get bored when they have to answer your basic qualifying questions. Use the "Help" technique: "I hope you can help me. So I'm better prepared when I speak with Ms. Big, there's probably some information you could provide me . . . ."
- Before cold calls, think of a good reason for needing to speak with the decision maker, and be prepared to sell this to the screener. What he's thinking about you is, "Does this person have anything of interest, or of value for the boss?"
- If leaving a message on voice mail, or with a screener, be certain it offers a hint of a benefit/result that sparks curiosity, but doesn't talk about products/services.

Interest-Creating Opening Statements

- The objective of your telemarketing opener is to pique curiosity and interest so that people will willingly and enthusiastically move to the questioning. You must answer "What's in it for me?" for the listener, or he will immediately begin the getting-rid-of-you process.
- Don't use goofy, resistance-inducing phrases on your telesales call, like "If I could show you a way to _____, you would, wouldn't you?" The only decision you're looking for in the opener is the one to continue speaking with you.
- When cold-call prospecting, don't start the call with, "I was just calling people in your area . . . ." People want to feel that they're the only person you're calling . . . not just one of the masses from a list of compiled names.
- Use what I call "weasel words" when opening cold prospecting calls: "depending on," "might," "maybe," "perhaps," and "possibly." These are nonthreatening words that intimate you might have something of value for them, but you really need to ask questions first. For example, "Depending on what you're now doing in the area of employee benefits, I might have something that could potentially increase the number of options you offer, while possibly decreasing your overall contribution. I'd like to ask you a few questions to see if this is something you'd like more information on."
- Have something of value to say on every telemarketing call, particularly those regular calls to existing customers. Avoid "Just checking in with you to see if you needed anything," and "Just calling to touch base." These are more nuisance than service. Be certain they're able to say they are better off

after your call than they were before it, even if they didn't buy anything. Call with news they'll have an interest in, ideas you've heard from other customers they might be able to take advantage of. Mention that you were "thinking of them" and tell them why. One of my printing salesmen called to say he "just came back from a trade show and saw something interesting, and thought I could benefit from it." It's little things like that that cause customers to say, "She always has something good for me when she calls," as opposed to, "Every time she calls, she's just looking for an order."

Effective Questioning

- Get information before you give it. How could you make an effective presentation otherwise?

- Don't use a "benefit list" to present from. Instead, use it to create questions to determine if those "benefits" truly are of value to your prospects and customers. Some "benefits" could actually be liabilities.

- Avoid asking go-nowhere questions like: "Is everything going OK?" "What are your needs?" "Are you having any problems now?" "How's service?" "What are you looking for in a vendor?" These all force the person to think too much. Instead, get her emotionally involved in seeing and feeling the pain or problem that can be solved with your product/service—especially problems you know she's likely experiencing. For example, "What do you do in situations when you need parts shipped overnight, but are unable to get them?"

- Ask one question at a time. That's how many they'll answer at a time.

- After asking, be quiet. Resist the urge to jump in if they don't answer immediately.

Don't be intimidated by silence. She's likely thinking about what they're going to say.

- After she's finished, count to two (silently, of course). This ensures she's done, plus she might continue with even better information.

- Have confidence in your questioning. One reason reps ramble with questions is that they're not prepared or confident. Prepare your questions. Role-play with yourself if necessary.

- Always know where you'll go with answers. Regardless of the answer.

- Follow-up answers with related questions. Too often reps work from a rigid list of questions, losing the opportunity to pick up on prospect statements that are just the tip of the iceberg of her real feelings. For example, if a prospect said, "I believe the main reason production isn't higher is a lack of motivation," the best move would be to follow-up with, "I see. What specific signs of poor motivation have you noticed?" Or simply, "Tell me more."

- Quantify the problem whenever possible. "How often does that happen?" "How much do you think that is costing you?" "How much time does that take?"

- Resist the tendency to present. Some reps get so excited when they hear the slightest hint of an opportunity that they turn on the spigot of benefits. Hold off, ask a few more questions, get better information, and you're able to craft an even harder-hitting description of benefits, tailored precisely to what they're interested in.

- Learn more about the decision-making process. There could be many behind-the-scenes influences on the decision. Ask about actual users of your products/services, anyone else who could influence the decisions, who has to sign off on the ultimate decision or OK the money for it, and perhaps people who would rather not see it happen.

Sales Recommendations

- You should only talk about your product/ service after knowing specifically how it will solve the problem, meet a need, etc. Then you can tailor your remarks specifically and personally for the listener.
- Get feedback during your discussion of benefits: "Do you feel that would work for you?" "How do you feel that would solve your problem?" Some trainers might tell you that this gives the prospect an opportunity to tell you "no." Precisely. And that's good. Because if there's a problem, and she doesn't see enough value in what you've presented, now is the time to find out.
- Avoid the question "Anything else?" when attempting to up-sell. Just like when a convenience store clerk asks the same question, the answer is usually, "No." Instead, give her a suggestion, and help her answer. For example, after she agrees to buy an item or a service say, "Many of our customers who get _____ from us also find that _____ is very beneficial for them. What are you now doing/using/buying in that area?"

Getting Commitment (Closing)

- This is not the major event in a telemarketing sales call. It's the natural, logical validation of the professional sales process up to this point. But you still must ask. Commitment must be gained on every contact in order to move the process forward. If there is to be a follow-up contact

and information is to be sent or faxed, there must be commitment on the part of the prospect regarding that material.
- Ask large. Think big. Buyers will often move down from a large recommendation, but they rarely move up from a small one. Those who ask the biggest have the largest average order size. Never suggest more than is in the best interest of the customer, but not making a large enough suggestion when appropriate is actually hurting the customer.
- When in doubt, ask. Do you have a foot-dragger in your follow-up file who is perched squarely on the fence? Ask for a decision! Get some movement. A "no" today is better than one six months and 15 additional calls from now. Move them forward, or move them out.
- If you're going to schedule a follow-up call, get a commitment of some type. Why would you call back otherwise? If she won't commit to doing anything—reviewing your literature and preparing questions, surveying their existing inventory, etc.— she'll likely have no interest.

Addressing Resistance (Objections)

- Objections can be avoided by doing everything else correctly up to this point in the call. When they do occur, resist the tendency to attack in defense. You must back up and revisit the questioning stage of the call. The voiced objection is simply a symptom of the real problem. Start by saying, "Let's talk about that."
- If you have an indecisive prospect, get her mind off the buying decision and on the problem or pain. For example, "Jan, let's look at this another way. What would happen if you did nothing about the situation?

Remember, we detailed the fact that you're missing sales opportunities every day. What will that amount to over just the next six months?"

- Most price objections start in the mind of the salesperson. Many sales reps aren't 100 percent sold on the value of their product; therefore, they're apt to offer price concessions even when the prospect doesn't flat-out ask, or they present price in a shaky tone of voice. Ask the right questions, present the results of what your product/service can do, and state the price boldly.

- Avoid common objections mistakes. Using slick, prepared, objection rebuttals that mainly tell people they're wrong and only serves to intensify the resistance. When this happens, neither sales person nor prospect can explore or understand the reason behind the problem.

Wrapping Up and Setting the Next Action

- When sending information, samples, demos, etc., know precisely how they'll evaluate the material. How will they know if they like it? What criteria will they use? This way, you'll both be clear as to what would need to happen in order for them to buy.

- When sending material, prepare prospects as to what they should look for. Otherwise, they'll get a package of materials and say, "Oh, there's a package of materials" and then toss it on the mountain of other stuff in their office. But, if you tell them to look for the catalog that will be opened to the page with the product they are interested in, and you'll have the three or four models highlighted that are most appropriate for them, there will be a greater likelihood they'll look at it.

Telemarketing laws have been in the spotlight of late. For up-to-date information on what laws protect you, and the ins and outs of the National Do Not Call Registry, consult the following:

- Toll-free Registry telephone hotline (888) 382-1222

- Online registration form, www.donotcall.gov

- http://www.privacyrights.org/fs/fs5-tmkt.htm

- The success of your follow-up call directly relates to what you accomplished, and how you ended the previous call. Never say, "I'll send you out some stuff, and we'll go from there." From where? Summarize agreed-to actions by both parties, including what happened, what they're interested in, and what will happen next. And set the agenda for the next call. That makes it so much easier to prepare for the follow-up call and helps you avoid starting calls with the useless questions, "I sent you the material, didja get it?" or "Whatdidja think?" For example, "OK, Pat, I'll send the proposal detailing the quantity price breaks. What you'll do is compare that to what you're getting now, and if we're within 5 percent, you'll agree to a trial order on our next call, is that right?"

Attitude and Self-Motivation

- You never have to experience rejection again. After all, what is rejection? It's not an experience—it's your definition of the experience. So, ensure that you accomplish something on each call, and you can hold your head high with a sense of achievement. Remember, a decision of any type is better than shadow-chasing someone who will waste your time with wimpy or misleading statements that cause you to believe there's a chance when, in fact, there's not.

- A good way to end a call in which you don't accomplish your primary objective (and to never experience rejection) is to plant a seed for the future. Give her something to look for, based upon what you uncovered during the call . . . something that might just cause her to call you back. For example, "Pat, it looks like we don't have a fit here, today, but I suggest that if you ever find yourself needing an emergency job finished, and don't have the staff to handle it, give us a call. We specialize in those type of projects, and would love to talk to you." Everyone has been surprised by those written-off prospects who later called to order. This is a way to proactively make it happen more often.

- Imagine every day is the end-of-quota-period day. I've noticed that reps tend to pick up the pace and behave like tornados in a hurricane when they reach the last couple of days of a quota period, doing whatever is necessary to squeeze out those last few sales. When you coast, you're going downhill. Get focused on a goal, and pursue it with single-minded determination.

- As a sales professional using the phone as your main method of communication, you perform a function that very few people in the world could do well, or would even want to try. And that's persuading someone to take action and make a decision, based almost solely on the words and ideas that come from your mouth. It's quite an awesome feat when you think about it. And do think about it. It takes a talented individual to be able to do that well. You are that per-

son. Feel proud of what you do, and always strive to get better.

Figure 3.6, the Telemarketing Checklist, assumes that equipment and personnel are in place and ready for program implementation. This checklist does not include anything to prepare equipment for a call center or a training program for a telemarketer.

DIRECT RESPONSE TV

More and more advertisers, including a large number of blue-chip companies, are using short-form Direct Response TV (DRTV) and infomercials to market their products and services.

DRTV is defined as media activity (TV) that permits and requests prospects to directly respond to the advertiser at the time of the advertisement viewing.

Products that have been marketed successfully by this direct marketing method have been those related to:

- Fitness equipment
- Financial programs
- Housewares
- Health and beauty products
- Collectibles

Here are 24 rules, tips, and techniques for making powerful, profitable, direct-response commercials and infomercials:

1. The more you tell, the more you sell. The most important thing to understand about DRTV is that each commercial needs to function as a complete, stand-alone sales presentation. This means that by the end of your spot, the viewer must have enough information to feel comfortable making a purchasing decision. It's your job to give that information. This means presenting as many features and benefits, answering as many questions, and overcoming as many

FIGURE 3.6	Telemarketing Checklist

❑ **Determine Telemarketing Objectives**
___ Sale
___ Lead
___ Follow-up
___ Fundraising
___ Other _____

❑ **Determine Business Objective**
___ Number of new orders
___ Sales dollars
___ Number of leads
___ Satisfaction rating upon follow-up
___ Other _____

❑ **Budget**
___ Cost per call
___ Cost per hour
___ Cost per caller
___ Sales per call
___ Sales per hour
___ Sales per caller

❑ **Script**
___ Introduction
___ Offer
___ Ways to develop rapport
___ Create interest and desire
___ Objection statements
___ Closings
___ Thank you/follow-up
___ Training of caller
___ Rehearsal
___ Feedback/adjustments to script

❑ **Measurement/Evaluation**
___ Cost per response
___ Sales per call
___ Costs per sale
___ Absolute sales $ increase
___ Profitability analysis

objections as possible in the allotted time. Don't cheat yourself out of a sale by leaving valuable information out of your spot.

2. The product is king, queen, and supreme ruler. Don't waste a second of precious airtime talking about anything except your product or service. Creative concepts that are not about extolling the virtues of your product or service are a waste of time.

3. Size matters. Forget everything you have been told about the tiny attention span of today's consumers. It's bull. Every test ever done shows that

the longer your DRTV commercial is, the more effective it will be. That's why 60-second DRTV commercials outperform 30-second DRTV commercials; 120-second DRTV commercials outperform 60-second DRTV commercials; and infomercials outperform them all. If you can't do a better job of selling your product in 30 minutes than you can in 30 seconds, stick with general advertising.

4. Focus groups will kill your commercial. Focus groups will happily tell you what they like or don't like about your DRTV commercial. Unfortunately, what they like or don't like in a commercial has nothing to do with what makes them buy from a commercial. Never confuse what a viewer likes with what makes him or her pick up the phone and buy. Save your money and skip the focus groups.

5. Show your product. TV is not a store or a showroom. The viewer can't reach up and squeeze the Charmin™ or take that shiny new SUV out for a test drive. You're going to have to show me how beautiful and irresistible your product really is. And by the way, with a little imagination you can also "show" the intangibles of products or services, like long-distance, financial planning, or even political ideas.

6. Demonstrate your product. Beauty shots are critical, but the viewer also needs to see your product or service in action. Remember this: Dynamite demonstrations have sold more products than any other DRTV technique. They captivate an audience and fuel the desire to purchase.

7. Use graphics to reinforce key selling messages. Study after study has concluded that people understand and recall information better when they hear it *and* see it. Therefore, make sure that all the key selling points are also written on the screen as graphics at the exact same time as they are being spoken by the talent.

8. Include a powerful offer. It is not absolutely essential to have an offer, but keep in mind that a good offer can transform an OK commercial into a runaway bestseller. Offers work because they make the viewer think about the cost of not acting, and nobody wants to miss out on a great deal. The better the offer, the better the response.

9. Value is in the mind of the viewer. The effectiveness of your offer depends upon its perceived

rather than its real value. That is why so many effective DRTV offers include inexpensive bonus items that boost the perceived value of the offer.

10. Talk directly to the viewer/buyer. I'm a big believer in dramatic re-enactments and good old-fashioned, slice-of-life creations. I think they add depth and realism to DRTV commercials. However, they should never replace having someone look the viewers right in the eye and tell them exactly why they should surrender their hard-earned money to buy your product or service.

11. Say it again, Sam. After you have read this list, see how many of the rules you can recall. Then you will understand why repetition is so important in a good DRTV spot. If you want people to remember your key selling points, repeat them over and over and over again.

12. Be passionate. Passion sells. That doesn't mean you have to be loud, cheesy, or over the top. However, if you can't get the viewers excited about what you're selling, you're going to have a hard time convincing them to buy. After all, if you're not pumped about your product and your offer, why should the audience get excited?

13. Be persuasive. It is one of the great truisms of life that no one sits down in front of the TV with their credit card, expecting to buy something. So, if you want people to purchase, you have to persuade them to do so. You have to convince them that your product really is as good as you say it is. You have to persuade them that their life is going to be more fun, more exciting, and richer if they buy, and definitely less rewarding if they do not.

14. Gold is in the details. You would be amazed at the number of tiny objections and misconceptions that can lurk in the viewer's mind, each powerful enough to derail the decision to purchase. Make a checklist of every possible reason someone might have for not making the purchase and try to answer as many objections as possible in the time available. In DRTV, there is no tomorrow. If viewers are is going to buy, they have to buy now.

15. Reason to believe. If your product or service is better than everyone else's is, tell the viewer why. What is the science behind this product? What technical innovation or recent discovery has made this miracle possible? Give them a reason to believe.

16. Establish credibility. It is critical to establish and maintain credibility. This can be done through testimonials, studies, or third-party endorsements.

17. Testimonials work. Consumers respond to hearing other consumers talk about how wonderful a product or service is and how much they love it. Especially if they happen to mention how skeptical they were before they tried it. To find out how well testimonials work, just try doing a successful infomercial without them.

18. Endorsements also work. Third-party endorsements, preferably from credible, respectable sources, also carry a lot of weight in DRTV.

19. Never give the viewer a choice. Consumers love choice, except in DRTV commercials. The reason is simple. As soon as you ask the viewer to think about whether they would prefer a red or blue car, guess what happens? That's right, they sit and think about it, instead of picking up the phone to buy. The viewer should only have one decision to make, and that is whether to call or not to call.

20. Ask for the order. Tell the viewers exactly what you want them to do, which of course is to call now and buy the product (or at least request more information).

21. The script is everything. If you haven't already noticed, DRTV is a scriptwriter's medium. If the script is written properly, using proven, time-tested DR principles, the phones will sing. If the script is not written properly, your commercial will die a silent death.

22. Test, test, test. The only way to be absolutely certain what price point, which offer, which demonstration is best, is to put them on air against each other and compare the response rates.

23. Use problem/solution. Showing the viewer a problem they can relate to and then showing how your product or service can solve that problem is never a bad idea.

24. Minimize the viewer's risk. The lower the risk, the higher the response. Ways to lower the risk include guarantees and refund policies.

There you have it: 24 rules for making phenomenal direct-response commercials and infomercials. (Reprinted with permission from Northern Lights Direct Response Television, www.nldrtv.com.)

Do you need to follow each of these rules to ensure success? Of course not. There are many successful DRTV commercials on the air that for one reason or another do not follow all the rules listed here. However, every rule you ignore decreases your chances of success, and every rule you follow increases your chances of success.

The entire response cycle to a direct-response television commercial is approximately 15 minutes.

If a phone line is busy or there is no answer, the sale is lost. Make sure your support systems are in place before embarking on your campaign.

Success Stories

DRTV campaigns work. Tim Hawthorne, founder, chairman and executive creative director of *hawthorne direct inc.* is considered by many to be the "Father of the Modern Infomercial" (www.hawthornedirect.com). He lists some especially successful campaigns.

- *Millionaire Maker.* Selling the home-study version of Beckley Seminars Real Estate No Down Payment live seminars product created $60 million dollars in revenue and $12 million in net earnings in just 18 months.
- *LifeSign Stop Smoking.* Health Innovations, a small start-up company with a unique stop-smoking program increased sales the first year of doing infomercials from $500,000 to $50 million, and by their second year to over $100 million. The product eventually was distributed internationally via DRTV.
- *RotoZip Tools.* A former dry-wall hanger in Wisconsin developed a new tool that cuts holes using a revolutionary rotary blade drill. His infomercial achieved record media efficiency ratings of as high as 17 to 1 ($17 in sales for every $1 media spent). The infomercial continues to run to this day, having grossed over one-quarter billion in sales.
- *Braun Hand Blender.* Braun, a major appliance manufacturer, saw its hand-held food blender languish on the retail shelves while a knockoff, priced twice as high, sold tens of millions of dollars of product via DRTV. An infomercial was produced and aired that sold Braun's like-styled product direct-over-TV successfully. The impact of the media campaign lifted Braun's in-store retail sales of the same product by 1,100 percent. Braun continued running this campaign for four years.
- *Oreck Air Purifier.* Oreck, a long-time and well-known direct-response marketer of vacuums via print and radio, also ventured into DRTV. In 2003, Oreck launched two separate campaigns for the Oreck vacuum and the Oreck Air Purifier. Both were successes, but the air purifier was exceptional. In 2004, Oreck purchased over $10 million of media time and in the first six months generated over $30 million in sales for the Purifier alone.

OTHER DIRECT MARKETING FORMATS
Sweepstakes

It is reported that in 1850 P .T. Barnum conducted the first recorded contest in the United States. By the turn of the century, there were more examples of prize promotions in advertising mail. In 1897, Eastman Kodak held a photography contest with the aim of increasing the public's interest in picture-taking. Sweepstakes as you know them began to be used more often in the early 1950s with the passing of legislation that allowed certain games of chance.

By the 1960s, with the increasing use of computers, prize promotions started to use preassigned winning entry numbers. With this development, prizes were now only awarded to those who returned winning entries. This led to an FTC investigation, which eventually resulted in sweepstakes sponsors agreeing to guarantee the awarding of all prizes in future contests.

Introduction of lotteries in the United States. The first recorded lottery in America was the Virginia

Lottery of 1611. Early lotteries fell into two broad categories: those organized by individuals for their own profit and those sanctioned by legislation for public benefit. These early lotteries were used extensively in marketing efforts, but as time went by, only those lotteries with legislative approval were allowed.

Today, a lottery is defined as a game of chance that includes the elements of prize, chance, and consideration. It is only legal to run a promotion that includes these three elements if there is specific legislative approval. It is a type of direct-response sweepstakes.

Overview of sweepstakes and contest legality. Currently, many sweepstakes and contests are legal in all 50 states as long as they do not contravene the lottery laws, FTC regulations, the truth-in-advertising laws, and each state's business practice laws.

In summary, to avoid contravening the lottery laws one must eliminate one of the three elements of a lottery (prize, chance, or consideration). Recently, a number of states have enacted laws to curb abuses in conducting sweepstakes, especially the "everyone wins" type of sweepstakes and those connected with time-share promotions. Unfortunately, some legitimate sweepstakes promotions have been adversely affected by this legislation.

Because an increasing number of states are enacting new legislation covering sweepstakes promotions, it is essential that an attorney who specializes in the area of sweepstakes laws approve all sweepstakes copy.

What sweepstakes and contests can accomplish
- Build retail traffic.
- Build sales.
- Increase customer involvement.
- Increase direct mail response.
- Increase coupon redemption.
- Increase questionnaire response.
- Reinforce the benefits of a product or service.
- Help build a database.
- Improve display compliance in retail outlets.
- Motivate salespeople.
- Reward excellent performance.

Mike Vos of Synergy Incorporated (www.synergyincorporated.com), who has granted reprint permission for much of this section on sweepstakes, says he has seen sweepstakes lift responses on average between about 30 percent and 50 percent and occasionally lift 200 percent or more. Sweepstakes may be used for merchandise offers, subscription promotions, catalogs, business-to-business promotions, and fundraising solicitations. Sweepstakes and contests may be used effectively by almost any business that is trying to elicit a response or establish a target audience.

Here is some background on this type of promotion, as well as a few tips on how to conduct a successful sweepstakes campaign.

Prize structure guidelines. The prize structure is one of the most important elements that will contribute to the success or failure of a sweepstakes or contest. The most important factor to bear in mind when developing a prize structure is the interests of your target audience. If you appeal to these interests, you will get their attention. When the prize has "hit this target," I have seen sweepstakes achieve a moderate-to-good success level even though there was only one prize with a relatively small value. Of course, the higher the perceived value of the prize in the eyes of the entrant, the more likely he or she will be to participate.

In order to achieve the highest-possible response, a prize structure needs to have a large grand prize (a dream prize) and a good number of lower-level prizes. If there is a large number of prizes to be won, this should be emphasized in the copy (e.g., a starburst graphic could be included, with the copy: "Over 100 Chances to Win!").

The importance of this combination of one big prize and a large number of smaller prizes cannot be overemphasized. An advantage of this prize combination is that the value of the grand prize does not have to be nearly as high as it does in a sweepstakes with just one prize. Despite the fact that the prize combination could have a lower total prize value, it is possible for the combination sweepstakes to garner a higher response rate than the single-prize sweepstakes.

The choice of which prizes to choose as mid-level prizes has not been proven to be critical to the success of promotions.

When cash is used as a prize in a sweepstakes, the copy should emphasize what can be bought with the cash. But in order for cash to work well as a prize, it needs to be a "dream" amount; if products that interest your audience are used as prizes, they will be more successful than the same (small or mid- level) amount in cash. For the major prize(s), build on your prospects' dreams and fantasies. Appeal to their needs and desires: to look and feel terrific, to suddenly strike it rich, to get a new lease on life, etc.

If your budget for prizes is not very high, you can increase the perceived value of the prize by including a choice. This does not increase your costs, but makes the prize seem more substantial.

Finally, celebrity prizes and trips do not pull as well as product or merchandise prizes. Cars and TV sets still create a high level of interest.

Suggestions for creative copy

- Make sure the sweepstakes copy reflects enthusiasm. Use simple yet strong action statements. Use the majority of the space available to "sell" the sweepstakes and not your product(s).
- Use the word "WIN" often. It is important that the headline should scream the word "WIN." A few states have made it illegal to use outer-envelope teaser copy with a "WIN" statement. Please bear this in mind if you want to conduct a nationally distributed direct mail campaign.
- Be sure to include at least one of the following in a subhead: "Enter," or "Enter Here," or "Enter for Your Chance to Win," or a similar statement. Emphasize the fact that entering is easy, and then simply explain how to enter. This basic formula works every time. And it's most likely to encourage an entry with an order.
- If there are a number of prizes to be won, this should be highlighted.
- Create a sense of urgency through deadlines. Don't hide the deadline statement; give it a prominent position.
- Use an involvement device that encourages purchase of your product.
- Where possible, use testimonials from past winners.
- Use an artist who understands how to make the graphics jump off the page or envelope.

If used correctly, a sweepstakes or contest can dramatically increase response and grab the interest of your target audience. Tim Hawthorne says he has seen this work for many different products and hundreds of different promotions. There's one caveat: Get good legal advice.

Bebe—sweepstakes with style. To see how this is done, here is a strong example of the fundamental use of the direct marketing sweepstakes vehicle, first presented in *iMedia Connection*, copyright 2003 (www.imediaconnection.com). Below is information from that article on how Bebe, the upscale women's retailer, crafted its sweepstakes campaign.

Conducting an average of two online sweepstakes a year, retailer Bebe has found what works and shares how the company has perfected its strategy to maximize results. The woman of today may be career-oriented, but every so often she still likes to play. Offering women the chance to do just that, bebe launched an online sweepstakes campaign titled "Bebe city chic." The winner was awarded prizes, including a trip to New York, a VIP invitation to the April 10, 2003, Bebe/*Vogue* party, two nights at the Bryant Park Hotel, $500 in cash, and a variety of other appealing prizes. The contemporary clothing company, meanwhile, enjoyed increased traffic to its web site, a rise in sales, and an impressive number of opt-ins from people requesting to receive future e-mails from the brand.

How the campaign worked. Partnering with Orbitz, Smashbox Cosmetics, Bryant Park Hotel, and *Vogue* magazine, bebe launched its 12-day online sweepstakes campaign. In an effort to spread awareness, the brand promoted the sweepstakes in a variety of ways. Messages on the brand's home page announced the sweepstakes and provided links for those interested in registering. Text links, flash, and different-size banner ads placed within the shopping section of Yahoo! enticed browsers to participate in the sweepstakes. The company also sent direct e-mails to 113,913 people who had previously opted to receive information on such promotions and distributed sales receipts bearing sweepstakes information and postcard bag stuffers in bebe locations across the United States, except for Rhode Island, Alaska, and Hawaii.

The results. With the hotel discounted and meals of the winner paid for, bebe was able to reduce the cost of the campaign with help from its partners. Even so, the brand ended up spending approximately $4,685. In return, 11,500 people entered the sweepstakes, and 8,366 opted to receive future e-mails. In addition, an average of 22,594 discrete visitors a day was recorded during the first week of the promotion, indicating a 4 percent increase from the week previous to the launch.

According to Julie Kessler, bebe's online marketing manager, it was the direct e-mails that produced the most entries. Of the 113,913 e-mails sent, 25 percent were opened. Kessler credits this high percentage to the fact that the e-mails were sent to consumers who had previously expressed interest through sweepstakes, magazines, mailing-list cards in the stores, and the web site. Therefore, the consumers who received the e-mail had already expressed interest in the brand. In addition, because the brand had conducted sweepstakes before, there was a certain level of trust, and people knew what to expect. Finally, the nature of the sweepstakes helped to attract entrants.

"Most of our customers are really into our brand, and a chance to win a wardrobe and a glammie trip is really appealing to them," Kessler says.

However, the results were especially noteworthy as they indicated an overall improvement over the online sweepstakes that launched in October, 2002, and lasted for 21 days.

Due to the positive results from the online sweepstakes, bebe continued these as well. Not only did they attract visitors to its site and encourage consumers to opt-in for information but they also built excitement around the events and parties. And for a contemporary women's apparel and accessories company such as bebe,

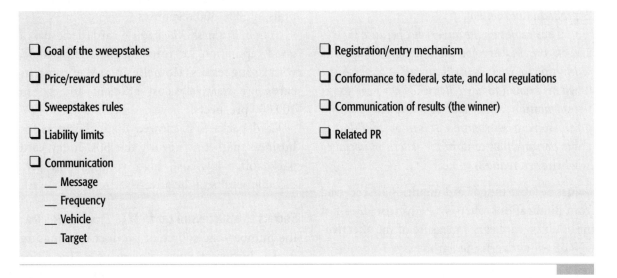

FIGURE 3.7   Sweepstakes Checklist

- ❑ Goal of the sweepstakes
- ❑ Price/reward structure
- ❑ Sweepstakes rules
- ❑ Liability limits
- ❑ Communication
  - ___ Message
  - ___ Frequency
  - ___ Vehicle
  - ___ Target
- ❑ Registration/entry mechanism
- ❑ Conformance to federal, state, and local regulations
- ❑ Communication of results (the winner)
- ❑ Related PR

the internet may be the most effective way of attracting modern women who, every once in a while, just want to have fun. (Reprinted with permission, www.imediaconnection.com.)

Use Figure 3.7, the Sweepstakes Checklist, to help you make sure you have covered all your bases.

Bingo Cards

Bingo cards, as they relate to direct marketing, are reply/response cards inserted into a publication as a vehicle to request information from advertisers in a particular publication. Said another way, a bingo card is a reply card inserted into a publication used by readers to request literature from companies whose products and services are either advertised or mentioned in editorial columns. They are also referred to as reader inquiry cards.

The response mechanism, usually on one side of the card and in the form of a postage-paid reply card returned to the issuer of the bingo card (often the publication). In turn, returns are

sent to the company supplying the information that is requested by the reader.

Sure, your ad in a publication will offer many other response mechanisms but not all readers will want to respond by phone, fax, online, or snail mail. Many find it efficient and easy to check off a box or circle a number on a bingo card as they read the publication.

Greg Jarboe of Ziff-Davis Publishing states that 20 percent of readers use bingo cards. One out of five of these 20 percent generally buys within 90 days. By direct marketing standards, this is a good response.

In the book, *Readings & Cases in Direct Marketing* (NTC Business Books, 1988) the article *"Bingo Card Junkies, Why They Could Be Your Best Prospects"* states:

> *Contrary to common perception, people who circle a large number of bingo card numbers are very important prospects . . . Heavy circling causes some marketers to think that the literature they supply is money thrown away, but not responding to such*

inquiries leaves vendors "unqualified" from the buyer's perspective when the buyer's problem does get hot.

They're not on the buyer's list because they took the inquiry too lightly. Sometimes a multiple circler is a "squirrel"—a person who is known to have files when the need for information arises, and is to provide problem-solving information. It is important that the person's files contain the seller's material when such requests come."

Just because bingo card inquiries are received from publications where you advertise does not mean bingo cards are a measure of the effectiveness of your advertising. Jarboe says:

Use bingo card leads to produce additional sales—not to judge advertising effectiveness. If you want to do research on how well your ads are working, and you can't get clear answers from your sales data, use focus groups or pay for some quality copy research. Don't make the mistake of using bingo leads volume as a measure of success. Bingo leads can make you some extra money but they can't help you draw fine distinctions between offers, creative concepts, positioning issues, etc.

Handling bingo card responses and leads aggressively and responding and fulfilling consistently can be a direct route to sales and profits.

Card Decks

Card decks are shrink-wrapped packages of advertising postcards. They let you reach hundreds of thousands of targeted prospects at a fraction of the normal cost of direct mail.

For example, Jeffrey Lant's long-running card deck program (WorldProfit.com) goes to 100,000 opportunity seekers and small-business people. You can get a one-line classified relatively inexpensively. A 5.5" by 3.5" card generally pulls in 50 to 300 responses.

Home Business Magazine's card deck has a good reputation for reaching the right people, with strong results (HomeBusinessMag.com). Its cards are relatively cost efficient and go to 100,000 prospects.

Card packs first showed up in business-to-business marketing in early the '50s. Today, card packs offer low-cost, high volume, and predictable results to the advertiser!

Secrets to a successful card. *D.C. Products Review,* the number-one source of product information in the chiropractic marketplace, offers these tips for a successful card that is part of a card deck mailing:

- *A horizontal layout is best.* Most recipients will not take the time to flip your card as they go through the "deck."
- *Add color.* Two-color is good, four is better. The more you can stimulate the senses, the better your response will be. Including a product photo is a must! Show the product's benefits in action!
- *Create a strong headline.* Make it a showstopper; use words like Free, Introductory Offer, and New!
- *Offer alternative ways to respond.* Include your free-toll number, fax, or web site address!
- *White space is good space.* Too much copy diminishes readability. Allow your message to breathe!
- *Make it easy to read.* Use at least 10-point type for main lines. Remember—it is natural to read top to bottom and left to right! Use lowercase letters! Research has shown that lowercase letters in headlines and text are easier to read than letters that are capitalized

- *Be clear and concise.* It should only take seven to ten seconds to read your main points and make your offer known; any longer and you risk losing your prospect! Keep it short!
- *Include a statement of satisfaction guaranteed.* This eliminates any feelings of risk. Gain their trust from the start!
- *Spark the reader's interest.* Offer a free product sample or free information!
- *Be user-friendly.* Make all your forms easy to fill out, and, of course, having a return-postage-paid card heightens your response!

Coupons

Coupons are both a response-generating direct marketing vehicle and a data collection tool. Coupons can be used to directly market and sell, and also represent an opportunity to find out more about your customers. Paying attention to and understanding the information gathered will guide you in reaching more prospects like your current customers and will show you how to get current customers to return more often. Sooner or later, as you accumulate more information from coupon responders, you can begin to segment your customer base and market accordingly.

Response Radio

David Oreck's voice on the radio:

> *Hi! I'm David Oreck, and I'm proud that over one million of my Oreck XL vacuum cleaners are . . . . Shoes don't ruin carpets, dirt does!*

Direct marketers using response radio can find themselves with spurts of flurried activity. The entire response time to a radio or TV direct commercial is 15 minutes. After that, you lose a prospect, either forever or until he is reminded by another commercial; most of the time, it's forever. You then have to make sure you are set up, using overflow systems during this flurried activity, to handle the responses generated. Not doing so is a cardinal sin in direct marketing and wastes a response.

Business Reply Card (BRC)

Including a business reply card (BRC) in your mailing is a surefire way of improving response rates. One of the fundamental rules of direct marketing is to make it easy for your prospect to act. Filling out cards, taking surveys, going online, and setting appointments can sometimes seem like too much for a prospect to go through, thereby diminishing response rates. It is much easier for an interested prospect to drop a BRC in the mail.

A business reply and permit can be purchased from the USPS. With the purchase, you're provided guidelines on how it is to look in its finished, printed state as well as guidelines for your printer. Once designed and printed, include it in as many mailings as you can. You can include it in an envelope package with a letter or make it a tear-off, perforated in a self-mailer.

Pay particular attention to the printing guidelines, as the position and clarity of the bar code is very important and will ensure delivery. Thickness and weight of the paper stock is also important, to ensure getting through automatic mail-processing equipment.

Newsletters in Direct Marketing

When you think of newsletters, you usually think about reading "news" about a particular company or organization. Feature articles about new products and services, personnel profiles of key employees, human-interest stories, and event information fill newsletter pages. In addition, newsletters usually announce, inform, entertain, and promote identity and awareness; all are related to relationship-building.

Is this direct marketing? The answer is usually no, if presented in the way that is described above. Let's review our definition of direct marketing to further answer this question.

Direct marketing is marketing that presents an offer with the intent of getting a response. In the description of newsletters above, there was no mention of an offer or a means of response. In the absence of these, a newsletter is not direct marketing. Sure, it keeps the company's name and identity in front of prospects and customers, but awareness is not the sole purpose of direct marketing.

If in your newsletter, you offer a special premium or discount just for readers by directing them to your web site for redemption, it starts to conform to the definition of direct marketing. A coupon with an offer, including a printed perforated border for clipping, would also make this newsletter more of a direct marketing vehicle.

Also consistent with the definition of direct marketing, by putting an offer in the newsletter, you now have the ability to measure the effectiveness of the vehicle; who reads it and how many respond to it.

You're spending money on marketing with this vehicle, so you might as well attempt to get it to pay for itself and more. Take advantage of this marketing touch and make it direct; make it an income-generating direct marketing vehicle. At least give customers a chance to place an order with you for your products and services.

What, at first, doesn't appear to be a direct marketing vehicle, can in fact be turned into one with just a few offers and a few response mechanisms, both increasing the efficiency of your marketing.

Much can be learned from what is being done, including the marketing you already are exposed to or are already receiving. Some of it will work; some won't. Some will stand out; some won't. In order to help you study this marketing, use the Direct Mail Audit Form (Figure 3.8) as a guide to make your direct marketing campaigns more effective.

| FIGURE 3.8 | **Direct Mail Audit Form** |

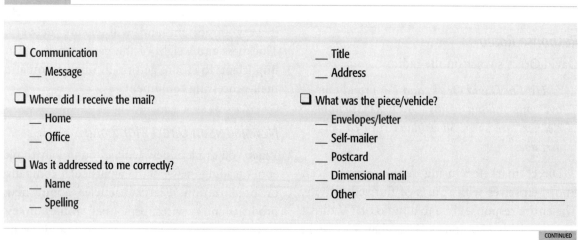

❑ Communication
  ___ Message

❑ Where did I receive the mail?
  ___ Home
  ___ Office

❑ Was it addressed to me correctly?
  ___ Name
  ___ Spelling

  ___ Title
  ___ Address

❑ What was the piece/vehicle?
  ___ Envelopes/letter
  ___ Self-mailer
  ___ Postcard
  ___ Dimensional mail
  ___ Other _____

CONTINUED

| FIGURE 3.8 | Direct Mail Audit Form |

❑ Did it immediately grab my attention? _____

❑ If yes, was the attention-grabber:
___ A picture?
___ A graphic/an illustration?
___ A headline?
___ A package?
___ Lots of color?
___ Creative copy?
___ An irresistible offer?
___ Something else extreme? _____

❑ Was it sent out with a stamp or permit indicia:
___ First-class?
___ Standard presort?

❑ Was there a call to action?
___ Where was it? _____
___ Was it easy to find/see? _____
___ Did you respond? _____

❑ Did you save the piece or discard it? _____

❑ Did it look like all the rest of your direct mail? _____

❑ If no, what made it different? _____

❑ Was there a special offer? _____

❑ What was being offered? _____
_____

❑ What part of the offer did you like? _____
___ Sample
___ Trial
___ Discount
___ Other _____

❑ Did the word free show up on the card? _____
_____

❑ Did the marketing leave you wanting more? _____
_____

❑ Did you have any questions that were left unanswered?
_____

❑ If this were your marketing, how would you change it to make it better? _____
_____

❑ How would you describe this marketing to someone in one sentence? _____
_____

— CHAPTER 3 SUMMARY —

▶ One of the four primary components of direct marketing is the marketing vehicle. Essentially, this is the component that defines how you will reach your targeted prospect.

▶ In order to qualify as a direct marketing vehicle, it has to be targeted for the purpose of soliciting a response. The different types of other direct marketing are only limited by a marketer's imagination.

▶ Direct mail is a means of direct communication involving the sending of a marketing message directly to a targeted list of prospects, most times using the U.S. Postal Service as the means of delivery

▶ Research from the Direct Marketing Association indicates that sales effectiveness of direct mail per-dollar-of-expenditure continues to grow and continues to outperform direct marketing overall, measured the same way.

▶ To prevent your mail from being considered "junk," you must send it as much as possible to recipients who you know will be interested in what you have to say.

▶ You must understand your prospect in all facets and segment your target into those interested in your offer.

▶ In today's increasingly cluttered marketing environment, direct mail continues to be one of the best ways to reach your target market and interact with them, seemingly on a one-on-one basis.

▶ Finding the right basic mailing format that consistently outperforms others will be determined by the amount of testing you do for your campaign.

▶ Choosing the format of your mailing is part of the creative process. It's crucial because it influences how the art, copy, and graphics will come into play and be used.

▶ One of the most popular direct marketing vehicles is the letter.

▶ Marketing with postcards is quick, easy, and, as you will find, less expensive than many of the traditional advertising, promotional, and marketing vehicles used today.

▶ Postcards are considered the fastest, easiest and most reliable way to dramatically increase your revenue and customer response.

▶ Dimensional-package mailings significantly impact response rates.

▶ Sweepstakes and contests may be used effectively for almost any business that is trying to elicit a response or establish a target audience.

▶ Bingo cards, as they relate to direct marketing, are reply/response cards inserted into a publication that serves as a vehicle by which to request information from advertisers.

▶ Card decks are shrink-wrapped packages of advertising postcards. They let you reach hundreds of thousands of targeted prospects at a fraction of the normal cost of direct mail.

▶ Almost anything may be sold through a catalog.

▶ Even with shoppers migrating to the internet, catalog marketing and selling is still strong.

▶ Catalogs represent a way a business can expand, either with new products or geographically.

▶ Consistent with the direct-marketing definition, telemarketing is the use of phone calls to prospects or customers for the purpose of generating a response. The response can be an order (the ultimate goal of any direct marketing) or another type of interested response as you have seen in other direct marketing applications.

▶ The reason these calls continue is because they work and produce results.

▶ More and more advertisers, including a large number of blue-chip companies, are using short-form Direct Response TV (DRTV) and infomercials to market their products and services.

Direct E-Mail Marketing

*A NEW COMMUNICATIONS TECHNO-
logy was developed that allowed
people to communicate almost
instantly across great distances,
in effect shrinking the world faster and
further than ever before; a worldwide
communications network whose cables
spanned continents and oceans, it revolu-
tionized business practice, gave rise to
new forms of crime and inundated its
users with a deluge of information.
Romances blossomed over the wires.
Secret codes were devised by some users
and cracked by others. The benefits of the
network were relentlessly hyped by its
advocates and dismissed by the skeptics.
Governments and regulators tried and
failed to control the new medium.
Attitudes toward everything from news
gathering to diplomacy had to be completely rethought. Meanwhile, a techno-
logical subculture with its own customs
and vocabulary established itself.*

At first glance, this looks as if it could have
come from yesterday's *New York Times* or
Chicago Tribune or even Yahoo online in a story
about e-mail, the internet, and other online
activity. It did not come from these sources. In
fact, this excerpt is from *The Victorian
Internet—The Remarkable Story of the
Telegraph and the Nineteenth Century's On-line
Pioneers* by Tom Standage (Berkley Books).
This description is the preface to a description
of how technology helped people tap a new
vein of optimism helped others find new ways
to commit crimes, start romantic relationships,
get rich quick, or at least start businesses.
Sound familiar? These same conditions exist
today with the internet that you now know so
very well. With e-mail the number-one application of the internet, it is easy to see how
direct communication can lead to direct-marketing applications. It happened with the telegraph. It's happening with the internet.

The first e-mail dates back to two programs developed by Ray Tomlinson of Bolt,

Beranek and Newman (BBN) that could send messages across the ARPANET. This was in 1971. The programs were SNDMSG and READMAIL for sending and reading, respectively. The first program that integrated sending and receiving was the BANANARD (it was first named as WRD), written by Marty Yonke. Mail addresses as we see them today were introduced in 1984.

In 1989, MCI Mail and CompuServe provided the first commercial e-mail connection to the internet through the Corporation for the National Research Initiative (CNRI) and Ohio State University, respectively. E-mail could then be accessed only through e-mail clients. Web mail was introduced in 1996 by companies like Hotmail, Four11, WhoWhere, and iName.

Today, direct marketers have the expertise and have been using the fundamental processes that are at the foundation of the internet's commercial application. With internet direct marketing, it's almost as if marketers have a head start. Just look at how communication is targeted, responses are solicited, orders are taken and fulfilled, databases are sorted, and customer-service systems take over. All are vital to e-commerce. Direct marketers are clearly poised to take full advantage the online vehicles available in the digital age.

Much of today's business is conducted via e-mail. Those not communicating via e-mail are deemed inefficient and inaccessible. Yes, there are a few exceptions, but their numbers are declining rapidly.

Ninety-seven percent of businesspeople use e-mail every day (Source: Pitney Bowes). IDC expects e-mails to exceed 35 billion by 2005. These developments are startling and are coupled with the fact that two-thirds of American citizens now use the internet (Source: *The Observer*).

Much like traditional direct marketing, direct e-mail marketing is the sending of e-mail to a targeted group of recipients for the purpose of response. As we learned in traditional direct marketing, response can take different forms.

E-mail marketing has hit the 21st century like a thunderbolt. Never has any marketing tactic become so widespread, so fast, so inexpensively. E-mail marketing can be done quicker, better, and cheaper than most other direct marketing. It should be the "no brainer" part of any marketing plan.

Where else in marketing can you do all this in one day, from start to finish?

- Think of what you want to market.
- Develop the communication.
- Send it to the targeted list of prospects.
- Measure the response.
- Process the responses.
- Fulfill orders.
- Evaluate the campaign.

The answer is direct e-mail.

This is not a recommendation to launch a campaign in one day, but it is theoretically possible,

▼ DIRECT E-MAIL DEFINITION

Simply put, direct e-mail marketing is a campaign of e-mail-formatted advertisements or messages sent to a targeted list of recipients via e-mail; it's very similar to the definition of traditional direct mail marketing. Direct e-mail marketing is sending e-mail to a targeted group of people, whereas spam is a mass mailing sent to a group of people with whom no previous relationship has been established.

where as it isn't generally possible with other marketing.

Although it is relatively easy to use and implement, it does have one characteristic common to all other marketing: It must be planned to be effective.

More and more companies are using direct e-mail every day. Effective planning is required to prevent shotgun efforts and getting lost in the competitive quagmire. With this rapid growth comes the need to stand out among the growing pool of participants. Just throwing e-mail messages out into the electronic community pool has a low probability of success. Planning the right message to the right people in the right way to stand out in this pool gives you a much higher probability of success.

MARKET STATISTICS BACKGROUND

At the time of writing, reports and research are pointing to increased spending by businesses on online marketing. This research also shows increased usage of e-mail promotions, web casts, and online newsletter advertising.

Some of the statistics reported were quite significant compared to the usage statistics for the previous year:

- The number of those who use e-mail promotions was up 83 percent.
- The number of those that will use web casts rose by 55 percent.
- The number of those planning on using newsletter advertising increased by 44 percent.

While the details and absolute information are not fully reported here, the general direction of these trends is obvious and underscores the importance of the direct marketing components of a business operation, especially direct online marketing.

In late 2004, Millward Brown reported in its "Marketing and Media Snapshot: 2004" report that marketing and media budgets continue to grow, with online budgets growing the fastest.

The report went on to further state that all channels of online marketing, advertising, search, e-mail, and promotions will grow at faster rates than other major media. This represents the feeling of those surveyed and is representative of the general marketplace, that online marketing is the most effective media for acquiring and retaining customers.

These statistics and research are supported by overloaded e-mail boxes—both legitimate commercial marketing messages and spam.

With a lot of direct marketing relying on numbers and probabilities, e-mail marketing can provide more numbers and more opportunities for viewing and communicating in a very cost-effective way. Of course, at the time of writing,

▼ TIPS FOR E-MAIL SUCCESS

Just like offline marketing, the success of direct e-mail marketing depends on many of the same variables. You still must have the right offer, supported by the right ad copy, offered to the right target group of people.

Direct e-mail marketing requires an attention-getting subject line.

An effective e-mail call to action is paramount and can be enhanced with a live link to a web site or to send an e-mail (hyperlink).

Frequency and timing are as important in e-mail direct marketing as for offline direct marketing.

thir cost effectiveness assumes there is no "e-mail postage."

With today's technology and the ensuing advancements, e-mailing can be done inhouse. No longer are expensive professional services required. This puts direct e-mail marketing efforts and costs in the hands of the marketer.

Direct e-mail marketing is highly effective in advertising, surveying, two-way communication, up-selling, cross-selling, making offers, and just staying in touch with customers and prospects. It is considered one of the most cost-effective ways to market, reaching many people at little or no expense. Compared to offline marketing, your messages reach your prospects at a fraction of the cost.

E-Mail Marketing Uses

- Single messages
- E-zines/newsletters
- Broadcast e-mails—sent to a wide distribution of targeted recipients for all the same reasons you would send traditional direct marketing. These can still be personalized and are still highly targeted.

Uses of E-mail Marketing

- Marketing to your own e-mail list
- Renting an opt-in e-mail address list
- Advertise in e-mail
- Links in e-mail
- Signatures
- Special offers only available via e-mail
- Announcement of new products/services
- Sales announcements
- Customer loyalty programs/frequent-buyer programs
- Contests/sweepstakes

- Referral programs—"send this to five friends to receive your free special white paper."

Using E-mail for Direct Response

Direct e-mail has many useful applications:

- Direct e-mail can reach a wide range of targets (businesses, consumers, opt-in, segmented, etc.).
- Direct e-mail can be linked to your web site to increase traffic.
- Information can be gathered through online e-mail surveys.
- Direct e-mail can be used to inform, announce, or generally stay in touch with clients and prospects.
- Direct e-mail can be targeted according to how you segment your e-mail list.

TYPES OF E-MAIL MARKETING

Direct e-mail marketing has many uses and, as the following describes, some cannot be done with traditional offline direct mail.

- *E-zine and online newsletters.* Although this is not direct marketing, online newsletters do allow you to continue an ongoing relationship with your customers, keep in touch with them, make special offers from time to time, and show prospects the benefits and value of doing business with you.
- *E-zine and online newsletters with embedded links.* This is where online communication stands out from offline communication. Adding a hyperlink to your communication directs readers to your web page for more information.
- *Automated e-mail messaging.* Databases can be created to allow for an unlimited number

of automated variable responses to be sent to your recipients. These can be set up months in advance and automate much of your online marketing.

- *E-mail presentations.* You can attach and send a presentation to your prospects to be viewed at their convenience or in conjunction with a phone presentation (webinar).

Advantages

The cost to you for e-mail has nothing to do with who receives it, where they are in the world, or how large a file you are sending. Most e-mail client charges are included in a monthly access fee. This may or may not depend on the number of hours you use the client server or how large your in-box capacity and usage storage is.

Direct marketing is being reshaped by electronic direct marketing. The very fact that campaigns are easily measured, created, and implemented makes it the direct marketing tactic of choice for most marketers.

Direct e-mail marketing fits the direct marketing framework. A compelling message with an attention-getting subject line can make an irresistible offer that can be responded to by a precisely targeted recipient and be measured—all quicker, better, and cheaper than via traditional direct marketing.

- *Targeted audience.* Because permission-based lists are used, your audience has already expressed an interest in you and in what you have to say. Legally, ethically, and theoretically, those receiving offers via this medium have given their permission to marketers. This increases response rates by five to six times compared to traditional direct mail.
- *Cost.* At the time of writing, there is no postage assessed to the distribution of e-mail.

For me to send you an e-mail message costs nothing. For you to send a message to your targeted, opt-in list costs nothing. No paper, no ink, no envelopes, no glossy cards, no postage is required for direct e-mail marketing. Compare this to the campaign you just sent out via regular post office processed and delivered mail.

There are costs, though, associated with creating the message/campaigns if an agency and a delivery service to distribute e-mails are used.

- *Speed.* Internet speed is virtually instantaneous; certainly speedier than any other form of marketing except direct sales calls and telemarketing. Click, send, and—depending on your internet service provider's server and your recipient's server—a message can show up instantly. Compare this to post office deliveries of one to seven days. Results of e-mail can be measured simultaneously as well. Real-time campaigns can be developed in a day.

The Bush campaign of 2004 collected much data upon its mandatory registration and used first-name personalization on all e-mails. The Kerry campaign only personalized if the registrant opted to become a campaign volunteer—a process that required submission of the registrant's first name (regular e-mail subscribers were not offered an opportunity to provide their first names, only their e-mail address and zip code). Kerry could have considered collecting a bit more information upon sign-up—even optional fields would have helped fill out their database and enabled more customized messaging.

With many e-mail programs it is possible to determine not only who has responded to a particular e-mail offer but also who actually opened the e-mail and did not respond. This could be as important for you to know as the former. You can't make this determination with traditional direct mail.

- *Personalization.* Customizing e-mails is as easy, perhaps more so, than traditional direct mail.
- *Testing ability.* E-mail has many trackable characteristics and is very conducive to quick tests.
- *Integrated.* E-mail marketing campaigns can support all marketing.
- *Instant calls to action.* Embedding a link in your message provides an instant response mechanism for your recipients, right at the peak of their interest.
- *Branding.* Even though I am emphasizing direct response, there still is a "look and feel" to your messages that recipients experience. Sometimes, this is all they experience, so use this advantage and promote your identity.
- *Faster campaign implementation*
- *Better response rates*
- *Immediate assessment of a campaign's effectiveness*
- *Interactivity.* The direct messaging of e-mail marketing also allows for two-way exchanges—truly a marketing dialogue, increasing the chance a good response. E-mails encourage this immediate interactivity with direct hyperlinks and return e-mails. Offers are usually crystal-clear—e.g., click here for the rest of the article, buy this, send for a free report, respond with your e-mail address, etc. This interactivity leads to purchases, a primary goal of any direct marketing.

- *High-impact contact*
- *Easily measured*
- *Versatile.* E-mail can be used to send all types of documents, including letters, memos, notes, photos, graphics, data, spreadsheets, artist and editor proofs, or reports. Applications are only limited by your actual e-mail program.
- *Noninvasive.* Sent e-mail may or may not interrupt your receiver. Usually mail will be saved in an unopened e-mail folder that the recipient can access at his or her convenience, without interruption.
- *Convenient.* Because you are not interrupted when e-mail arrives, you can read it or work with it when you make the time. The sending of e-mail can also be treated the same way. You can send it at a convenient or designated time. It doesn't have to be written or sent at a time when you know the recipient will be available.

E-MAIL LIMITATIONS

E-mail isn't necessarily private. There are many issues with hacking, identity theft, and related corruption. This is as rampant online as it is offline. The many networks involved that carry e-mail messages make them vulnerable and not as private, many times, as snail mail. True, there are more and more security systems being built into and implemented for e-mail messaging, but each time there is a new system, there is a new hacker trying to violate the security it offers. Being aware of this is the first step toward security.

All e-mail systems are not created equal. Some systems can communicate, send and receive text-only files. Some programs cannot show the pictures, graphics, or complex files that may be sent. Some systems cannot accommodate HTML e-mails that are becoming more and more popular.

It's possible to forge e-mail. E-mail is not like the written word. My typed word looks just like your typed word. On top of this, there are ways to forge the address of the sender.

It's difficult to express emotion using e-mail. Just as with all other written communication, it is hard to read between the lines without the benefit of body language, facial expressions, or voice inflection. Because of this, what you think might be humorous might not be received in the same way, and vice versa.

You can receive junk e-mail just as you receive other types of junk mail offline. But junk e-mail can overload a system and cause inefficient use of your time as you try to sort through the volume of messages you receive. It can be safely said that if you have an e-mail address, you will receive junk. In many cases the volume of you receive far outweighs the unwanted mail you receive offline.

Lack of identity of the sender can be a problem; with traditional offline direct mail you usually know who the sender is. With e-mail, you may not know. This is another strong contributor to corruption online.

HOW DIRECT E-MAIL MARKETING DIFFERS FROM TRADITIONAL DIRECT MARKETING

As a traditional direct mail package is received, a reader (prospect) can riffle through it, pick and choose what looks interesting, and read it or not. This might be a letter with a fact sheet, a brochure, and a few testimonials. Direct e-mail marketing can't be sifted through from piece to piece in arbitrary order. Your prospect must read it top to bottom.

The marketer has a bit more control over the prospects' viewing. The drawback is not being able to fit as many components into an e-mail message. However, with today's hyperlink technology, you can direct readers to other links with other information or a series of e-mail marketing messages can be sent over time consisting of one component at a time. The series approach helps to tell the marketer's story but becomes less direct if a purchase depends on hearing the whole story.

E-MAIL MARKETING MISTAKES

As you watch your own e-mail in-box pile grow daily, you continue to get frustrated with the junk received. Yes, I said *junk* because it is not intended for you, you are not interested in it, and you won't respond to it—much less read it. This amount of junk frustrates you every day. You can't help but wonder: Why am I getting so much junk? Why won't these people stop? If I continue to delete it unread, won't they just go away?

Unfortunately, as things stand now, these marketers, or spammers, will not be going away anytime soon. If 4 percent of e-mails in total are responded to, spammers and mass e-mail marketers are willing to accept you hitting your own delete buttons. Someone, somewhere will actually read their e-mails. Regardless of your stance, feelings, or practices, there is a right way to market by e-mail and there are mistakes that many freelance marketers make.

Here is a list of definite "don'ts" when using e-mail marketing. This will help keep you out of the junk pile and greatly reduce the number of frustrated prospects.

- Don't buy arbitrary e-mail lists that haven't been tested or aren't even billed as opt-in. Purchasing any e-mail list and marketing to it is still not a high-success activity even if it is billed as opt-in. The best list to market to is *your own* list of opted-in prospects and customers. This way you know for sure that they are interested and are part of your target market. You take huge chances with purchased lists of any kind. Related to this is the general principle of not sending out massive untargeted spam mailings.

- HTML e-mails do have some advantages and disadvantages. Do not send out an HTML e-mail as text, otherwise you get an e-mail full of code that only the geekiest of geeks will read and be interested in. If you send out HTML e-mails, make sure your hyperlinks link to something. Broken links in an e-mail are a no-no.

- Don't send out e-mail marketing messages with huge attachments. Many recipients won't even open any attachment unless they know you positively and trust you beyond all doubt. For who that will open an attachment, limit yours to less than 5 MB.

- As you offer your privacy, opt-in, and unsubscribe policies and procedures, you will surely get those asking to be removed from your list. This happens inevitably as people change their jobs, their goals, and their attitudes. This is OK because it makes your marketing more efficient. When this does happen, respect it, remove the names, and don't make the mistake of sending out another e-mail to those names. Make a folder in your e-mail program to capture all remove requests and act on them immediately so you don't forget to do it before your next mailing goes out.

- E-mail marketing should be tested just like traditional direct mail marketing. Testing a portion of your list will provide valuable information related to openings and responses. When testing, use a small portion of your list, not the whole list. Also, don't wear out the same portion of your list with test after test after test.

The key to e-mail marketing is respect for your prospect. Much as in traditional direct mail, you want to keep your mistakes to a minimum. An offended or perturbed prospect usually has no inclination ever to become a paying client. An offended or perturbed customer usually just leaves, ending their lifetime of value to you. You don't want your marketing campaigns to turn into antimarketing or sales prevention campaigns! Repeated mistakes can be very harmful to your business. E-mail is an incredibly effective tool, but only when used correctly. Show respect for the individuals on your e-mail lists, and pay close attention to the details of the mailing itself. You can then reap the benefits of e-mail marketing.

HOW TO IMPROVE YOUR E-MAIL MARKETING

- *Don't be tempted to mass e-mail.* Do not use e-mail as a mass marketing medium. You may be tempted to do this because it is so inexpensive. Why not blast to the world? If direct marketing is a numbers game, why not go for as many numbers as possible? Don't do it. There is so much spam today that direct marketing is being threatened by the delete key on many computers. Direct e-mail marketing is quickly becoming more junky than traditional direct mail because of those treating it as a mass marketing medium. Don't do it. Read the sections on opt-in lists. Make sure your message and marketing are important and of interest to a potential prospect. When in doubt, don't send.

- *Are your opt-ins really interested?* Even those who have opted in to your list may not necessarily be interested in your product or service. Many opt-in lists are developed through the enticements of sweepstakes and other promotions where the recipient is only interested in the sweepstakes prize or promotional offer, not the actual product or service. Know who is on your list and the source of your list. Determine if they are really as interested a prospect as opt-in suggests.

- *Direct mail objectives.* What are you really trying to do with your mail marketing? Just because there is no or little cost associated with e-mail doesn't mean you should abuse the frequency of sending it. You want to be very careful not to fall into the annoyance category. Discriminate just as you do with traditional direct mail. Every 30 days keeps you out of the annoyance category. Testing frequency will also help you know how often to market without annoying a prospect. Measure the response rate, not the complaint rate.

- *What is the effect on your bottom line?* You will know the answer to this question by measuring and analyzing. Here are a few thoughts to help you understand the effect of this type of marketing on your bottom line:
  - What is the conversion rate of responders to paying customers?
  - How many interested prospects can you add to your list and market to in the future?
  - What is the lifetime value of those who buy from you?

- *Don't forget to respond.* You worked hard to create a campaign and craft an offer to elicit response. When someone does respond, don't ignore that response. You might think it is common sense to mention this. Responding may be common sense; its just not common practice. Just handling responses in an efficient, timely

manner may be enough to give you a competitive edge.

- *Get help if and when you need it.* You have your area of expertise. Creating direct marketing campaigns may or may not be one of them. Regardless of your expertise, you can't be an expert in everything and get everything done by yourself. Use the pros. There are copywriters, graphic designers, printers, mail processors, and list vendors who offer their assistance. Let the pros do what they do best so you can do what you do best. Don't be afraid to ask for help, and certainly don't be afraid to admit that you are not an expert in everything.

- *Use HTML in your e-mail.* Take advantage of the fact that most e-mail programs today are able to read HTML. Use HTML in your e-mail messages. This will pop the color, show the photos, and professionalize your message. In addition to the aesthetics, you can insert links and forms in your messages to make them interactive and very conducive to direct response.

- *Automate wherever possible.* Some e-mail programs allow you to specify the date and time for e-mails to be sent. This allows you to set up a whole campaign's set of messages in advance. This campaign management feature saves you lots of time, while keeping your campaign on schedule. There are both programs and services that do this.

> Some e-mail programs, such as older AOL programs, can't read HTML messages.

SURVIVABILITY OF YOUR E-MAIL MESSAGE

Your e-mail in-box has become a focus of sender's attention, much like other marketing arenas. There are eight ways to increase the "survivability" of your message/e-mail:

1. One-to-one communication wins out every time. Know your recipient; know what they want and need. Know what they are interested in. Know why they have given you permission to be on your list. Know what they do, how they react certain things, and why. The more you know about your prospect, the more you can craft a message that encourages response and effective interaction and marketing success.

2. Opt-in permission doesn't always guarantee readability and attention, but nonpermission increases, significantly, the potential for your e-mail to be deleted.

3. Some e-mail marketers will segment their e-mail lists to make sure their marketing message is appropriate for the group they are sending it to.

4. Personalization helps achieve one-on-one marketing. Bulk e-mail recognized as such slides into the junk mail category quickly. Personalization will avoid the bulk look. Using the recipient's name in salutations strengthens your connection with them. The ultimate in personalization is the e-mail reply. This shows attention to one person and creates a customer dialogue and relationship that is vitally important to your marketing and your business.

5. Motivate to action! I'm talking about direct e-mail marketing here; therefore, you want your recipient to take action. In order to make this happen, you have to tell your prospects what action you expect them to take. Be clear here and identify all ways to respond. In addition to telling them exactly what to do, you should clearly communicate what they get in return for taking such action. This is basic direct marketing messaging.

6. Fill in the blanks wisely. The blanks here refer to the sender's field and the subject line field. In the sender field, use your name or the name that people recognized when they opted in to your list. The subject line is more important than a salutation or a headline because people see it before they open an e-mail. Use this powerful marketing tool to your advantage. You have 30 to 40 characters to grab attention and motivate your recipient to open and read your message.

7. Testing applies as much, if not more, to direct e-mail marketing than to any other kind of marketing. Measuring responses, click-through rates, and returned e-mails will show the effectiveness of your campaign and/or variable tested.

8. One of the advantages of e-mail messages is that you can use photos, images, graphics, and links to communicate your message. Don't overload your message with these. Think of your images and graphics supporting the context of your marketing message. Having banner ads and "advertisement-looking" graphics is the quickest way to the delete file.

Direct marketing fundamentals apply. A highly targeted audience coupled with low or no-cost delivery and high response rates to an irresistible offer account for e-mail marketing's high degree of effectiveness and very high ROI.

E-MAIL LISTS

Just like traditional direct mail, there are list brokers for opt-in e-mail lists.

Opt-in e-mail lists are usually offered by category. These lists are compromised of people who have expressed an interest in something.

This adds another dimension to the further defining and refining of your target audience and ideal client. What category best describes them? Refining can be done by defining more categories for the list member to belong to. Adding more to the interest category starts to narrow the universal list further. Adding more categories substantially reduces the number available but narrows the list closer to your defined target audience. A refined list will win out over quantity every time.

Some vendors offer list selects to help in this process. This further segments the category list by gender, industry, geography, or other specifications. Keep in mind that you pay a premium for applying selects to a list.

Note: E-mail address lists are proprietary even when offered by an e-mail list vendor or broker. Unlike traditional direct mail lists, the vendors send out your promotion to the people on the lists you've purchased or rented. You do not get the list for your own e-mailing directly to the addressee. This is different than traditional direct mail list rentals.

DATABASE E-MAIL MARKETING

Database marketing can be done within the context of e-mail messaging. You can use the same database-marketing techniques of sorting and segmenting to refine your lists to your precise target. This, of course, assumes that you have all the information necessary to sort and segment. Sometimes you only have an e-mail address—not enough to segment. The same rules, however, apply. Narrow your target, find your niche, make your offer, collect responses, measure, fulfill, repeat, and most of all, test, test, test. The good news is that all phases of database e-mail marketing can be carried out much quicker than in traditional database marketing.

E-MAIL DELIVERABILITY

Not every e-mail sent is delivered. There are many reasons they never make it to the intended recipient's inbox. The biggest reason today is the smart spam filters that are increasingly used. Another reason is the high turnover in accounts and the number of e-mail users who change companies or e-mail accounts. The old addresses become undeliverable. This is happening at a higher rate then ever.

Once an e-mail bounces back as undeliverable, it is very important that you remove that bad address from your e-mail marketing list. This will make your marketing more efficient and your measurement and testing processes more accurate.

Here are the different reasons why e-mail messages bounce back as undeliverable:

- An e-mail box does not exist for a particular domain.
- An e-mail box is full.
- A sender's e-mail server is slow or still attempting delivery.
- The e-mail address is wrong.
- Spam filters mistake your message for spam.
- Restrictions placed on received e-mail by a recipient.
- Away/idle notifications.
- An opt-out request automatically or manually sent back.
- A virus has corrupted the file or message.
- A challenge by today's spam filter software.

All these reasons are incentive enough to keep your lists up-to-date, permission-based, and cleaned. A valuable, deliverable list is the key to achieving your direct-mail marketing objectives.

E-MAIL COSTS

Wait. I thought you said e-mail marketing had no costs attached to it? This is generally true for the sending and delivering of e-mail compared to the postage on a letter. Other direct marketing costs can still apply and should be managed accordingly. Creative work, copywriting, list acquisition, and design can all be outsourced and should be if that is not your area of expertise. Acquiring an opt-in list in your area of concentration can be obtained for $180 to $500 per thousand e-mail addresses. If lists are offered for less than this, be careful. They might not truly be opt-in. They may be just harvested e-mail addresses with no permission granted for their use—which turns into major spam. Pay attention to these as they can quickly eat up a marketing budget.

MEASURING E-MAIL MARKETING

How well is your direct e-mail marketing working? If you have used it, you know the answer to this question. How do you know the answer? Are you just watching sales increase, thinking it's attributable to this one marketing tool? Are you watching clicks or visitors to a link from an e-mail? Do you know when you send out your messages and when your sales increase? The answer to all these questions is, you measure it. Tracking performance over time will tell you whether to repeat a particular message or campaign, fix it, or get rid of it and try something else. This sounds real familiar. The more marketing that can be measured, whether online or off, the more your chances of gaining profits, not just sales and certainly not losses.

E-mail is conducive to tracking, making measurement and analysis sometimes easier than with other forms of marketing. There are primarily five measurements: How many messages are sent, how many get opened, how many links get clicked on (click thrus), how many e-mails don't get delivered, and how many list members asked to be removed from the list and subsequent marketing. Overall, total sales is the ultimate measurement.

Deliverability is a measure of how accurate an e-mail list is. This is the complement of how many e-mail messages bounced back from the total sent. List activity is another way to describe how many e-mails are getting opened, assuming delivery. Response to the offer is measured by click thrus or even sales (although as expressed earlier, this is also indirect measurement). Negative response is how many people contacted you as a result of the e-mail asking to be taken off the list. Again, this is measured from the total e-mail messages delivered and opened.

There are several conditions that affect the number of responses to a direct e-mail marketing offer. First, the e-mail has to be direct-marketing-oriented. Information and awareness-building will not usually generate a response. This makes it really tough to measure the effectiveness of such marketing. There are different ways to gain permission and different levels of relationship that you have with prospects and customers. Both affect response rates. Accuracy of the list and the absence of bad addresses or duplicate recipients affect response rates. Once all of these are cleaned and refined, you will see improvement in your e-mail marketing response rates.

Regardless of how well you clean or how well your message is developed, there still will be bounce-backs, unopened e-mails, undeliverable e-mails, and e-mails that don't get a response. Remember a 5 percent response rate means a 95 percent failure rate. Setting realistic objectives and expectations and measuring against these will help establish your control, baseline situation. It will also help you troubleshoot your mailings when expectations are not met.

Testing is done with a portion of your list. After testing, you are ready to send out to your whole list. As in all marketing, repetition is key. To get the optimum response, you will need to send two or three multiples of your e-mail marketing campaign. You may or may not use a variation of the original offer each time.

Testing is critical to optimizing any direct marketing campaign, and the same goes for your e-mail marketing campaigns. In order to test, you have to measure. Make sure you have a way to collect detailed information about your mailings so that the proper analysis can be done. You'll need this information to optimize and improve upon your direct e-mail marketing campaigns.

TESTING YOUR E-MAIL CAMPAIGNS

Sending out a direct e-mailing and getting 100 percent response is a maximized direct e-mail campaign. Although I won't say this never happens, I will tell you that it hardly ever does. Throughout this book, you are reading how direct marketing is very much a numbers game. Theoretical delivery percentages, theoretical open percentages, theoretical response percentages, and so on make up the game. It is because of the absence of the perfect, maximized situation that direct mailers concentrate on optimizing their campaigns.

Webster defines *optimize* as making as effective as possible. As a direct marketer, that is what you do with each and every campaign component, and you do it on an ongoing basis. In other words, if something works, you strive to find something that works even better. The best way

to do this is to continually test different variations of your campaign, one variable at a time. The variables to test are much like the sections of this book: the target (list), the vehicle (in this case, e-mail), the message (copy and offer), and the frequency (follow-up, continual marketing).

Vehicle

The vehicle is an e-mail message, but within that message there are format types, layout, and other creative elements that can also be tested. You will find that different target markets respond differently to each of these. Finding the one that continually beats your control will lead optimization. There are certain recipients who may respond to text and interactive e-mails; others won't. Some will respond to a highly creative campaign that has lots of bells and whistles. Only testing will determine who will, and who won't and the corresponding rate.

Message

When looking at your message, consider the headline, the body copy, the offer, the benefits, and the calls to action. Small subtle variations in wording can make a big difference. This also includes the look and feel of your message, communicating your identity, and making the right impact on your audience. Each of these message components can be tested one at a time until you feel your message is optimized.

Timing and Frequency

The time of day or day of the week can have a big impact on the results of your e-mail marketing campaigns. Although the industry as a whole has done extensive testing in this area, conditions tested may not be exactly like yours. By now, you know that the best way to determine the day of the week, the time of the day, the point of a season, or the time of the year to communicate via e-mail is to test each of these variables. You are searching for optimum, and you can only do it by testing.

Actual Testing

The actual testing can be done using small portions of your large list. The tests can run parallel to each other as you evaluate each variable. This will help speed things up. Once you learn which component works best, you can move on to another category of testing until you are ready to launch what you think is the optimum marketing message.

It is recommended that you use 10 to 20 percent of the total addresses for testing. Don't keep using the same segment. You will create prospect annoyance, chance their opting out of the list, and get invalid test results.

Only through testing can you get the information necessary to analyze the results. You then can determine what is working well, what isn't, and what needs to be changed or eliminated in your campaigns. All this information and execution leads to optimization and eventual improvement in profitability.

RICH MEDIA

Rich media is as a new media that offers an enhanced experience relative to older, mainstream formats. Rich media is a "produced" message. In actuality, rich media, although rich in effect, may be less effective than a text e-mail message. This is primarily because text e-mail doesn't scream "Advertising" right away, as do rich-media messages.

New formats of rich media are regularly being introduced as old formats become part of the mainstream (or disappear altogether). Standard graphics format such as JPEG and GIF would not be considered rich media. Some popular formats commonly considered rich media are Macromedia Flash and Shockwave, along with various audio and video formats.

Still, some pretty heavy-hitters in the rich-media technology field have difficulty agreeing on a coherent and all-encompassing definition of rich media. One tactic is simply to enumerate all the different technologies that are currently being used by the major rich-media ad formats; these include video, audio, vector graphics (i.e., flash), DHTML, cursors, Shockwave, and Java.

The experts and users have kicked around a few terms such as "interactive" and "click-within" to convey the abilities of certain rich media ad technologies. But these are, at best, terms that only incompletely define what rich media is about. Most have finally agreed on the descriptive phrase for rich media as *enhanced experience*.

What they're really saying is that the subject of rich media is too big and too important to be summed up in a simple catch phrase or definition.

Here's another quote, this one from Jim Nail of *Forrester Research*: "The web is a dress rehearsal for interactive TV."

No form of traditional media—TVs, radios, newspapers, even billboards—will be left untouched by the "internet in the background" ghost in the back of your computer.

What you will find is that this thing called rich media that is so difficult to define today will be absorbed into the very fabric of all media in the very near future.

ELECTRONIC NEWSLETTERS AND E-ZINES

In the other Ultimate Series books, in *Guerrilla Marketing*, and in this book, "standing out" is always discussed. With today's flood of electronic

▼ AUTO-RESPONDERS

Auto-responders are programs set up to automatically respond via e-mail when triggered. Most are triggered by a blank e-mail sent to the auto-responder e-mail address (e.g., "For information on marketing coaching send a blank e-mail to gmcoach@market-for-profits.com").

When someone sends an e-mail to that auto-responder address, the sender receives an already prepared e-mail message with the requested information. This happens automatically and almost instantaneously, depending on the internet and e-mail servers.

Auto-responders are e-mail on demand, making your information available to your prospect and customer 24/7. They can significantly increase sales with little work because of this automatic nature. Your costs remain low and your profits soar to the Guerrilla Hall of Fame when automating any of your marketing. Auto-responders may be your ticket.

What to offer in an auto-responder message:

- Free report
- Checklist
- Top-ten list
- Article
- Free book chapter
- Recipe

- Guide
- Booklet
- E-book
- Charts
- Worksheet
- E-course

Some auto-responder programs can be set up to send a series of e-mails back to a requester. E-courses are an example of this. A blank e-mail is sent to a designated address, and a preplanned, already written series of e-mails is sent at designated intervals, all automatically.

Remember how many times it takes for your marketing message to be exposed to a prospect to get him into a state of purchase-readiness. Auto-responders ensure a consistent and frequent communication tool to touch prospects the sufficient number of times.

Source: *Guerrilla Marketing in 30 Days* by Jay Levinson and Al Lautenslager (Entrepreneur Press, 2005).

newsletters and e-zines, the concept of standing out surely applies. Five years ago this was not as much an issue as e-zines were in the early stages of popularity.

An e-zine, or electronic newsletter, is still one of the best direct marketing vehicles to build an audience of interested prospects and the associated following, many of whom will eventually become customers.

Call them electronic newsletters. Call them e-mail newsletters. Call them electronic magazines. They all mean the same thing, and most are now just referred to as e-zines. The following definition reflects this:

An e-zine is an electronic newsletter sent out via e-mail or linked from a web site, available at regular intervals to a list of opt-in subscribers.

Here is one company's stated purpose for having an e-zine:

. . . to build a customer mailing list for our products and services. Our goals are to stay in touch with our customers on a regular basis and give them information about our products and services, new and existing. We also expect to offer to our list members only, "private offers" and specials. The communication related to all of these will be done through our e-zine.

It's already been pointed out that awareness is a by-product of direct marketing. In looking at the above e-zine purpose statement, however, there are two points related to direct marketing.

The first part of the statement relates to the all-important, most important component of direct marketing—the target, which is "to build a list." Using an e-zine to build a list is a very good way to make sure your list is qualified and full of the most interested prospects.

Many people think of newsletters, online or off, as a keep-in-touch vehicle. By including special offers, coupons, and other response mechanisms, you can turn this vehicle into a direct marketing workhorse. The purpose statement above reflects this.

Assuming your customers have opted in to your e-newsletter list, they will consider your e-newsletter less intrusive than advertising. Most, if not all, traditional advertising cannot be opted in to. An e-newsletter presents value to your customer and prospect. It is valuable because you are an expert and have something to offer that they don't have. They have indicated to you (opt-in) that they want to receive the information from you. Consistent with all direct marketing, an e-newsletter's readership and interaction can be tracked and measured. You can track which article of an e-newsletter is most read by your audience. Most e-newsletters approach a 50 percent or more open-rate compared to a lot less for traditional print marketing. Use Figure 4.1 to help you make certain you have covered all the angles.

FIGURE 4.1 E-Zine Checklist

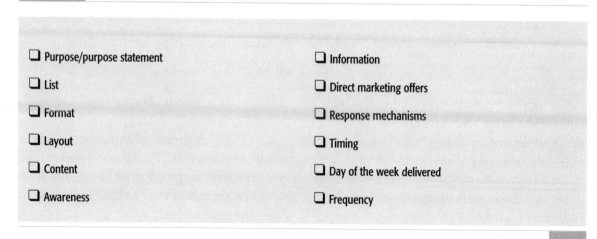

❏ Purpose/purpose statement

❏ List

❏ Format

❏ Layout

❏ Content

❏ Awareness

❏ Information

❏ Direct marketing offers

❏ Response mechanisms

❏ Timing

❏ Day of the week delivered

❏ Frequency

E-MAIL CAMPAIGN PLANNING*

Before blasting e-mails to your target world, do the following:

- Develop your campaign strategy, much like your printed direct mail campaign strategy.
- Develop content and copy. Remember AIDA and value. Keep in mind that the attention span of a Web browser is much shorter than a print reader.
- Make sure your list is targeted and permission-based.
- Offer a marketing hook for a better response rate. This could be free information, a report, a download, a CD, or an e-course.
- Make sure you are reaching your target audience. Do they even use the internet? Interested prospects buy. Noninterested prospects will skip over you.
- Plan your measurement and track where your browsers come from. Understand what they do once they get to your site. What pages do they land on? How long do they stay there? What do they click on?
- Follow up and plan subsequent e-mails. Remember how many times it takes to get a prospect to purchasing mode.
- Have a follow-up system. Know exactly what you are going to do when you get a response to your marketing.

*Source: *Guerrilla Marketing in 30 Days* by Jay Levinson and Al Lautenslager (Entrepreneur Press, 2005).

YOUR DIRECT E-MAIL CAMPAIGN

There are four main considerations in developing your e-mail marketing campaign. They are very similar to all marketing campaigns:

1. Who are you targeting?
2. What do you have to say?
3. What is the best way to say it?
4. What response do you want?

The answers to these questions come from your careful effective planning. Use the following points to help you map out your plan.

Setting the marketing objectives. These should be specific and measurable. Are you trying to elicit a certain level of response to a certain offer? Are you building awareness? Are you soliciting for direct orders? These and other objectives are the first steps in your campaign planning. You won't know if you are there if you don't know where you are going.

Determining the target of your campaign. Soon you will be determining what to say in your e-mail marketing messages based on the campaign objectives. Before doing that, you want to determine your audience. This is typically known in marketing circles as your target market. Specifically in the world of e-mail marketing, this is really your list, the list of e-mail addresses you will send your campaign messages to.

There are many ways to develop lists to send to, but you want to make sure they are comprised of those who you are trying to serve with your product or service, just as in traditional marketing your target is made up of those possessing a certain set of characteristics and conforming to certain demographics. Never target e-mail addresses that you have no information on. You should know before sending whether addresses belong to your target market or not.

What's in it for the receiver? This planning step is worded this way to keep your messages benefit-oriented. Prospects don't care about the features of your product or service. Their only concern is, "What's in it for me?" In other words, what are the benefits to them? Furthermore, reasons should be given as to why they should read your e-mail and respond to your offer.

If your benefits are the same as everybody else who is sending your prospects e-mail, what is your competitive advantage? Remember that the benefit you offer that your competition doesn't (or can't) is your competitive advantage. Keep this in mind when crafting your direct e-mail marketing campaign.

What are you going to say? This is where you seriously plan content and copywriting. What specific message are you trying to plant in your prospect's minds? What do you want them to respond to? What is your call-to-action? What do you want them to remember once they finish your e-mail? These are content-related questions you'll need to answer early on. You are appealing to as many senses and emotions as you can, and pushing for direct response or sales. More about this in the section on copywriting.

E-mail format. This goes way beyond typing a message in your e-mail program and hitting send. Not only are you planning what to say and to whom to say it, you also have to plan how you will say it. In its two generic forms, you have an HTML option and a text option. You then have to plan if you are going to send a newsletter, a letter, a press release, an announcement, a survey, an article, or a series of highly commercialized advertising messages. Different formats serve different purposes for different targets, all depending on your marketing objective and quality of copywriting.

The technology involved. There are technical considerations for your e-mail marketing campaign. What e-mail program will deliver the messages? In what form will the target list be compiled and managed? Are there other software and/or hardware concerns? Is your list maintained and of the size and format you need

for an inhouse e-mailing, or will you need to employ outside service professionals? Don't overlook the technical component of your campaign. It is analogous to the postal system for distribution and delivery of traditional offline direct mail.

Budget. "But I thought the appeal of e-mail marketing is the fact that it is free?" Sending e-mail is generally free, but from a budgeting and planning standpoint you may have expenses associated with outside services, including copywriting, graphic design, programming. You also have to understand how this budget component fits into your overall marketing budget.

Timing. Most mass e-mail communications are scheduled to be delivered in a particular series in a particular sequence. This sequence needs to be scheduled. All the above planning steps leading up to this delivery also need to be scheduled.

Response fulfillment. As you receive responses to your messages, you must be prepared to address those responses. You might have to deliver a particular report, an electronic product like an e-book, or some other information. You may have to answer questions or deliver more sales information. Be ready for this, and plan accordingly before sending out the first message. Nothing will lose a prospect quicker or blow a sales opportunity quicker than being unprepared when addressed by a potential buyer.

An e-mail campaign doesn't just happen, it truly is work. Plan your work, and work your plan. Many parts seem like common sense and deliberate activity. Most of it is, if done completely and correctly. Forgetting one or two details can make your campaign incomplete and ineffective. Planning overcomes this.

SIGNATURES

The e-mail signature is a two- to three-line message under the last part of an e-mail message. Usually the signature consists of your name and contact information. The e-mail signature is one of the most underrated marketing tools in online direct marketing. You can put a short sales message, a link, or an offer in your signature. It's called a signature because it's unique to you and is usually on all your e-mail messages, much like a written signature on a printed letter.

Some people put a favorite quote in the signature area. Others include a call-to-action. Alternatively, a signature can be customized, depending on your targeted recipient and the purpose of your e-mail. Signatures can offer information, announce events, promote products and services, communicate a special offer, or direct people to a web site.

The signature on an e-mail is underutilized. Watch the e-mails you receive and see who is marketing with them. Also take note of those that stand out from others. Remember to include your signature when replying to a message that you have received or when proactively sending e-mails in your own campaign.

PERSONALIZATION

Personalization of your e-mail marketing messages will increase response. Many of the mass mail e-mail programs allow for customization. Just like traditional, offline direct marketing, personalization makes it sound like you are speaking directly to your customer or prospect—a true one-on-one marketing communication.

Beware of the mechanics of the automated programs. You don't want a message to go out with a "Dear___, Thank you for taking the time . . ." if there is no data field available for the recipient's personalized information.

FORMATTING E-MAIL

Just as you take care to produce an attractive sales letter or direct mail package, you want to make sure your e-mail message looks professional and readable.

Formatting is important because the e-mail program your recipient uses to receive your e-mail may be different than yours, causing the message to look different from what you sent.

In traditional direct mail or direct response advertising your eyes guide you through the marketing. You skip around from graphics to headlines to subheadlines to bullets of information and finally to text. This may or may not be in linear order on a marketing piece from top to bottom. E-mail marketing is different. It is always read in linear fashion. This works to a marketer's advantage because you know how the reader will follow your message. Although long sales letters work in many cases, this is not a suggestion that you cram as much as you can into one e-mail message.

Wrapping is the term applied to what happens with each line of an e-mail—the truncation. If your recipient's e-mail program does not allow the wrapping you sent, your message will look like this:

. . . because your lines are too long, they will

be cut off
and formatted in a way that is
unsightly
and unprofessional. The lines actually look

chopped up. This is due to the different wrapping
settings for the length of each line in the e-mail.

The effect of this is worse than poor copy. Your e-mail will not get read. And if it doesn't get read, you have no chance of getting a response.

Most programs will open an e-mail to the line length of 65 characters, by default.

The way to wrap a line shorter is to hit a hard return (enter key) at the end of each sentence. Typical wraps to prevent the problem formatting are about 60-65 characters per line. There are programs available that will allow you to cut and paste your message into the program and automatically let it wrap at a specified number of characters per line.

Messages should be direct and to the point. Short paragraphs also improve the look and formatting of your e-mail. This provides adequate white space, will be easy on your reader's eyes, and increases the probability that your message will get read. The general rule of thumb for paragraph size is five to seven lines of text.

E-mail messages also can be composed as HTML messages or plain text. HTML has many advantages such as color, photos, and links. Plain text, although without these features, has also proven to be effective.

Fonts also can look different on a recipient's computer, depending on the fonts within their computer system. Most e-mail programs, by default, will use "fixed-width" fonts to display e-mails. Using a nonfixed-width font in your message will almost guarantee that your message will look jumbled on the receiver's end.

The best thing to do is stick to simple fixed fonts and not stray to proportional or nonfixed-width fonts.

OPT-IN

Opt-in is derived from the word option, meaning to choose. In the case of e-mail marketing, it means that a subscriber has chosen to be part of a list that receives communication from the list owner. Conversely, opt-out means choosing to NOT be on the list.

Opt-in means that the subscriber has given permission to the list owner to communicate and, more specifically, market to the subscriber.

Seth Godin made permission marketing famous with his book of the same title. He declared that most marketing is "interruptive." Marketing that is not an interruption and directed to an interested prospect who wants to be marketed to has much more success in generating responses and sales.

Opt-in e-mail marketing is sending e-mail marketing messages only to people who have "agreed" to receive them. What this agreement consists of is up for much debate in the e-mail marketing community.

If a prospect/customer corresponds with you or asks for more information, you generally have permission to reply. To continue to send information requires permission, the whole basis of opt-in lists.

Opt-in marketing is synonymous with permission-based marketing. Permission in this sense is also defined as a request. Technicians and purists define opt-in as not only permission granted—an agreement—but an actual request to be on a particular e-mail marketer's list.

Many opt-in list providers suggest some kind of messaging in an offer letter that reminds the targeted recipient why they are receiving the e-mail message, or reminding them that they opted in to receive the marketing message. For example:

You are receiving this message because you expressed an interest (granted permission) to receive additional offers and information related to electronic sound systems.

Another way to say it is to constantly remind the recipient of your relationship with them.

Once you get prospects to a web site, you want them to enter their e-mail in response to an online offer or you want them to buy something.

FIGURE 4.2	Opt-In Policy

By submitting this information I confirm that I am acting on behalf of an e-mail address that I own or over which I have authority over.

By submitting this request I agree to accept e-mails from you. I understand that I may unsubscribe and revoke my permission at any time.

I also understand that this permission is not transferable and my address will not be sold.

Don't lose sight of the last part of this direct marketing goal. Some direct marketers spend so much time generating a nonpurchase response that they forget about actually asking for the sale. After all, this is the ultimate response, and the one you are really going after with all of your direct marketing.

Early adopters of the simple checkbox on a web site that allowed targeted offers to be sent could not foresee the revolution this would start. Little did they know that this simple application would revolutionize the world of direct e-marketing as we know it today. If only traditional, printed direct mail worked the same way.

You see a request, many times, on online forms that are filled out by interested Net surfers:

- ❏ Yes, keep me up-to-date with the latest version of your catalog.
- ❏ Let me know of future special offers.
- ❏ Alert me to news relating to your product, service, and company.

These are all permission-based requests and will become part of an opt-in list.

Permission cannot be assumed. It must be granted. Just because you receive a business card from someone does not automatically grant permission to you to add that person for your opt-in list.

By no means should you share a permission-based e-mail list with anyone. This includes selling it. Permission cannot be transferred.

Opt-in e-mail has been endorsed as a best practice for marketers by the Internet Direct Marketing Bureau (IDMB).

Some web sites will show an opt-in policy or opt-in terms right on the sign-up form page. Figure 4.2 gives you an example of what the terms or policy might look like:

E-MAIL ETIQUETTE

It is amazing to find that in this day and age, some companies still don't recognize how important their e-mail communications are. Many companies send e-mail replies late or not at all, or send replies that do not actually answer the questions that were asked. Dealing professionally with e-mail will provide your company with that all-important competitive edge. Moreover, by educating employees as to what can and cannot be said in an e-mail, and what should and should not be said, you protect your company from awkward liability issues and situations that may offend a prospect or customer. This section discusses the main etiquette rules and provides advice on how employers and companies can ensure that they are implemented.

By requiring employees to use appropriate, businesslike language in all electronic communications, employers can limit their liability risks and improve the overall effectiveness of the organization's e-mail and internet copy in the process.

Why Do You Need E-Mail Etiquette?

A company needs to implement etiquette rules for three reasons:

1. *Professionalism.* By using proper e-mail language, your company will convey a professional image.
2. *Efficiency.* E-mails that get straight to the point are much more effective than poorly worded or rambling e-mails.
3. *Protection from liability.* Employee awareness of e-mail risks will protect your company from costly lawsuits.

What Are the Primary Etiquette Rules?

There are many etiquette guides and many different etiquette rules as they relate to business communication. Some rules will differ according to the nature of your business and the corporate culture. Below are what I consider to be the 32 most important e-mail etiquette rules that apply to nearly all companies, businesses, and professionals. (Reprinted with permission from www.emailreplies.com).

1. Be concise and to-the-point. Do not make an e-mail longer than it needs to be. Remember that reading an e-mail is harder than reading printed communications, and a long e-mail can be very discouraging to read.

2. Answer all questions, and preempt further questions. An e-mail reply must answer all questions and preempt further questions. If you do not answer all the questions in the original e-mail, you will receive further e-mails regarding the unanswered questions, which will not only waste your time and your customer's time but also cause considerable frustration. Moreover, if you are able to preempt relevant questions, your customer will be grateful and impressed with your efficient and thoughtful customer service. Imagine, for instance, that a customer sends you an e-mail asking which credit cards you accept. Instead of just listing the credit card types, you can guess that their next question will be about how they can order, so you also include some order information and a URL on your order page. Customers will definitely appreciate this.

3. Use proper spelling, grammar, and punctuation. This is not only important because improper spelling, grammar, and punctuation give a bad impression of your company; it is also important for conveying the message properly. E-mails with no full stops or commas are difficult to read and can sometimes even have the meaning of the text changed. And if your program has a spell-checking option, why not use it?

4. Make it personal. Not only should the e-mail be personally addressed, it should also include personal (i.e., customized) content. For this reason, auto replies are usually not very effective. However, templates can be used effectively in this way.

5. Use templates for frequently used responses. Some questions are asked of you over and over again, such as directions to your office or how to subscribe to your newsletter. Save these texts as response templates and paste them into your message when you need them. You can save your templates in a Word document or use preformatted e-mails.

6. Answer swiftly. Customers send an e-mail because they wish to receive a quick response. If they did not want a quick response, they would send a letter or a fax. Therefore, each e-mail should be replied to within at least 24 hours and preferably within the same working day. If the e-mail is complicated, just send an e-mail back saying that you have received it and that you will get back to them. This will put the customer's mind at rest and usually customers will then be very patient.

7. Do not attach unnecessary files. By sending large attachments, you can annoy customers and even bring down their e-mail system. Wherever possible, try to compress attachments and only send them when they are productive. Moreover, you need to have a good virus scanner in place because obviously your customers will not be very happy if you send them documents full of viruses!

8. Use proper structure and layout. Because reading from a screen is more difficult than reading from paper, the structure and layout are very important for e-mail messages. Use short paragraphs and blank lines between each paragraph. When making points, number them or mark each point as separate to keep the overview.

9. Do not overuse the high priority option. We all know the story of the boy who cried wolf. If you overuse the high priority option, it will lose its function when you really need it. Moreover, even if a mail has high priority, your message will come across as slightly aggressive if you flag it as "high priority."

10. Do not write in CAPITALS. The use of all caps in your communication is equivalent to shouting online. This can be highly annoying and might trigger an unwanted response in the form of a flame mail. Therefore, try not to send any e-mail text in capitals. This is usually considered impolite unless emphasis is really needed in your message. Even then, there are other ways to emphasize your points without SHOUTING.

11. Don't leave out the message thread. When you reply to an e-mail, you must include the original mail in your reply. In other words, click "Reply", instead of "New Mail." Some people say that you must remove the previous message because this has already been sent and is therefore unnecessary. However, I totally disagree. If you receive many e-mails, you obviously cannot remember each individual one. This means that a "threadless e-mail" will not provide enough information, and you will have to spend a frustratingly long time to find out the context of the e-mail in order to deal with it. Leaving the thread might take a fraction longer in download time, but it will save the recipient much more time and frustration in looking for the related e-mails in their in-box!

12. Add disclaimers to your e-mails. It is important to add disclaimers to your internal and external mails because this can help protect your company from liability. Consider the following scenario: An employee accidentally forwards a virus to a customer by e-mail. The customer decides to sue your company for damages. If you have a disclaimer at the bottom of every external mail, saying that the recipient must check each e-mail for viruses and that the company cannot be held liable for any transmitted viruses, this will surely be of help to you in court. Another example: an employee sues the company for allowing a racist e-mail to circulate through the office. If your company has an e-mail policy in place that includes an e-mail disclaimer to every mail saying that employees are expressly forbidden make defamatory or racist statements, you have a good chance of proving that the company did everything it could to prevent offensive e-mails.

13. Read the e-mail before you send it. A lot of people don't bother to read their e-mails before they send them out, as may be seen from the many spelling and grammar mistakes contained therein. Apart from this, reading your e-mail through the eyes of the recipient will help you send a more effective message and avoid misunderstandings and inappropriate comments.

14. Do not overuse Reply to All. Only use Reply to All if you really need your message to be seen by each person who received the original message.

15. For mailings to many people, use the Bcc: field or do a mail merge. When sending an e-mail mailing, some people place all the e-mail addresses in the To: field. There are two drawbacks to this practice: (1) The recipient knows that you have sent the same message to a large number of recipients, and (2) You are publicizing someone else's e-mail address without their permission. One way to get around this is to place all addresses in the Bcc: field. However, the recipient will only see the address from the To: field in their e-mail, so if this was empty, the To: field will be blank and this might look like spamming. You could include the mailing list e-mail address in the To: field, or even better, if you have Microsoft Outlook and Word you can do a mail

merge and create one message for each recipient. A mail merge also allows you to use fields in the message so that you can, for instance, address each recipient personally. For more information on how to do a Word mail merge, consult the Help in Word.

16. Take care with acronyms and emoticons. In business e-mails, try not to use acronyms such as BTW (by the way) and LOL (laugh out loud). The recipient might not be aware of their meanings, and in business e-mails these are generally not appropriate. The same goes for emoticons, such as the smiley :-). If you are not sure whether your recipient knows what it means, it is better not to use it.

17. Be careful with formatting. Remember that when you use formatting in your e-mails, the sender might not be able to view formatting or might see different fonts than you had intended. When using colors, use a color that is easy to read against the background.

18. Take care with rich text and HTML messages. Be aware that when you send an e-mail in rich text or HTML format, the recipient might only be able to receive plain text e-mails. If this is the case, the recipient will receive your message as a .txt attachment. Most e-mail clients, however, including Microsoft Outlook, are able to receive HTML and rich text messages.

19. Do not forward chain letters. Do not forward chain letters. I can safely say that all of them are hoaxes. Just delete the letters as soon as you receive them. Many times they are spam anyway, and you would just be re-spamming.

20. Do not request delivery and read receipts. This will almost always annoy your recipient before he or she has even read your message.

Besides, it usually does not work anyway because the recipient could have blocked that function or his/her software might not support it, so what is the point of using it? If you want to know whether an e-mail was received, it is better to ask the recipient to simply let you know.

21. Do not ask to recall a message. Chances are that your message has already been delivered and read. A recall request would look very silly in that case, wouldn't it? It is better just to send an e-mail and say that you've made a mistake. This will look much more honest than trying to recall a message.

22. Do not copy a message or attachment without permission. Do not copy a message or attachment belonging to another user without the permission of the originator. If you do not ask permission first, you might be infringing on copyright laws.

23. Do not use e-mail to discuss confidential information. Sending an e-mail is like sending a postcard. If you don't want your e-mail to be displayed on a bulletin board, don't send it. Moreover, never make any libelous, sexist, or racist comments in e-mails, even if they are meant jokes.

24. Use a meaningful subject. Try to use a subject that is meaningful to the recipient as well as yourself. For instance, when you send an e-mail to a company requesting information about a

> For many Internet Service Providers (ISP), the lack of a subject line is indicative of junk e-mail, and may be filtered out or deleted before it is sent or received.

product, it is better to mention the actual name of the product, e.g., "Product A information" than to just say "product information" or the company's name in the subject line. Always use a subject line. If you are marketing or selling, this is a powerful opportunity to communicate something that will get read. The absence of one could signify laziness, lack of knowledge of internet marketing, and lack of interest or care on the sender's part, even if not intentional. Keep your subject line short and sweet, yet compelling.

25. Use active instead of passive. Try to use the active voice of a verb wherever possible. For instance, "We will process your order today" sounds better than "Your order will be processed today." The first sounds more personal, whereas the latter, especially when used frequently, sounds unnecessarily formal.

26. Avoid using URGENT and IMPORTANT. Even more than the high-priority option, you must at all times try to avoid these kinds of words in an e-mail or subject line. Only use these words this if it is a really, really urgent or important message.

27. Avoid long sentences. Try to keep your sentences to a maximum of 15 to 20 words. E-mail is meant to be a quick medium and requires a different kind of writing than letters. Also take care not to send e-mails that are too long. If a person receives an e-mail that looks like a dissertation, chances are they will not even attempt to read it!

28. Avoid illegal or offensive messages. Don't send or forward e-mails containing libelous, defamatory, offensive, racist, or obscene remarks. By sending or even just forwarding one libelous or offensive remark in an e-mail, you and your company can face court cases resulting in multimillion-dollar penalties.

29. Don't forward virus hoaxes and chain letters.

If you receive an e-mail message warning you of a new unstoppable virus that will immediately delete everything from your computer, it is most probably a hoax. By forwarding hoaxes you use valuable bandwidth. And sometimes virus hoaxes contain viruses themselves, which attach via the file to stop the dangerous virus. The same goes for chain letters that promise incredible riches or ask your help for a charitable cause. Even if the content seems to be bona fide, the senders are usually not. Because it is impossible to find out whether a chain letter is real or not, the best place for it is the recycle bin.

30. Keep your language gender-neutral.
In this day and age, avoid using sexist language such as, "The user should add a signature by configuring his e-mail program." Apart from using he/she, you can also avoid gender all together: "The user should add a signature by configuring the e-mail program."

31. Don't reply to spam.
By replying to spam or by unsubscribing, you are confirming that your e-mail address is "live." Confirming this will only generate even more spam. Therefore, just hit the delete key or use e-mail software to remove spam automatically.

32. Use cc: field sparingly.
Try not to use the cc: field unless the recipient in the cc: field knows why they are receiving a copy of the message. Using the cc: field can be confusing because the recipients might not know who is supposed to act on the message. Also, when responding to a cc: message, should you include the other recipient in the cc: field as well? This will depend on the situation. In general, do not include the person in the cc: field unless you have a particular reason for wanting this person to see your response. Again, make sure that this person will know why they are receiving a copy.

Other E-Mail-Related Etiquette Tips

- Never send e-mail to a recipient who has not granted you permission to communicate with them. Follow what is written in this book about permission-based marketing, spam, and opt-in lists.
- Target your e-mails and only communicate with a purpose. Just because someone has given you permission to communicate, doesn't mean that you can blast arbitrary marketing messages at them. Target interests and interested prospects wherever possible.
- Communicate via e-mail much as you would when speaking face-to-face. Reacting emotionally in an e-mail message and pressing the send key cannot be undone. Think twice before writing and sending your message, especially if is an emotional response to something.
- Don't put your whole mailing list in the To: field of your e-mail program. This shares your list with everyone who receives it, and is no longer private or secure. The same goes for the cc: field, unless there is a purpose for showing who else received your mail. Use the Bcc: field to keep your list hidden (private and secure).

Enforcing E-Mail Etiquette

The first step is to create a written e-mail policy. This e-mail policy should include all the dos and don'ts concerning the use of the company's e-mail system and should be distributed to all employees. Secondly, employees must be trained to fully understand the importance of e-mail etiquette.

YOUR E-MAIL POLICY

Before you start creating an e-mail policy, do some investigation into already existing company policies, such as guidelines on writing business letters, access to confidential information, personal use of the telephone systems, and sexual or racial harassment at work. It is important that your e-mail policy be compatible with your company's existing policies. You will also need to decide whether your company is going to allow personal use of the e-mail system, and if so, to what extent.

The e-mail policy should be drafted with the help of human resources, IT, and the board of directors in order to reflect all viewpoints in the organization. It is also advisable to have several employees look at the policy and provide their feedback. Make sure that your policy is not so restrictive that it will compromise your employees' morale and productivity.

What Should Be Included in an E-Mail Policy?

For the policy to be effective, the document should use clear and simple wording and not be longer than three to four pages. You cannot expect employees to read a long complicated document, and you want them to remember what it says. List short bullet points so that employees can easily find rules in they are unsure about.

How to Write Effective E-Mails

- Establish e-mail style (formal/informal). This could include guidelines on salutation and the ending of messages.

- What kind of signatures should be used—i.e., should signatures include company name, job function, telephone and fax number, address, web site, and/or a corporate slogan?
- Provide basic rules on how to write e-mail messages.
- What is the expected time in which e-mails should be answered. For example, you could set a general rule that each e-mail should be answered within at least eight working hours, but that 50 percent of e-mails should be answered within four hours.
- How will you determine which e-mails should receive priority?
- Determine when to send cc: or Bcc: messages, and what to do when you receive them.
- Set guidelines on how and when to forward e-mail messages, and how you should handle forwarded messages.

Productivity Issues

Will personal e-mails be accepted and if so, to what extent? For instance, you could limit the number of personal e-mails sent each day, or you could require that they be saved in a separate folder. You could also limit or eliminate certain e-mail attachments from being sent or received, and include rules on sending chain letters. Include examples and clear measures taken when these rules are breached.

- Set policy use of newsletters and news groups. For instance, you can require a user to request permission to subscribe to a newsletter or news group.
- Warn users that they should not engage in nonbusiness activities that unnecessarily tie up network traffic.

Legal Risks

- Include a list of e-mail risks to make users aware of the potentially harmful effects of their actions. Advise users that sending an e-mail is like sending a postcard: if you don't want it posted on a bulletin board, then don't send it.
- The policy should expressly state that the e-mail system is not to be used for the creation or distribution of any offensive or disruptive messages, including those containing offensive comments about race, gender, age, sexual orientation, pornography, religious or political beliefs, national origin, or disability. Advise that employees who receive any e-mails with this content should report the matter to their supervisor immediately. Furthermore, mention that employees should not use e-mail to discuss competitors, potential acquisitions or mergers, or to give their opinion about another firm. Unlawful messages, such as copyright-infringing e-mails, should also be prohibited. Include examples and clear measures taken when these rules are breached.
- If you are going to monitor the content of your employees' e-mails, you must mention this in your e-mail policy. (In most countries/states you are allowed to monitor your employees' e-mails if they are made aware of it.) Warn that employees should have no expectation of privacy in anything they create, store, send, or receive on the company's computer system and that any of their messages may be viewed without prior notice.

Finally, include a point-of-contact for questions arising from the e-mail policy.

Publishing Your E-Mail Policy

When you have formulated an e-mail policy, you should make sure that all employees are made aware of it. You can do this by handing out printed copies, publishing it on your intranet, and including it in staff handbooks. Also, when a new employee starts at your company, he or she should be given a copy of the document as standard policy.

It is a good idea to include the most important points of the e-mail policy in the employment contract, so that employees must sign that they have read, understood, and acknowledged receipt of policy. Cover the most important issues, such as the personal use of e-mail, possible e-mail monitoring, and the prohibition of defamatory, sexual, and racist remarks in e-mails, in the employment contract. Also expressly state that breach of these rules can lead to termination of employment.

Furthermore, you could organize e-mail trainings to explain the risks to users and why the policy is so important. If users understand potential offenses, most of them will understand why the rules need to be set up and will have less difficulty in applying them. A training will also help you obtain feedback to ensure that the policy is feasible and can actually be put into practice.

Updating Your E-Mail Policy

Because e-mail and the internet are changing rapidly, it is important to review the e-mail policy at least once every quarter. Keep an eye on new developments in e-mail and internet law so that you are aware of any new regulations and opportunities. When you release new updates, it is advisable to have each user sign an acknowledgment of receipt of the policy.

Enforcing Your E-Mail Policy

Finally, when you have created your e-mail policy, you must monitor your e-mails to ensure that your users follow the rules.

PRIVACY POLICY

The difference between a privacy policy and the above stated e-mail policy is that the e-mail policy is for internal company use and the privacy policy is for publication to outside contacts, telling them what you will do with collected e-mail addresses.

Privacy is a strong consideration and imperative all direct e-mail marketing today. As you collect information, even beyond e-mail addresses, you should let all know that you respect their privacy in return for their giving you information. Many e-mail marketing messages will have a privacy policy embedded right into the message or at the end of a message in a footer.

Your privacy policy should tell prospects how and why you collect information. You should state how you will use the information. You also disclose whether or not you plan on renting or selling the accumulated names and addresses. As you communicate your privacy policy, you should also identify a point person or contact who is responsible for it. This person can be the one with whom prospects can follow up if there are questions or concerns. An unsubscribe method or procedure should be included in the policy as well.

If you don't want to embed a privacy policy in each and every e-mail message, add a link to one that is posted on your web site (this also gets prospects back to your site).

Here are two examples of e-mail privacy policies embedded in an actual e-mail message:

- The information transmitted is intended only for the person or entity to which it is addressed and may contain confidential and/or privileged material. Any review, retransmission, dissemination, or other use of or taking of any action in reliance upon this information by persons or entities other than the intended recipient is prohibited. If

you received this in error, please contact the sender and delete the material from any computer.

If you are not the intended recipient, you are not authorized to forward or otherwise distribute this e-mail unless specific approval is given above.

- This e-mail, including attachments, may include confidential and/or proprietary information, and may be used only by the person or entity to which it is addressed. If the reader of this e-mail is not the intended recipient or his or her authorized agent, the reader is hereby notified that any dissemination, distribution, or copying of this e-mail is prohibited. If you have received this e-mail in error, please notify the sender by replying to this message and delete this e-mail immediately.

SPAM

Spam is unsolicited, nonpermission-based e-mail that is usually sent as part of a mass marketing campaign. The recipient doesn't know, has never heard of, nor is interested in the sender or the sender's product or service. Spam is the junk mail of the internet.

The first spam message dates back to 1978 and was sent by a marketer for DEC (now owned by Compaq Computer, a division of Hewlett Packard). In 1978, the internet was known as ARPANET. At that time, there was a printed directory of everyone in the ARPANET system. The unsuspecting marketer copied the directory and sent a notice to everyone on the West Coast that was in the directory. The message announced a DEC open house to show off new models of a DEC mini mainframe computer.

ARPANET had an official "acceptance use policy related to research and education" that the DEC message clearly violated. Although not known by the term which came into use ten years later, this was spam.

▼ SPAM STATISTICS

14%	The percentage of spam messages that do not have an operational opt-out capability. (MailFrontier Research)
27%	The percentage of spam messages that use a hidden "Customer ID" to determine if you have opened a given spam message. (MailFrontier Research)
81,000	The number of computer viruses in existence today. (McAfee)
2 billion	The estimated number of spam e-mail messages sent each day.
500	The average number of new viruses discovered each month. (McAfee)
$11 billion	The 2002 to 2003 increase in the annual cost of spam to U.S. corporations. In 2002, U.S. companies spent $8.9 billion handling spam. In 2003, they spent over $20 billion dealing with spam-related issues. (Ferris Research)
$874	The average annual cost in lost productivity to spam per employee. (Nucleus Research)
$60 billion	The cost of identity theft to U.S. corporations over the last five years. (Federal Trade Commission)
79%	The growth in identity theft from June 2002 to June 2003. (Gartner)
$500	Cost for one spammer to send out one million spam messages. By comparison, sending one million letters via U.S. mail would cost at least $240,000.

Spammers generally send out a large number of e-mails, banking on the small percentage who will respond even though the messages were unsolicited.

There are attempts at legislating against the high volume of unsolicited commercial e-mails, and at the time of writing, the subject was up for debate. The CAN-SPAM Act of 2003 (Controlling the Assault of Non-Solicited Pornography and Marketing Act of 2003) attempts to regulate and control:

The CAN-SPAM Act requires that unsolicited commercial e-mail messages be labeled and that they include opt-out instructions and the sender's physical address. It prohibits the use of deceptive subject lines and false headers in such messages. The Federal Trade Commission is authorized, but not yet required, to establish a "do not e-mail" registry. State laws that require labels on unsolicited, commercial e-mail or prohibit such messages entirely are preempted, although provisions merely addressing falsity and deception can remain in place. The CAN-SPAM Act took effect on January 1, 2004.

These are the actual words from the Act. This and more related information can be found at www.spamlaws.com.

Has this act eliminated spam? One year later, the answer is clearly no. Just look in your own e-mail in-box. Has it slowed down the spam? Maybe it

> In May 2004, it was reported that more than 80 percent of all e-mails in the United States were spam. For this information and a comprehensive report on False Claims in Spam, a report by the FTC's Division of Marketing Practices, visit: www3.ftc.gov/reports/spam/030429spamreport.pdf

- *Hot XXX action* (also: *teens, porn*)
- *Lowest insurance rates* (also: *lower your insurance now*)
- *Lowest mortgage rates* (also: *lower your mortgage rates, refinance, refi*)
- *Online degree* (also: *online diploma*)
- *Online pharmacy* (also: *online prescriptions, meds online*)
- *Viagra online* (also: *Xanax, Valium, Xenical, phentermine, Soma, Celebrex, Valtrex, Zyban, Fioricet, Adipex*, etc.)
- *Work from home* (also: *be your own boss*)

Karyn Greenstreet, of the small-business consulting firm Passion for Business (www.passionforbusiness.com), offers yet another list (see Figure 4.4). But as she noted at the time of writing, by the time of publication the list will have changed, and it will continue to change. Hackers will work to fool spam filters, spam filters will get smarter, and it will continue to be an endless question as to what spam is and what it is not. The key is to use as much opt-in communication and personal relationship communication as possible so your recipients know you, know about you, and know how, when, and why you communicate with them.

has just a tiny bit. Although the law promises big penalties and fines to violators, enforcement agencies lack sufficient resources to effectively prosecute and convict violators. The legislators knew that the Act wouldn't eliminate spam, but they did hope to provide a tool that ISPs and consumer protection agencies like the FTC could use to protect you against spammers.

Why is this important to you, the direct e-mail marketer? Depending on your message and your delivery, legitimate marketing by you could be confused for spam if safeguards are not put in place. Just consider the list in Figure 4.3. This list, offered by www.surferbeware.com, exposes common words used by spammers. These words are ones commonly flagged by spam-filter programs. Words used in "adult" e-mails have not been included here but do exist. This list is by no means exhaustive, but will serve as a guide for the development of your own legitimate e-mail marketing messages and help to spam-proof them, wherever possible.

AOL reported the subjects of the spam most widely sent to its members during 2003. Here they are in alphabetical order:

- As seen on *Oprah*
- *Get bigger* (also: *satisfy your partner, improve your sex life*)
- Get out of *debt* (also: *special offer*)

OPT-OUT

Recipients need the ability to be removed from your list. A method/procedure for this should be included in any outbound e-mail marketing message to a prospect. The easier and clearer you make this process, the more loyal your recipients and list members will be to you.

Opt-out also is a technique in which e-mail messages are sent unsolicited (no permission, no opt-in, basically spam), allowing the recipient to request to be removed from any future communication. This is done by marketers routinely, but is still considered unsolicited and without permission.

FIGURE 4.3   Some Common Words Used by Spammers

thousands per day	if you wish to be removed	remove in the subject line
thousands per month	Increase sales	remove in the subject line
thousands per week	Largest payoff	REMOVE in the subject line
Act now	Liens	remove me
affiliate program	life insurance	remove yourself
all rights reserved	limited time offer	removed from future mailing
An invitation to	Look younger	Removed in subject line
any future mailing	Loosest slots	reply to this message
Bad credit	Lose 10 pounds	reply with
Bankruptcy	Lowest mortgage interest rates	retirement business
be a millionaire	mailing list	Second mortgage
big money	mailinglist	sign up today
Broadcast E-mail	Major credit cards	Single deck black jack
Burn fat	make money	Stop balding
Call now	Mlm	stop future mailing
Cash back	Money problems	Student loans
Chain letter	No more debt	subscribe
claim your	no obligation	subscription
click this link	No obligation	This E-mail complies
Consolidate today	Non secured	this is not spam
Credit approval	not mlm	to be removed
Credit counseling	Not mlm	To be removed
Debt consolidation	Not multilevel	trial offer
Doctor approved pill	Not multi-level	Try it for free
E-mail marketing	offer only available	unsubscribe
Equity line of credit	Online casino	Vacation giveaway
follow the link	opt out	very low-cost
For only $	opt-out	Viagra
free sample	optout	Video pOKer
Free to the first	Order by fax	web cam
Full refund	Order by phone	webcam
get a free	Order now	Why wait
Get rich	Order within	write in subject line
Hair loss	Over weight	write remove in the subject line
Herbal remedies	please read the following	you win
home based business	Rate quote	you won
home business	Rates slashed	You're already approved
Home equity	referring url	

FIGURE 4.4 Other Words Used by Spammers

4u	confidential	free hosting
50 percent off	congratulations	free installation
accept credit cards	consolidate your debt	free investment
act now	copy accurately	free leads
act now don't hesitate	credit	free membership
additional income	credit bureaus	free money
addresses on CD	credit card offers	free offer
all natural	cures baldness	free preview
all new	dear e-mail	free priority mail
amazing	dear friend	free quote
amazing stuff	dear somebody	free sample
apply online	different reply to	free trial
as seen on	dig up dirt on friends	free web site
auto e-mail removal	direct e-mail	free!
avoid bankruptcy	direct marketing	full refund
be amazed	discount	get it now
be your own boss	discusses search engines	get paid
being a member	listings	get started now
big bucks	do it today	gift certificate
billing address	don't delete	give it away
billion dollars	double your income	great offer
brand new	drastically reduced	guarantee
bulk e-mail	earn	guaranteed
buy direct	earn per week	hidden
buying judgments	easy terms	hidden assets
cable converter	eliminate bad credit	home employment
call free	eliminate debt	human growth hormone
call now	e-mail harvest	HGH
calling creditors	e-mail marketing	if only it were that easy
cancel at any time	expect to earn	in accordance with laws
can't live without	fantastic deal	increase sales
cash	fast Viagra delivery	increase traffic
cash bonus	financial freedom	information you requested
casino	find out anything	insurance
cell phone cancer scam	for free	investment decision
cents on the dollar	for instant access	it's effective
check or money order	for just 10$	join millions
collect	free access	laser pritner
collect child support	free cell phone	limited time only
compare	free consultation	loans
compare rates	free dvd	long distance phone offer
compete for your business	free grant money	lose weight multi level

CONTINUED

FIGURE 4.4 Other Words Used by Spammers

marketing	one hundred percent	shopping spree
lose weigh spam	one time	sign up free today
lower interest rates	one time mailing	social security number
lower monthly payment	online biz opportunity	special promotion
lowest price	online marketing	stainless steel
luxury car	online pharmacy	stock alert
mail in order form	opportunity	stock pick
marketing solutions	opt-in	stop
mass e-mail	order now	stop snoring
meet singles	order status	strong buy
member stuff	outstanding values	stuff on sale
million dollars	pennies a day	subject to credit
mlm	please read	subscribe
money back	potential earnings	supplies are limited
money making	print form signature	take action now
month trial offer	print out and fax	terms and conditions
more internet traffic	produced and sent out	the best rates
mortgage rates	profits	the following form
multi level marketing	promise you	they're just giving it away
name brand	pure profit	this isn't junk
new customers only	real thing	this isn't spam
new domain extensions	refinance home	time limited
Nigerian	removal instructions	university diplomas
no age restrictions	remove in quotes	unlimited
no catch	remove subject	unsecured credit
no claim forms	removes	urgent
no cost	removes wrinkles	us dollars
no credit check	reply remove subject	vacation
no disappoint	requires initial investment	Viagra
no experience	reserves the right	we hate spam
no fees	reverses aging	we honor all
no gimmick	risk free	weekend getaway
no inventory	round the world	what are you waiting for?
no investment	safeguard notice	while supplies last
no medical exams	satisfaction guaranteed	while you sleep
no middleman	save $	who really wins?
no obligation	save big money	why pay more?
no purchase necessary	save up to	will not believe your eyes
no questions asked	score with babes	winner
no selling	search engine listings	winning
no strings attached	see for yourself	work at home
not intended	sent in compliance	your income
off shore	serious cash	you're a winner
once in a lifetime	serious only	you've been selected

DOUBLE OPT-IN

Double opt-in is giving permission twice or confirming the fact that you really did give permission in the first place. Double opt-in guards against an inadvertent agreement or reply for permission. Double opt-in is enhanced permission. In the double opt-in process, a name is not added to the list until a confirming e-mail is sent by the marketer and replied to by the recipient. If no e-mail is received back from the recipient, the second step of the double opt-in process, the name does not get added to the list.

This process ensures that there will be no false opt-ins and is truly a safeguard agains being accused as a spammer. The process can make it longer to build a list but the quality of a double op-in-list will be higher, therefore generating more response.

ONLINE COPY

Now that more technology is being understood online, now that programmers have done their thing, and now that design is easier for the do-it-yourselfer, online copy has risen in importance. It is now at to the point where that people are persuaded by many of the same things online that persuade them offline. Many offline direct marketing techniques are now being tested and used successfully online. Online copywriting is vitally important. Online copy can now be as much a king as it is offline. Marketers still market, and target markets still buy, online or off. Because of this, offline copy and online copy are similar. Consider the following:

- You still have to deliver a message from the perspective of the reader or your target audience. Benefit orientations answering the reader's question of "What's in it for me?" still need to be present. Benefits still do the selling, even online. Whether reading an e-mail or visiting a web site, the readers want to know first why they should start reading and secondly, why they should keep reading. Once the online copy passes this test, the readers must then be convinced, via online copy, why they should respond or order your product or service, just as with offline copy.

- Messages still need to be targeted. Target those who are most likely to respond to what you write. Again, this is a consideration that applies online and offline.

- The rules of Attention, Interest, Desire, and Action apply to online or off copy. Grabbing a web browser's attention is still as critical as getting a direct mail envelope opened. Keeping the attention is just as challenging and important online as it is offline.

- Because there is so much information available online, it is more important than ever to offer answers, not just a lot of extraneous information. Focus on your subject and what you think your reader wants and needs. Information that leads a prospect through the purchase process or through a marketing process to the point of response is the goal online as well as offline.

- Credibility is as important online as offline. This stresses the need for using testimonials and offering references. Case studies that cause a reader to identify with a situation and then a solution will generate responses and purchases.

- Offers and calls to action are other similarities between online and offline copywriting. Making these clear and easy to respond to is the goal of both.

There are, however, some differences between online and offline copywriting as they relate to direct marketing. The following points are examples of this:

- Length of copy is still debated both online and off. Because of the way you read web pages and e-mail messages, you have the ability to delete, scan, and ignore quicker. Attention spans are at an all-time low online, suggesting shorter copy.
- Communication online is done by its own set of rules. You don't hear much about spam in your direct mail pile at home. There seem to be way more rules and etiquette guidelines for online communication than offline.
- One of these rules often talked about is opt-in lists or permission-based marketing. This is much more prevalent in the online world. How many times have you contacted a direct mailer to ask them to remove you from their list?
- Hyperlinks provide the greatest interactivity ever in copy. You can't click anywhere on a printed letter, but on an e-mail or web site you can choose to go somewhere else. This level of interactivity enhances the direct marketing experience online compared to offline, nonlinked communication.

There are more differences; there are more similarities. The bottom line is to understand your target, choose the best vehicle, optimize your message, and apply all the pertinent direct marketing rules that make your campaigns effective, whether marketing online or offline.

Online Copy Process

When discussing online direct marketing copy, people tend to to talk about the same things that are important in offline direct marketing copy. There are some times though, when online copy is longer, more comprehensive, or more attuned to taking a reader or prospect through a process, from start to finish, with more elements in between. The key points to this process in total are still:

- Grabbing the attention of the online reader/prospect
- Communicating from the perspective of the prospect
- Benefit orientation and emphasis
- Why they must buy from you and you only
- Offer testimonials and credibility.
- Create, offer, and continue to build value.
- Use a call to action to tell the prospect what to do.
- Build a sense of urgency in the message to act now, instead of later.
- Provide reasons for the reader, prospect, or customer to return again after this visit or reading.

These fundamentals provide the proper recipe for all your online communication in both e-mail messages and online sales letter communication.

Adapting Offline Copy to Online

Many times the first step in direct marketing is taken through traditional, offline means. This marketing is then used online and needs to be adapted. Aside from the technical transfers of scanning and input, three key things need to happen:

1. Copy needs to be edited for the online reader's eyes. Many times this means catering to those short attention spans and shortening the amount of copy.
2. Most internet browsers and online prospects are used to getting more information online than just promotional information. This is different than offline marketing, so copy needs to be beefed up with more information while being toned down from a promotional perspective.

3. Interactivity options via proper hyperlinks must be placed into online copy. Sometimes interactivity will take the shape of an online form.

DIRECT E-MAIL COPY

As early as 2000, direct marketing executives determined that the marketing objective for e-mail should be direct sales as opposed to reinforcing brand and identity, collecting data, or initiating a customer dialogue. This belief is still dominant today.

Direct E-Mail Format

There are two types of e-mail format: HTML e-mails and straight text e-mails. The basic format for a text e-mail message has similar components to a direct mail printed letter but some very different, unique to e-mail components. Here are the major components to a direct e-mail text message.

From. This is simply who the e-mail is from. It can be an e-mail address or a name. The name can be a person, a company, or a nickname. It is the primary identifier that shows up in the recipient's inbox "from" field.

Subject line. This tells what the subject of the e-mail is. It is not to be taken lightly. It can make the difference between a recipient opening your e-mail or not. It can determine whether a spam filter rejects your e-mail or not. It can mean the difference between interest and disinterest. Imagine all your traditional printed direct mail at home coming with a printed subject line on it. It would make sorting quicker and easier. Here are a few rules that apply to the subject lines of e-mails:

- Make it benefit-oriented.

- Make it from the recipient's perspective.
- Don't use more than 30 to 40 characters.
- Motivate to action.
- Make it a promise.
- Don't exaggerate or YELL.
- Use a question to be different.
- Be aware of the most common spam words.
- Use words that create interest and desire and that challenge the recipient.
- Avoid annoyance and exclamations.

The words *free* and *first time offered* stimulate great response in e-mail subject lines. Today, however, many spam filters pick up on these words and deem the message unsolicited, or spam. There are ways around this. You can substitute words or rewrite the actual messages. Instead of "free" you can say, this won't *cost you anything*. This usually will get around a spam filter. For "first time offered" you can say that this offer is not available to anyone else yet or available only to you until next week.

Opening statement. Because most online readers and prospects are presumed to have short attention spans, the first sentence or two of your opening paragraph is very important. It tells the reader whether the e-mail is of interest to them or not, immediately.

Response mechanism. In the online world, the call to action can be "click here." The click here is a hyperlink that takes the reader to another Web page. It can be a form page, an order page, or another response-oriented, electronic link. This is the primary response mechanism online; however, the traditional ones are still pertinent. You can still ask someone to call your toll-free number, send for information, or redeem a coupon.

E-mail body. Much like traditional offline direct marketing copy, the main copy is the body of the

PROS AND CONS OF HTML

PROS	CONS
• Use of color	• More resources/more bandwidth needed
• More variety of fonts, layout, and graphics	• Large file sizes
• Increased readability/response	• Deliverability problems as spam filters filter out HTML
• Graphically pleasing	• Must serve a variety of e-mail client servers, creating the potential for a corrupted look.
• Better attention getter	• HTML readily classified as junk or spam by the reader
• A picture is worth a thousand words	• Content is still king, not design.
• Becoming a significant reader preference	• Can't view HTML e-mails in AOL (yet)
• Surveys are saying more and more that HTML is more user-/reader-friendly.	• Older versions of e-mail clients can't read HTML messages.
• A better customer experience	• Mobile devices at the time of writing couldn't read HTML messages.

Usually any e-mail service provider or even your own program gives you a way to do either. (HTML is by far the e-mail format of preference as indicated.) Through testing, you can determine what format works best with your message and with your audience.

communication. In the online world, with less initial attention given by prospects, you want to construct shorter paragraphs, bulleted information, or lists. Again, this applies to text-based e-mail communication. HTML will utilize graphics, photos, and illustrations for this.

Privacy statement. This is where you give the online reader the opportunity to not receive online communication from you in the future. This is the opt-out mechanism and policy.

USING E-MAIL MARKETING TO SELL

Direct e-mail marketing is designed and used to gain a response from your recipient. It would be nice if that response was an actual sale. That's the best kind of response there is. Thinking in terms of gaining a sale can be the best marketing decision you make in your direct e-mail campaign. There are certain ways to achieve this objective, especially if your prospect list is your current customer list. Let's look at a few.

Sales Conversion

In Sales 101, it is taught that at some point in the conversation with a prospective buyer you have to ask for the sale. You want to "convert" the prospect into a paying client. Just as in traditional direct marketing, this motivation is helped along with a call to action. Calls to action have been discussed in this book; they must be specific and clear to the prospect. Prospects will often only do what you ask them to do. They also will many times not do something without being prompted. The more your e-mail can focus on this one specific action, the higher probability that you will gain conversion. Don't forget to include incentives, discounts, freebies, and bonuses to encourage the conversion process. Always craft your message with the prospect in mind, not you. The "what's in it for me?" motivation exists here as well. Let your best benefit address this on your way to conversion. Construct your e-mail message accordingly.

Upgrades

Once customers get a taste of your product or service, it's likely they'll want more, want a better version, want the best of the best. Upgrades are a common way to increase sales from a customer. One of the best ways to do this is to send them an e-mail offering to sell them the new version, or renew their service, even if it is in advance of their need. This is often done by magazine companies asking for extended subscriptions. I just noticed the same technique being used by domain-name registrars asking for URL renewals. The upgrade is a request for two or more years instead of just the one-year version. Providing some extra incentive for doing so can increase sales and promote incremental profits for the upgraded products or services.

Follow-Up

Your best prospect is a current customer. If they bought from you once, there is high probability that they will buy from you again. Continuing the direct approach, soliciting responses or purchases still works once a prospect enters the paying-customer category. Sending follow-up e-mails in

direct fashion will increase sales to current customers. Following up the purchase can be direct. Checking on their satisfaction while suggesting add-ons or complementary products or services can be done with direct follow-up messages.

Private Notice of a Sale or Offer

One way to encourage people to join your list is to provide notice of advance sales or offers. This can take the form of a special member sale, a private sale, or some other incentive to include only those in a special community. This is a very powerful e-mail marketing technique. Putting customers into a category of their own provides value: "As a valued and respected customer or member, we want to extend a private offer that is for a special exclusive group and not the general public." This also tells your customers that you value their business and their loyalty to you as a paying customer. You will see higher response rates doing this because your current customers already know you and trust you. You have an established relationship with them. A direct approach to someone you already have an established relationship with makes your target very precise and your response higher.

These e-mail marketing techniques are best when combined with other direct e-mail marketing or integrated into a company's total marketing campaign. It is one more way that direct e-mail marketing can significantly increase sales, almost at no cost. You've made up your mind to employ direct marketing. You might as well have a direct-sales attitude while you are doing it.

WRITING EFFECTIVE E-MAIL

In days of yore, you would hear, often around the office, "Have you seen the memo yet?" or "I haven't gotten the memo on that yet." Today those common phrases are still about; however, tho word *e-mail* is substituted for *memo*. "I'll send an e-mail out on that," or "Send me an e-mail to confirm our discussion." Although e-mail communication is similar the old memo mode, communicating by e-mail is different than other forms of communication. It's now used in all aspects of our lives: personal, professional, and business. People never used to send a "memo" out on something personal! Because this form of communication is becoming more all-encompassing, it's important to think about how to communicate effectively using e-mail.

E-Mail vs. Other Communication

Sometimes e-mail simulates conversation. How many times have you sent an e-mail to someone only to get an almost instantaneous response or at least a response within minutes? Usually when communication is spoken, it tends to get informal and personal, which is usually very acceptable during quick exchanges with another person. However, when using written communication, e-mail in this case, it's hard to show body language, facial expressions, nods of approval, or questioning expressions the way we do when communicating face-to-face. People try, but it's not always possible to "read between the lines" of an e-mail message.

E-mail is another form of written communication, but it's a different medium than traditional written communication and, as we've just read, conversation. E-mail isn't bound by the physical limitations of a page of paper. E-mail can be sent and received almost instantaneously, and a single message can be sent to a group of several people as easily as it can be sent to one or two people. Because of all these conveniences, it is in your best interest to communicate in a way that is easy to read and easy to understand.

There's no substitute for a well thought-out, well-expressed, efficiently communicated message. Care should also be given to spelling and grammar, whether in professional, business, or social situations. E-mail is most effective when written clearly, taking into account that people will likely be reading your message on a computer screen or some other electronic device (PDA).

Here are some tips for effective e-mail communication:

- *Choose the subject line carefully.* Make it brief, descriptive, and to the point. In many cases, the subject line is the first thing that will get a reader's attention or make the reader delete your message. Readers have to decide in a matter of seconds if your message is important enough to keep, open, and read. Also pay attention to the smart spam filters that exist today. They primarily look at subject lines and sender information.

- *Keep your messages short.* Remember the attention spans of typical e-mail readers. People online are busy; don't waste their time. Also remember that the view screen in many e-mail programs shows only part of what is on the "page"—many times half of a hard-copy page. You can always link to your web site for the rest of the message. Tell the who, what, where, when and why as soon as possible, or supply a summary paragraph before or after your message.

- *Use a spell-checker, if possible.* Proofread your work. True, you are in a hurry, too, and have the same exigencies of as your recipient. Simple typos can miscommunicate your messages, make you appear less than professional, and make your reader really wonder if they should pursue reading your message or not.

- *DON'T SHOUT.* That's what writing in all caps is equivalent to online. There are plenty of other ways to show emphasis. Don't use all capital letters. On the same hand, don't write in all lowercase letters either. This makes it appear that you are too lazy to hit the shift key on your keyboard and

- *Not sending an e-mail reply is the same as not returning a phone call.* Consider how your prospect thinks and feels before ignoring messages.
- *Craft messages that are clear, complete, accurate, concise, and to the point.* Violating the rules of English grammar and usage makes it difficult for your reader to read, understand, and act appropriately. Keep the body of the message succinct. Limit a message to one or two screens.
- *Be careful not to fire off a reply or e-mail message without giving it proper thought.* Emotional, quick replies may come across even worse on the other end. Just because you can send information faster than ever before doesn't always mean that you should send it back just as fast. Understand the situation and reply accordingly.
- *The written word is permanent or permanent until it is deleted or the printed version is destroyed.* The point here is that if you don't want it recorded or possibly be made public, don't put it in an e-mail.
- *E-mail is not necessarily confidential or private.* Some employers will monitor employees' messages.
- *Some e-mail programs have a preference to include the original message in your reply.* You don't always need to include the whole message. E-mail messages can be more effective and efficient if only a portion of the original message is included in a reply.

The secret to direct e-mail copy lies in the testing. What works for one audience may or may not work for another e-mail audience. The only way to find out what works is to stick to some fundamentals and test different variables of the message copy.

What are those variables? I'm glad you asked. Whatever they are, the key is to write, test, rewrite, test, and rewrite some more until your message is just right. How do you know what is just right? When your campaign returns the results that you expect.

Prospects read e-mails almost as scans across or down the page. E-mail copy should reflect this. Key words should appear in bold, paragraphs should be short, and headlines should be noticed.

Most e-mails get opened because of the subject lines. Don't waste this precious space with hype, exaggerations, or spam-filled phrases. Load it with benefits and action words.

"Prevent sore eyes with our nonglare computer screen," sounds much better and will get opened more than "Our new computer screen will help your eyes." The first subject line is short, sweet, and to the point, with no of exaggeration. Notice the position of the benefits—first, in the subject line.

The first line and paragraph shouldn't be overloaded with facts, figures, and background information about you, your company, products, or services. Start with benefits as soon as you can here too. Most readers won't go past the first couple of lines, so you want to hook as many readers as you can early on.

> *Dear friend,*
>
> *Our new computer screens prevent sore eyes and improve readability by 15 percent. They are pleasing to the eyes and will allow you to work longer at your computer.*

Writing copy like this will help to get your message communicated. Save the details for later; your customer/prospect may not read that far.

The way the human eye/mind works when reading e-mails (or web sites or direct mail or advertising) is to notice graphics, photos, and images first, headlines second, bulleted information third, and plain text fourth and last.

Bulleted information will get your points across and still be in scannable form for an e-mail reader. These digestible bits of information are easy on the eyes:

> *Our new computer screen has many benefits:*
> * *No glare*
> * *Easy to clip onto your current screen*
> * *Washable*
> * *Enhances color*
> * *Soothes the eyes*

Do not use a lot of hype in your e-mail copy. Just look at how it is presented and the effect it has on you:

> *This is AWESOME! Never have I seen anything like this. You have to go get this NOW! HOT! HOT! HOT!*

It wears thin quickly, as you can see. Don't oversell. The best rule of thumb is to write like you talk. And in the case of e-mail copy, the shorter the better; the less copy it takes to get your points across, the better.

Along with no hype goes the rule of no lies. Don't put deceptive, leading words in your subject line that have nothing to do with your product. If you're selling computer screens, don't fill your subject line with something related to "getting rich quick!"

Think in terms of reaching customers and prospects with your information as if e-mail didn't exist. The customers, prospects, and targets haven't changed with the advent e-mail. Only the medium has. Herschell Gordon Lewis, author of *Effective E-Mail Marketing—The Complete Guide to Creating Successful Campaigns*, says it best:

> *Whether by e-mail, direct mail, television, or on the inside of matchbook covers, success comes from reaching and influencing—at the lowest possible cost—the largest number of people who can and will respond to your offer.*

EMBEDDED LINKS WITHIN E-MAIL COPY

Within your e-mail message, it is easy to add a link for your prospect to click through. This embedded link, also known as a hyperlink, can take your prospect to a page with more detail on your offer and a data collection form that resides on your web site. This helps to move the prospect

---

THE E-MAIL STORY

When you turn on the computer you *expect* e-mail.

The subject line will determine if your e-mail is *welcomed* or not.

Your first sentence and opening paragraph will determine if your e-mail is *liked* or not.

Get to the point and do it quickly. Of course, this assumes that there *is a* point. And that point better be perceived as a benefit to the reader.

to the next step of response. Make snail mail and a toll-free phone number an option when possible. If a prospect clicks through to this point, chances are they will end up completing the response online instead of using another response mechanism. Use Figure 4.5 to make sure all aspects of an e-mail campaign are covered.

GETTING E-MAILS OPENED NOW!

Getting e-mails opened is always the challenge of the direct e-mail marketer. Because many people use their e-mail programs as an "electronic filing cabinet," many e-mail messages are put aside. This further challenges the direct marketer to get e-mails opened, NOW. Most e-mail results and responses occur within one to two days of being received. If people procrastinate beyond this, action may never happen.

Incorporating deadlines and a sense of urgency in a subject line as well as the actual copy can help. Here are some examples:

- 4 reasons to subscribe today
- If you haven't received money by the end of the day, you need this.
- Private offer only for those signed up to receive e-mails from us.
- Come see now what the general public has to wait two days to see.
- Only 4 left to be sold today.
- This offer expires at midnight and will no longer be online.

A NOTE ON JUNK E-MAIL

When direct mail or direct e-mail is recognized immediately as advertising, it could be a good thing or a bad thing. The effect depends upon the relationship you as the marketer have with the recipient. A good way to preliminarily determine this is to consider how and where you got the targeted recipients' e-mail addresses.

FIGURE 4.5 E-Mail Campaign Checklist

❏ Is your target a business or consumer? _____

❏ E-mail campaign objectives:

   __ Number

   __ Targeted

   __ Conversion rate

   __ Average order size

❏ Response required to meet profit objective _____

_____

❏ Client LTV

❏ List source

❏ List specs

❏ List cost

❏ Outsourced components:

   __ Design

   __ Copywriting

   __ Delivery

   __ Tracking

   __ Database management

   __ Fulfillment

❏ Create your budget

❏ Establish your time line and schedule

── **CHAPTER 4 SUMMARY** ──

▶ More and more businesses every day are turning to e-mail marketing.

▶ E-mail marketing has hit the 21st century like a thunderbolt. Never before has any marketing tactic become so widespread, so fast, so inexpensively.

▶ E-mail marketing can be carried out quicker, better, and cheaper than most other direct marketing. It should be the "no brainer" part of any marketing plan.

▶ A company needs to implement etiquette rules in the interests of professionalism, efficiency, protection from liability, and common courtesy.

▶ The difference between a privacy policy and an e-mail policy is that the e-mail policy is for internal company use and the privacy policy is for publication to outside contacts, telling them what you will do with collected e-mail addresses.

▶ Spam is unsolicited, nonpermission-based e-mail that is usually sent as part of a mass e-mail marketing campaign in which the recipient doesn't know, has probably never heard of, and is not interested in the sender or the sender's product or service. Spam is the junk mail of the internet.

▶ A method/procedure for a recipient to request removal from an e-mail list should be included in any outbound e-mail marketing message to a prospect.

▶ In the double opt-in process, a name is not added to the list until a confirming e-mail is sent by the marketer and replied to by the recipient.

▶ Online copy can now be as much king as offline is.

▶ Direct e-mail marketing is designed and used to gain a response from your recipient, with the best response being an actual sale.

Planning a Direct-Mail Campaign

DIRECT MARKETING VEHICLES HAVE BEEN looked at in detail. You've decided to use direct mail as one of your marketing tactics. With a good understanding of vehicles, you can now plan and execute your marketing campaign. It's time to start your campaign. Now what? You write a letter, place it in an envelope, stick a stamp on it, and mail it to someone, right? If only it were that simple. This might work for a target list of one, using a single mailing piece. There is much more to a campaign! What steps do you take? What has to be considered? Where do you start and what has to be implemented and managed? The answers to these are probably part of the reason you bought and are now reading this book. The answers will elevate your marketing to a new level.

Just like any other component of marketing, an effective campaign is the result of effective planning.

KEEPING THE END IN MIND

Borrowing a Stephen Covey idiom, effective direct-mail campaign planning starts with the end in mind. It actually starts with several "ends in mind."

1. Why are you conducting a direct mail campaign?
2. Whom are you sending it to?
3. What are you sending?
4. What will you say?
5. When will you send it?
6. How frequently will you send your mail?
7. What can you spend on a campaign?
8. What will the actual mailing piece look like?

Once these "ends in mind" are determined, the consequent action can then be planned.

The following section will provide you with a planning guide for Figure 5.2, the Direct Mail Checklist.

- *Why are you conducting a direct mail campaign?*

   Checklist Item Covered Here:
   ❑ Define overall direct-mail campaign objective

Effectiveness is a function of your precision and your marketing objectives. Some likely marketing objectives related to direct mail targeting and making an offer are as follows:

- Finding interested prospects and generating leads
- Acquiring new customers
- Building customer loyalty
- Taking advantage of the direct marketing by-product of awareness
- Announcing new products and services
- One-step order-taking/direct purchases
- Building in-store traffic
- Sending people to your web site
- Announcing a test drive or free sample
- Keeping in touch
- Showing customer attention
- Providing information, tips, and ideas
- Asking for referrals

Understanding what direct mail can do for you, your knowledge of your prospects and your imagination will lead you to establishing these marketing objectives.

Your objectives will determine the offer and message of your direct-mail piece. Don't always think of your piece as being a letter or postcard. There are other forms of direct mail, such as catalogs. I have even seen a night-deposit bank bag sent in the mail as a special promotion. The forms promotions take are only limited by your imagination (and postal regulations).

- *Whom are you sending it to?*

    Checklist Items Covered Here:
    ❑ Define target-market characteristics.
    ❑ Include as much specific and quantitative information as possible.
    ❑ Include geographic area in target-market definition.

The more precisely you define your target for direct mail, the greater chance of response. The specifics referred to here are things like demographics, characteristics, and geographies. When compiling or purchasing a list of contacts, these elements will determine who is on that list. Taking time to define and refine these specifications will be worth your effort in the long run. Consider the following target markets:

Target Market A: Everyone who lives within a five zip code area.

Target Market B: Homeowners who live in a five zip code area, have children, make over $75,000 a year and take a vacation once a year.

If you are selling family vacation packages for spring break, which target market will you have greater success with? The answer is Target Market B, because it is more specific. There are people in Target Market A who may not have children or may not go on vacations. These people are not your target; your mailing to them would fall into their junk-mail category.

At the risk of sounding like a broken record, put some real thought into defining your target market. It will not only pay off in terms of number and quality of response, but will make for an efficient mailing—a mailing that hits the mark. Junk mail is inefficient, expensive, and lowers your return on investment.

More on targeting appears in Chapter 2, "The Marketing Target."

> **Checklist Item Covered Here:**
> ❑ Based on your quantitative campaign objective, determine the number of pieces to mail. (Assume a response rate of 0.5 to 1.0 percent.)

As you plan who to send the marketing pieces to, you should estimate the number of pieces based on required responses to generate a profit. Here is a simple calculation to help determine the size of your mailing:

- Number of pieces to be mailed

- Total costs of the campaign
- Expected percentage of response
- Expected percentage of conversion
- Expected average order

From these numbers you can calculate how many people will respond to your mailing, how many will be converted to buyers, and what the total revenue is likely to be from your campaign. Knowing the total costs of the campaign will then give you the cost per response, cost per actual purchaser, and the resulting return on investment.

Example:
- Number of pieces to be mailed: 1,000
- Total costs of the campaign: $500
- Expected percentage of response: 0.8%
- Expected percentage of conversion: 15%
- Expected average order: $500

Given these numbers, you then end up with:

- Number of responders: 8
- Number of buyers: 1.2
- Total campaign revenue: $600
- Return on investment: 20%

If you want a higher return on investment, you can adjust the total quantity sent, assuming your response rate and conversion stay the same. You can test the results of different assumptions by varying the number in the respective calculation for ROI. This is a good calculation to run through, certainly after the campaign to measure your assumptions but also at the beginning of a campaign to estimate the size of your mailing.

- *What are you sending?*

  Checklist Item Covered Here:
  - ❏ Determine if your target market prefers a letter (many professionals such as doctors, lawyers, consultants, etc., prefer letters over other vehicles).

For many businesses and consumers, direct mail advertising is informative and provides

> ### ▼ BONUS RESOURCE
>
> For an automatic online calculator to instantly provide the resulting numbers and allow you to test different scenarios and assumptions, visit Experian BizInsight's Resource Center online at:
>
> https://www.experianbizinsight.com/biz insight/resource_center/index.jsp

value and convenience. Yet, there are still some people who do not like to receive direct marketing advertising mail. Some prospects react to postcards that stand out in their daily mail pile. Others prefer full-line catalogs listing item after item category of interest. Businesses and professionals many times will react mostly to letters that appear to be from other businesses and professionals. Guessing what your target market will respond to is one way to determine what you will mail. Asking a representative sampling of the group what they prefer is the more sure way of knowing what will generate a response. This is an important step in your direct mail campaign so you can estimate costs and plan production and fulfillment.

Checklist Items Covered Here:
- ❏ What budget have you allocated for the design and production of the mailing piece?
- ❏ If using a letter, do you have the budget for printing, folding, inserting, sealing, and the envelope itself?

It costs money to put ink on paper. Printing is just one component to consider about a mailing. With printing comes many other cost variables. In the Printing Production Costs of this book, the subject will be covered in more detail.

FIGURE 5.1   Mailing Cost Worksheet

Printing and design costs _____

List acquisition costs _____

Mail prep, sorting, addressing costs _____

Postage costs _____

Total costs for the mailing _____

In addition to printing, there are costs for mail processing. If you are sending your mail via standard presort (bulk-mail), there is the cost of addressing, sorting, and the cost of the bulk mail permit.

Other fulfillment and processing costs are associated with the folding of letters, stuffing envelopes, and sealing the envelope itself. Make sure when working with a printer or mail house that these costs are itemized and included.

Add to this the cost of your list rental or purchase and postage. All of these together represent the total cost of your mailing campaign (see Figure 5.1). There are many ways to economize with some of these variables, which will be covered later.

Once you assess the potential costs of a mailing you can then calculate your potential ROI as I did in the previous discussion.

Once you know your total costs, you can then factor that into your total marketing budget within your total company budget to see if you can afford a mailing, how many mailings you can

afford, and if this is the most cost-effective marketing you can employ.

Checklist Item Covered Here:

❏ Can the direct mail vehicle be produced within the time line you have established for your campaign?

Planning with your printer is key for more than just planning costs. Timing of the production of the pieces has to be considered. Most printing companies can help you with this by estimating lead times for a particular job to be produced. This is done after carefully planning the individual specifications of a particular job. Take into account the design of the piece, the typesetting or layout, the proof approval process, the printing time, and any converting time (folding, cutting, perforating, etc.) after the ink has dried on the piece.

In addition to the time it takes to produce and convert a mailing piece, you now must consider the mail processing time. If stuffing and sealing are required, that adds to the process time. Addressing and sorting for bulk mail takes additional time that has to be factored in. Considering how long it will take the postal service to deliver your mail in addition to the production and processing time will allow you to plan accordingly for the delivery of your mailing piece to your prospect.

Checklist Item Covered Here:
❏ Are postcards more effective for your target?

Postcards are considered the fastest, easiest, most reliable way to dramatically increase your revenue and customer response. Next to e-mail, postcards are the most cost-effective marketing vehicles to generate customer response. This, of course, is because, your target market looks at postcards. The direct-marketing credo that applies here is test, test, test. If you test a postcard program vs. a letter program, be sure to calculate the cost differences between the two.

Obviously, one advantage of postcard marketing is that you don't have the expense of an envelope and the subsequent stuffing and sealing. There are many other advantages that are covered in the postcard section of this book, but none of them matter if the target market doesn't respond to postcards. Most target markets will, but using as little guesswork as possible will ensure your campaign's success.

Checklist Items Covered Here:
❏ Are you really trying to stand out in the mail pile and need to send dimensional mail (also known as lumpy mail or 3-D Mail)?
❏ Will your mailing piece change the postage rate that you have planned and budgeted, and can you afford it?

Lumpy mail is a direct marketing piece that is three-dimensional in nature. An advertising item being mailed is what makes it lumpy: a pen, a key chain, a novelty item, or other advertising premium. This technique is used to get the attention and interest of the recipient/prospect by standing out from all the other mail. The ultimate goal is to generate a response or a purchase. Gaining the attention of the prospect and standing out from the crowd leads to this.

Adding an item to a letter or parcel will increase its weight. Because one of the determinants of postage is weight, find out if the inclusion of the item puts you into a different weight range and a different postage bracket. This is still OK if you include the increased cost in your ROI estimates. In many cases, if you assume a higher opening/delivery rate, it will more than offset the higher postage.

- *What will you say?*

Checklist Item Covered Here:
❏ What action/response will achieve your marketing/ campaign objectives?

Think about your "calls to action". Do you want your prospect to pick up the phone to call you, send in for information, visit your place of business to redeem a coupon, visit your web site and put in credit card information for a purchase, or send in a faxed order? All are examples of direct marketing response that is generated from a direct marketing piece. Telling your prospect what to do is part of your planning process. If you don't tell a prospect to take action, chances are they won't.

Checklist Item Covered Here:
❏ How can you get the attention of your targeted prospect?

There are many ways to get the attention of your prospect. You must do this so your piece won't blend in with all other mail. You want your marketing message to be noticed, read, and eventually acted upon.

Here are different attention-getting mechanisms to consider as you plan your direct mail:

- A strong headline
- A plain question
- An inspirational quote

- A startling statistic or fact

In addition to getting attention you have to excite enough interest enough to create a desire, which is a motivation to take action. This is the whole formula for direct marketing. Attention-getting devices are ultimately directed to response and/or purchase. The offer is what sparks interest, desire, and action. The strongest direct mail pieces offer what an interested prospect wants and needs. Wanting and needing something will produce action in an interested prospect.

Checklist Item Covered Here:
❑ What can you fit on the printed piece?

In the world of direct marketing, you want to do as much of the sales job as possible. Many times this means long copy. If you have to consider a headline or some other attention-getting device on your piece and craft an ingenious offer, you must plan how to fit it, while being graphically pleasing, on the particular direct mail vehicle. A four-page double-sided letter can offer a lot more information than a standard-size postcard. Knowing your space limitations and the message you really want to get across will help you to prioritize your information. Prioritizing and planning within your space limitations will give your offer the greatest impact possible given the amount of space that you have to communicate your message in.

Sometimes calls to action can refer the prospect somewhere else for more information, like to a web site, a recorded phone call, or a direct-response fax number. This, of course, is adding a step to the whole direct marketing process, but it is an alternative to providing more information when space is not available.

Checklist Item Covered Here:
❑ How will your message complement or interfere with the design, or vice versa?

Direct marketers are mainly concerned with the message to their prospects. Awareness and branding are by-products of any direct mail message. Awareness and branding are best built by graphics, pictures, and eye-catching design. Effective messages are best communicated by attention-grabbing headlines and compelling copy. Let the marketing piece do its job in communicating, and don't let it be overwhelmed with design. Overwhelming design is a distraction to an effective marketing message. True, there is an optimum balance that can be achieved. Copy is king in direct marketing and should take precedence over anything else in a direct mail piece.

- *When will you send it?*

Checklist Item Covered Here:
❑ By what date would you like it to reach your target?

As a marketer and planner, you have control over the date that you send out your direct mail. Unfortunately, that is where your control ends. You don't have control over the postal system. You don't have control over companies' internal incoming-mail-processing centers. You don't have control over the in-box on someone's desk, and you don't have control over whether your piece will get opened or looked at. Despite these considerations, you can still approximate when your piece will reach your target.

Third class or presorted bulk mail can take anywhere from two to ten days to be delivered according to the USPS. Generally speaking and not during the heavy October catalog season, estimate three to five days' delivery time. You can estimate times for internal mail processing and other things beyond your control to probably within a day's time. Depending on the type of recipient that is on your list, your mail piece will delivered, most likely, within a range of four to six mail days. That means postal holidays and

Sundays have to be factored into your time line as well.

> **Checklist Item Covered Here:**
> ❑ Will you be mailing third-class bulk mail or first-class? (Think budget and timing here.)

There are many reasons to use third-class bulk mail or presorted mail (as the post office now refers to it). The primary reason is cost. The post office offers reduced rates if the mail is presorted by you or your designated mailing house. You get this reduced rate because you are effectively doing work that would normally be done by postal employees. If they don't have to do the work, you don't pay. Third-class mail raises the question of whether you can stand the time range that delivery might take place in or whether you need it there quickly and within a tighter day range.

Studies suggest that mail with a first-class postage stamp on it will get opened more often and receive more attention than presorted bulk mail. This is another consideration you must take into account when deciding how your mail will be sent.

The whole decision here boils down to budget and timing. Once these two matters are decided, you can choose how your mail will be sent.

> **Checklist Item Covered Here:**
> ❑ How long will it take to produce the mailing pieces?

You just learned how to estimate delivery times, depending on the type of mail service you use. This is assuming you have your mail piece in hand, produced and processed, and ready to send. Another important consideration in your time line of planning is how long it will take to produce your piece.

Most printers and converters can estimate that time fairly accurately when you place your printing order with them. If your piece has a special die cut or some other nonstandard converting or printing, your production time may increase. With an accurate projection from your production company, you can then estimate, along with the delivery time, how long your campaign will take from the idea stage to the point of appearing before your prospects' eyes. Take this into consideration when planning the total campaign. Don't think of an idea today and expect to have it in your prospects' hands in three days. This is too tight of a time frame. If you are not satisfied with the quoted time for production, consider another printing and mailing company and see what its turnaround time is. Planning and prioritization lead to effectiveness.

> • *How frequently will you mail during the campaign?*

> **Checklist Item Covered Here:**
> ❑ What other marketing will complement a direct mail campaign? (What other ways are you talking to your prospect? Remember the six to eight times here.)

Direct marketing should be part of your total marketing program. If you rely only on direct marketing, keep in mind that it normally takes take six to eight contacts for a prospect to get into purchase-readiness mode when they want or need what you are offering. Because direct mail and direct marketing are trying to activate that impulse to buy or respond, awareness build-up is not primary but a by-product of the campaign. Your marketing efforts are also enhanced by other touches to your prospect. If a prospect has heard of you, seen you or your marketing, and receives your direct marketing mail piece, they may be more inclined to respond or purchase. Marketing is made up of many, many, many things that support each other, whether direct response or not. This is a good time to plan your total mailing campaign, looking at what complements what and the total costs of your program. It may yield information to increase your direct marketing efforts while spending less money and time.

- *What can you spend on a mailing campaign?*

   Checklist Items Covered Here:
   ❏ What is the break-even point and return on investment?

   ❏ Have you considered the lifetime value of your client in your income projections?

When we reviewed costs, we examined various cost variables. In order to calculate your break-even point for a campaign, at a minimum, you must know:

- Number of pieces to be mailed: _____
- Total cost of the campaign: _____
- Expected percentage of response: _____
- Expected percentage of conversion: _____
- Expected average order: _____

If your total campaign cost is $1,000, then your average order times the number of converted responders must equal at least $1000 to break even. You can meet this break-even point and possibly exceed it by converting more respondents into paying customers or by having a higher average-order income. Knowing the break-even point will set your expectations and measure the success of your campaign. Paraphrasing from *Alice in Wonderland*, "If you don't know where you are going, how will you know when you get there?"

One important note about this calculation: The break-even analysis shown here is for one mailing. If you do more than one mailing in your campaign, which you should, you have additional costs and consequently a higher break-even point. This break-even point is calculated based on the responses from the particular mailing being measured. If the responding customer continues to buy from you on an ongoing basis, your campaign return will compound and actually be higher. This ongoing purchase situation during the lifetime of the customer is called the lifetime value of a client. Many direct mail campaigns that initially appear to break even actually yield far greater returns when taking into account these lifetime values.

Checklist Items Covered Here:
❏ What other marketing have you budgeted?
❏ What percentage of your total marketing budget is for the direct mail campaign? (Is this the only marketing you are doing, or are you funding more marketing?)

Marketing is made up of ever so many things. Direct mail is an important part of your marketing portfolio. Many of the items like PR and networking will be free. Other aspects of your marketing will cost money. At the beginning of your business planning cycle, you budget all the expenses and investments over the ensuing business year.

Your marketing budget will actually be made up of many smaller component budgets, such as what you will allot for direct mail. If direct mail is the foundation of your marketing, it should be the main focus of your marketing budget.

Checklist Item Covered Here:
❏ How much can you/will you spend on design, production, fulfillment, and postage?

Knowing the cost of all campaign components is important when trying to estimate the most realistic budget numbers. Overlooking just one of those components will result in your spending more than planned on your campaign.

There are more costs to consider than just printing and postage. The piece has to be designed if you don't do it yourself. There is also converting and fulfillment. Does the letter need to be folded, inserted into an envelope, and then the envelope sealed? How is the envelope or postcard going to get addressed? Is your list an inhouse list, a rented list, or a purchased list? Each of these factors adds one more cost component to your total campaign costs.

- *What will the actual mailing piece look like?*

  Checklist Items Covered Here:

  ❑ How much will you budget for design, printing, and production?

  ❑ What resources do you have for design (e.g., graphic designer—inhouse vs. outsourced)?

Jay Conrad Levinson, the father of guerrilla marketing and coauthor of *Guerrilla Marketing in 30 Days,* advised marketers to launch their marketing attacks according to what they can financially and mentally afford. The same credo applies to your direct mail campaign. Don't overwhelm yourself with so much activity and so many details that nothing gets carried to completion or done right. This is the emotional part that he speaks of. If you can't afford it financially, don't do it unless you are assured of response and conversion.

Aside from this overall attitude, you must look at the resources you have at your disposal to take a campaign from start to finish. You might be creative in terms of ideas but need the outside help of a graphic designer to take your ideas to print. You may have an assistant or coworker who can do that. Evaluating your resources will lead to what can be done inhouse and what must be outsourced.

Don't think about design only in terms of graphic design. Even if you have a text-intensive direct mail piece/campaign and an attention-getting headline, it still must look graphically pleasing and professional. Graphic designers work with layout as much as they work with graphics and pictures.

Outsourcing will generally involve a cash outlay and probably be more expensive. This is a key factor in your budgeting analyses. The same goes for printing, production, fulfillment, and processing.

Checklist Item Covered Here:

❑ What is the impact of design and format on postage and other costs?

A postcard requires different postage than a letter, whether sent via presorted bulk mail or first class. A single-page letter mailed in an envelope requires different postage than an eight-page booklet. The design of your mailing piece will have a direct impact on your postage costs and should be considered when planning and budgeting. Anything inserted into an envelope will also affect the cost of the envelope. A postcard mailing does not incur envelope costs. If you design a letter to be folded vs. a letter that is mailed unfolded, you have postage differences and the cost of the folding to consider. Keep postage and other costs under consideration when designing your direct mail piece and your total campaign.

Checklist Items Covered Here:

❑ Will the piece stand out or look like everyone else's direct mail campaign?

❑ Can the production, fulfillment, and mailing dates be met with the design that is chosen?

The ideal outcome for any direct mail campaign is that the pieces get opened, read, and responded to. There are many design considerations that can contribute to this. The cost of extra design has to be factored in as well as extra postage and extra production time. All these things come into play when planning the design of the direct mail campaign. Usually the printer you contract with will be able to define the extra costs and the extra time.

When you work with your printer, you will be quoted a production time. Anytime you add another design component that requires another converting, fulfillment, or production operation, time is added to the schedule. Some fancy printing can add days to a standard printing schedule. Things like die-cuts, special folds, and varnish coatings can add time to a job. Designers typically like to be very creative. Remember: The art of direct marketing has more to do with results than how creative a piece is.

Checklist Item Covered Here:

❑ What format will work for your target (letter, post card, 3-D mail, etc.)?

We discussed this above when thinking about what your target market might prefer in its direct mail advertising. But it's not just your target market that determines the format of your mailing. Design considerations also play a role. We have already discussed cost considerations and postage implications. Keep in mind the format and all these other considerations also play a role when designing your piece and total campaign.

Answering each and every one of these questions fully, completely, and as accurately as you can, will define your total campaign. The complete form is in Figure 5.2. Your answers will allow you to assign dates for each step of the way. This is your campaign plan. This is your accountability tool. The more complete it is, the more chance of success you have for your campaign, and the easier it will be to measure its effectiveness.

Campaign Summary

Just like any other part of a marketing plan, the direct mail component must be thoroughly planned. These components are covered throughout this book and comprise all the steps necessary for a successful campaign.

- Designing a direct mail campaign
- Pinpointing your target/list
- Concept/copy development
- Printing, letter-shop, fulfillment
- Mail prep and processing
- Best postage rates/budget
- Tracking and analyzing results
- Internet/e-mail support
- Follow-up

FIGURE 5.2 Direct Mail Checklist

Here are the vital questions and corresponding answers that can lead to success in any marketing campaign:

- *Whom are you sending it to?*

  ❑ Define overall campaign objective.

  ❑ Include as much specific and quantitative information as possible.

  ❑ Define target market characteristics.

  ❑ Include geographic area in target-market definition.

  ❑ Based on the quantitative campaign objective, determine the number of pieces to mail. (Assume a response rate of 0.5 to 1.0 percent.)

- *What are you sending?*

  ❑ Determine if your target market prefers a letter (many professionals, such as doctors, lawyers, consultants, etc., prefer letters over other vehicles).

  ❑ What budget have you allocated for the design and production of the mailing piece?

  ❑ If using a letter, do you have the budget for printing, folding, inserting, sealing, and the envelope itself?

  ❑ Are postcards more effective for your target?

  ❑ Are you really trying to stand out in the mail pile and need to send dimensional mail (lumpy mail or 3-D mail)?

CONTINUED

FIGURE 5.2	Direct Mail Checklist

❑ Will your mailing piece change the postage rate that you have planned and budgeted, and can you afford it?

❑ Can the production of the direct mail vehicle be produced within the time line you have established for your campaign?

- *What will you say?*

  ❑ What action/response will achieve your marketing/campaign objectives?

  ❑ How can you get the attention of your targeted prospect:

  ❑ Strong headline

  ❑ Plain question

  ❑ An inspirational quote

  ❑ A startling statistic or fact

  ❑ What can you fit on the printed piece?

  ❑ How will your message complement or interfere with the design or vice versa?

- *When will you send it?*

  ❑ By what date would you like it to reach your target?

  ❑ Will you be mailing third-class bulk mail or first-class? (Think budget and timing here.)

  ❑ How long will it take to produce the mailing pieces?

- *How frequently will you mail during the campaign?*

  ❑ What other marketing will complement a direct mail campaign? (In what ways are you talking to your prospect? Remember the six to eight times here.)

- *What will you spend on a mailing campaign?*

  ❑ What is the break-even point and return on investment?

  ❑ Have you considered the lifetime value of your client in your income projections?

  ❑ What other marketing have you budgeted?

  ❑ What percentage of your total marketing budget is for the direct-mail campaign? (Is this the only marketing you are doing, or are you funding more marketing?)

  ❑ How much can you/will you spend on design, production, fulfillment, and postage?

- *What will the actual mailing piece look like?*

  ❑ How much will you budget for design, printing, and production?

  ❑ What is the impact of design and format on postage and other costs?

  ❑ What resources do you have for design (e.g., graphic designer—inhouse vs. outsourced)?

  ❑ Can production, fulfillment, and mailing dates be met with the design that is chosen?

  ❑ Will the piece stand out, or will it look like everyone else's direct mail campaign?

  ❑ What format will work with your target (letter, postcard, 3-D mail, etc.)?

PRODUCTION COMPONENTS OF DIRECT MAIL

There are many cost components to a direct mail campaign. The largest is postage, followed closely by the cost of printing and production.

In looking at budgeting and planning, there will be times you're tempted to cut costs to manage your campaign optimally. Postage costs can be reduced by going through the whole "presort" process regulated by the post office. There are certain guidelines to follow and processing functions to perform. The postal service spells these out in detail, with the associated postage reductions. It's a very clear structure.

Managing the costs of printing and production is not as clear-cut. Costs are important considerations for your direct mail campaign but not the only consideration and sometimes not even the primary ones consideration.

In this book, the primary components of direct marketing are pared down to the vehicle, the message, timing and frequency, and the target.

Of these four, the vehicle has strong cost considerations associated with it. And the printing and production component of the vehicle is the greatest part of that cost.

If you choose a postcard as your direct mail vehicle over a four-page letter inserted into a 9" by 12" envelope with an accompanying catalog, your costs of printing and production will be considerably different. If you choose an elegant invitation instead of a flier, your direct mail printing and production costs will be significantly different. These formats are determined by factors other than just cost. Your choice of marketing vehicle depends on your marketing objective, your target, and how you want your message to be communicated. Just because you have 1,000 printed postcards left over from a previous campaign doesn't mean that those postcards should be your vehicles of choice for

your next campaign. It may be that they are still useful, but leftover material should not affect your vehicle decision. Consider everything mentioned above before deciding to use them.

Direct Mail Printing and Production Planning

The following section will provide you a quick-glance planning guide for Figure 5.3, the direct-mail planning checklist. Most of the topics covered in this section and on the checklist are detailed in other sections of this book.

Choose a printing company to work with. You don't ordinarily wake up in the morning and say that you need to find a printing company to work with . . . unless you have a direct mail project to complete. Once you have this need, you will start to see them everywhere. You may drive by and suddenly notice some of the smaller commercial/direct-mail printing companies right in your own neighborhood or you may talk to others who have dealt with these companies. You have to find a printing partner who is right for you.

There are many ways to find a printing and mailing company:

- *Yellow Pages.* Although most people now consult directories online, the Yellow Pages still have a listing of commercial printing and mailing companies. The listings will vary, but more than likely appear under: Commercial Printer, Printer, Mail House, Quick Printer.
- *Online/internet.* More and more people are consulting online directories for things they used to look up in the Yellow Pages. Search engines have replaced the thick paper directories. Use the same search terms as you would use in the Yellow Pages lookup. Searches online allow you to refine

your search by adding additional terms or descriptors that pinpoint your needs: Direct Mail Printing, Color Printing, Printing and Mailing, Direct Marketing Printing.

Note: Be careful about using just the word printer in the search engine. You will end up with a listing of desktop, office, and computer printing equipment.

- *Referrals.* If you know others who have used printers for marketing projects like yours, you can ask them who printed for them. You can also ask the senders of direct mail that you have received and liked what printing company they worked with. Maybe you received a direct mail piece that is similar to what you want to produce. Finding the company that printed that piece would be ideal for you.

It's best to find a printing company experienced in printing direct mail projects and the components involved. This includes the printing of envelopes, letters, postcards, self-mailers, and other marketing material.

Quality of work, professionalism, attention to detail, ease of doing business with, price, and service are all value considerations, regardless of the type of outside supplier you are seeking.

Make an appointment to meet with the printing company you choose. Once you have found a few companies that might suit your needs, call and make an appointment with them. Ask to speak with the marketing or sales manager if they have someone in that position. If that position doesn't exist or the person is unavailable, any sales representative will do. Operations managers sometimes take the time to meet with customers about project work. The company you choose will become a partner in your campaign. It is important that there be a "fit" between you, your project, your timing, and budget.

Note: If the company you choose does the actual processing of the mail, you may also speak with their direct mail specialist. They can, many times, offer tips to hold down expenses and speed up production while meeting the proper postal regulations for mailings.

At the appointment, discuss your overall marketing objectives, your direct-mail objectives, and your ideas. If the company or person you choose is to be a "partner" in your campaign, it's best to communicate as completely as possible. This includes discussion of your overall marketing objectives, any ideas you may have for format, or any other direct mail ideas. Just like the direct mail specialist in the company, other company representatives that you work with will be able to offer shortcuts and efficiencies to help you and your campaign. The goal here is to establish trust and exchange information. Once that is done, you will find that the printing company will actually be an extension of you, your staff, and your company—a very valuable partnership.

Discuss target audience quantity (the list) and frequency of mailing to determine final quantity. Very simply, the number of pieces in your campaign depends on the size of your list and the frequency of your mailings. If you have a mailing list of 4,000 and you want to mail six times to that list (the same piece), your total quantity for the campaign is 24,000. This is an important variable in the pricing of the printing and your overall campaign.

Note: It is better to favor frequency over quantity when determining final quantity and budget. Mailing 6 times to 4,000 people will produce a higher response than mailing once to 24,000 people.

Propose direct mail format ideas. During the conversation with your printing partner, you will want to start proposing **direct mail** format ideas, almost a "what if" discussion. If your printing partner is a trained and experienced marketing expert, that is a bonus. You can then evaluate different scenarios from a cost, design, and mailing standpoint. Sizes, colors, and other specifications can be discussed in an effort to reach final format decisions.

All specifications mentioned will eventually need to be determined to arrive at cost estimates and production-time estimates. The more defined your campaign and components, the more efficiently your time will be spent.

Decide on all printing variables. The price of printing is depends on six variables: paper, ink, size, quantity, prepress, and any postconverting that is needed.

1. *Paper.* Consider weight, thickness (pay attention to postage regulations here), color, and size.
2. *Ink.* How many colors (full-color is made up of four colors—blue, yellow, red, and black), how many sides are printed, and the amount of coverage.
3. *Quantity.* How many finished pieces do you want? Let the printing professional determine how many "finished pieces" can fit on a particular-size sheet, or how many will be printed at a time. Printers talk to customers in terms of finished quantity, not sheets printed.
4. *Size.* Size will determine the printing company's efficiencies which translate into cost effectiveness for you. If your finished piece will measure 8.5" by 11" and a printer has the capability of printing an 11" by 17" sheet, the printer can print two finished pieces at a time, doubling the productivity and passing the economies on to you, the customer.

5. *Prepress.* In today's digital printing environment there is still preparation that has to be done before ink hits paper. This is often referred to as "prepress" work. Graphic designers, many times, have to manipulate files to get to a point of print readiness. This includes color enhancement, color separation, the stepping-up of forms, digitizing, application of halftones, and more. In most cases, you won't need to worry about what all this means and the related details; your printing partner will assess what needs to be done and charge you accordingly.
6. *Postconverting.* It is often said by commercial printers that printing is the easiest and quickest part of a direct mail job. Once printed, your job may require some type of postprinting converting: folding, die-cutting, wafer-sealing (for self-mailers), cutting, trimming, and packaging.

Defining each of these six variables will lead you to the point of not only project definition but identifying the components needed by the printing company to estimate total costs.

Obtain printing cost/price estimates. Having identified all necessary components that printing costs are based on, you can now request an official price estimate from your printer. It is at this point that you can compare estimates to your budget. If costs exceed your budget, your printer is well trained to discuss the giving and taking necessary to bring your project within budget.

Place printing order. After establishing costs, quantities, and all other specifications, you are now in a position to place your order with the printing company. This is your agreement with them to pay for products and services rendered.

You may or may not be asked for a deposit or a credit application upon placing your order. You will then be quoted a completion date and a shipping/pickup option.

Choose a mail processing company/mail house, if different from the printing company.

Depending on the printing company you choose, they may or may not be involved in direct mail processing. It is quite advantageous to you if they are. If they aren't, it's not a show stopper for your project. To find a mailing company, you simply go through the same process you used to find a printing company. Mailing companies that are stand-alone businesses are often referred to as "mail houses." Use this search term when using search engines. Another term you will hear is a "letter shop." In addition to functions related to direct mail processing, a letter shop can perform mail merging—personalized letters in matching personalized envelopes.

Once you have chosen the mail processing company, you can then schedule your mailing based on the completion date your printer gave you.

Approve a printing proof sample.

Because printing cannot be undone and so much goes into a print job up to the point of putting ink on paper, printers want to make doubly sure that what they print is exactly what you want. Because of this, they will offer you a "proof" to approve before printing. The proof is a facsimile or replication of your finished printed piece. Your job is to make sure the layout, spelling, fonts, photos, and other creative features are as you specified. You can still make minor corrections at this point but not complete redesigns. Complete redesigns may constitute another order, with additional costs.

If the proof is as you specified, sign and date it and return it to the printer.

The printer uses your approved proof to compare to the finished product coming off of the printing presses.

Provide a mailing list/database to the printing company/mail house.

After printing, the printing company (and/or mail house) will be ready to address each individual mailing piece that is printed. The names and addresses come from the list that you supply. The list will be an electronic file attached to an e-mail, an electronic file on a disc, or some other digital transport device. The list will be assembled in some type of file application, usually Microsoft Excel, Access, or other spreadsheet program.

Many data programs and business application programs handle and process many different mail list file formats. Common ones are:

- Fixed length
- Comma-delimited
- DBASE. This is the best way to send mail list data. DBASE is the most structured and the easiest to recreate.
- Delimited Text. This format is easy to handle. It uses less disk space because it lacks the structure that dBASE files have. Any ASCII character may be used as a delimiter (separator). The standard for IBM is the comma and for Macintosh it is the tab.

Other file formats are also available, such as Excel; however, these programs have file-size limitations (up to 65,000 entries) that can present problems with some clients. It is, therefore, recommended that files be sent in one of the supported file layouts, described above, that allow an unlimited number of records.

Common file extensions for the above formats:

- Excel (.xls)
- Tab or comma-delimited text (.txt)

Database (.dbf)
- Comma-delimited ASCII (.csv)
- Microsoft access database files (.mdb)

Almost all database-management programs such as Access, Excel, ACT, GoldMine, etc., will allow you to export or save your data in one of these formats. DO NOT upload in label format. For most individuals using spreadsheet software such as Microsoft Excel, you can use the Excel format simply by selecting File/Save As, then selecting Microsoft Excel as the format. If Excel is not your forte, it is best to consult the local mail house or printing company that processes direct mail.

The direct mail specialist then sorts the list according to postal regulations and postage method. This also is the time each individual address is imprinted onto each piece. In some cases, the addresses are printed on a label and the label is affixed to the mailing piece. All data for the address come from your database.

Use the database to do any sorts you want for testing or segmenting of your mail campaign.

Provide a postage check to the mail house, printing company, or directly to the post office. Most printing companies and mail houses will deliver your finished, addressed, and sorted mail pieces directly to the post office for you.

Because the postage is paid to the post office and is not a marked-up, value-added item in a mailing job, payment of postage is requested directly from you at this time, usually in the from of a check. The postage check should be made payable to the U.S. Post Office or U.S. Postmaster or just Postmaster.

Note: Beware of mail houses that mark up postage amounts. You are already paying a processing fee so there is no reason to add it again.

Establish a "send" date with the mailing company. While it's hard to predict the exact time your recipient will receive your mail, you still want to target a range of time for sending it. This will include the day the mail house "drops" your mail at the post office.

This should be clearly communicated by your mail house based on your specifications, the actual time lines of production and processing you established, and the mail house delivery schedule.

The worst thing that could happen is that you start getting responses to your direct mail campaign and you aren't prepared to respond to the prospects or fulfill their responses. You did all that work so don't blow it with a poor response system or lack of response!

Planning your response, having materials already prepared, knowing next steps, and understanding the scripts to be followed are the final parts to planning your campaign. And be sure to cheer for every response! You will be more than ready when responses start to pour in, if you take this step.

Plan the next mailing. Plan your campaign. Execute it in the way that this checklist suggests. Send it out. Sit back and watch all the responses roll in. Fulfill the orders quickly and collect the money.

If only that were all there was to it! Inevitably, more marketing and more mailing will be done. Whether carried out simultaneously with another campaign or right after the mail-drop date of your most recent campaign, you have to go right back through this whole process to plan the next campaign.

It's important to look forward and plan your next step of growth. Forgetting to plan for the future spells doom to your ongoing success.

| FIGURE 5.3 | Direct Mail Printing and Production Planning Checklist |

❑ Choose a printing company to work with.

❑ Make an appointment to meet with the printing company you choose.

❑ At the appointment, discuss your overall marketing objectives, your direct-mail objectives, and your ideas.

❑ Discuss target audience quantity (the list) and frequency of mailing to determine final quantity.

❑ Propose direct-mail format ideas.

❑ Decide on all printing variables.

❑ Obtain printing cost/price estimates.

❑ Place printing order.

❑ Choose a mail processing company/mail house, if different from the printing company.

❑ Approve a printing proof sample.

❑ Provide mailing list/database to the printing company/mail house.

❑ Provide a postage check to the mail house, printing company, or directly to the post office.

❑ Establish a "send" date with the mailing company.

❑ Make sure follow-up, response fulfillment, and tracking systems are in place.

❑ Plan your next mailing.

DIRECT MARKETING AT WORK

Just pick up the latest issue of *Home and Away*, the bimonthly publication of AAA Chicago Motor Club, and you will see direct marketing hard at work. For example:

- Four pages into the magazine, you see a full-page ad from Bose. It seems like Bose advertises everywhere. It really doesn't. I notice it because I am in its target market and happen to read the publications Bose has identified that hit its target market. This particular ad is benefit-laden with offers for free shipping, a guarantee, and information. It offers a web site and a toll-free phone number as response mechanisms for its offers. This is direct marketing at its finest.

- Two pages after Bose hits you, Select Comfort Direct strikes you with a double whammy. It is at this point in the publication that a business reply card (BRC) is inserted between the pages. The card is simple with lots of white space and communicates several direct calls to action:
  - Mail this card today.
  - Call toll-free.
  - Rush me a brochure.
  - Send a free sleep video or DVD.

  Right under the reply card is a full-page, full-color ad for the same mattress product that is advertised on the BRC. Here, a few benefits are expounded upon, but the same direct-reply options are also present. The toll-free number is also highlighted on a clip-out coupon to send in for the free video. It is stated that the video also gives details about a 30-night, in-home trial.

- On the following two pages, direct response ads for two different products/companies appear. One is for a scooter wheelchair device, complete with a toll free number and web site address. The offer is a free, over-the-phone, mobility consultation—no pressure, no obligation, according to the copy.

- The other is a direct, in-your-face, full-page ad for official government-issued $5 gold coins. A huge headline and a picture of our nation's capitol grab the reader's attention. There is a call-to-action to call a toll free number and to do it *now* . . . because "they will not last long." Another reason for of urgency is built in to the ad:

    Beginning today, telephone orders will be accepted on a first-come, first-served basis according to time and date of the order!

    The ad looks official, is attention-grabbing, tells the whole story, lays out the benefit, and instills a sense of urgency to buy now. This ad is direct!

- Half way into the publication is a two-thirds page full color ad for the Talking Road Whiz. The offer is an AAA member special, with a full guarantee. There are testimonials and benefits galore. One thing of note, in this ad you can respond by purchasing the item/product and only by a toll-free number; no web site, no address, no coupon for more information. It's only a direct-sale offer.

USPS: Customized Market Mail (CMM)

Much has been said about the volume of mail, the marketing messages consumers and businesses receive, and how to stand out from the crowd. Looking different and not the same as everyone else's mail is key.

Sometimes being different is cost-prohibitive. On top of that, postal regulations don't always allow for absolute creativity. Both of these hurdles can now be overcome with an innovative new offering from the USPS: customized market mail (CMM).

CMM offers direct marketers a standard mail vehicle that allows him or her to send a highly targeted, unique piece of mail of any shape or design without the use of an envelope. Now, nonrectangular, circular, oblong, triangular, or any die-cut shapes are allowable under the new program offered by the Postal Service. The mail pieces may now include die-cuts, voids, and holes. They can be made from a variety of materials to create different thicknesses and textures, all in an effort to stand out, make impact, and increase response rates from your direct mail efforts.

There are still weight and size restrictions for CMM. They can weigh no more than 3.3 ounces and may range in height from 3.5 to 12 inches with widths of 5 to 15 inches. The .007-inch minimum thickness still applies with the maximum being .75 inches.

In a world of consumers and businesses being bombarded constantly by thousands of marketing messages a day, this is clearly one way to stand out in the crowd.

An example might be a hot dog restaurant sending out a postcard in the shape of a mustard-covered hot dog, or a pet store sending out a notice and offer in the shape of a fuzzy dog or a bone—all without an envelope.

Shapes don't have to be exotic and fancy. Consider what Rosenfeld, Raymon, Pielech did.

Rosenfeld, Raymon, Pielech is a public accounting firm in New Bedford, Massachusetts. Its campaign consisted of a target of just over 1,000 business-to-business prospects in Massachusetts. Its goal in this direct marketing endeavor was to acquire new customers. Rosenfeld, Raymon, Pielech decided to present something different from the rectangular, full-color glossy pieces often found in direct mail piles and direct mail trash cans and opted for a simple black-and-white piece with no photos or graphics. Best of all, the piece was in the shape of a circle.

The CMM rules allowed this piece to be mailed as is, clearly standing out in any mail pile full of rectangular, and square pieces.

Odd shapes increase response rates, and that certainly was the case with this mailing. The campaign achieved a 20 percent response rate, representing approximately 200 requests for an appointment. Leads were generated so quickly and in such quantity that Rosenfeld, Raymon, Pielech had to schedule meetings far in advance to keep up with demand.

It experienced its best mail campaign ever and achieved goal of cutting through clutter, communicating a simple message, and acquiring new customers, all while making a profit.

A similar campaign was undertaken by Palmetto Bay Village Center, a commercial office complex in Miami, Florida.

A die-cut 12" by 10" cardboard Boston terrier dog shape was printed and mailed to a targeted commercial audience of 12,000. The campaign had the objective of enticing businesses to relocate their offices to the new commercial complex. Imagine the mail sort that happened with a cute Boston terrier staring people in the face amongst their many direct mail rectangles. The piece stood out. It got read, and response was much greater than a letter in an envelope.

EXTREME DIRECT MARKETING EXAMPLES

As you've seen, direct mail makes up a large part of the thousands of marketing messages people are bombarded with every day. Standing out and being unique in this bombardment is essential for successful direct marketing. Bill Glazer, direct marketing guru, and owner of Gage Menswear, Baltimore's world class men's stores, works on this continually with his own retail store direct marketing and as consultant to others. Below are descriptions of campaigns that have yielded, in some cases, double-digit response rates or rates significantly above average for direct mail campaigns. Look at the unique individual components that have helped achieve the direct mail goals of getting opened, responded to, and converted into a sale.

All direct mail campaigns for Gage Menswear and Bill Gazer's BGS Marketing, described below, were sent to existing clients and have two things in common. The first is that all campaigns truly cut through the clutter that is in all of our mailboxes each day. This was done by being different, unique, and sometimes extreme, significantly increasing the chances of getting the piece opened. The second common factor is that each campaign/piece tells an interesting story of some kind, holding the interest of the client.

Because Gage Menswear had an existing relationship with the targeted clients, the campaign built on the "stories" of Bill Glazer, the high-profile, popular, and well-known owner in each tale. Clients love to be entertained; they looked forward to receiving the pieces in the mail just to see what Bill's next story would be. Each piece has a very unusual look, and most were either oversized pieces, allowing them to stand out in mail piles, or were sent in a blank Number-10 business envelope, providing that curiosity factor that increases open-rates.

All these samples are part of Gage Menswear's "prospecting funnel." Attention-getting entertainment blended seamlessly with deadlines, testimonials, sense of-urgency messages, and lots of calls to action. It's always easy with Gage's pieces to find a convenient way to respond—a great characteristic of direct mail.

Bill Glazer knows that people like to be amused. With all the marketing messages bombarding people each day, it is common for them to get bored or overwhelmed with advertising. Making things outrageous in Bill's case is a way to get mail into the must-read pile.

All the pieces have provocative headlines, captions below photos, quick expiration dates, and lots of P.S.'s. Because the P.S. is one of the most read parts of any letter, second only to the headline, it is used to restate the offer and deadline, and to suggest one more place for a call to action.

All of the Bill Glazer examples are reprinted with permission (www.bgsmarketing.com and www.dankennedy.com).

A Shiny Authentic Nickel

In a two-page printed letter, Gage Menswear sends lots of information, packing into those two pages more direct marketing techniques than most marketers use in an entire campaign.

On top of the letter is a glued nickel. Now *that* will certainly get your attention. The headline is personalized: "Why is this Menswear Retailer Sending Beth Fitzpatrick a Shiny Authentic Nickel?"

Throughout the letter, Glazer uses printed handwritten notes to draw attention to appear more personal. Circled items, checked items, and arrows pointing the reader elsewhere appear throughout. A picture of Bill laughing hysterically and entitled Crazy Bill uses humor to warm the client and extend the relationship-building qualities of Bill and Gage Menswear.

Extreme offers, more personalization, deadlines galore, and lots of tie-ins to the nickel theme pervade. Not only does he use a P.S.— this letter has five P.S.'s!

There are free gift offers, and if anyone skips everything and just reads the last P.S., he asks for a return of the nickel (if the reader is not going to use it). If you decide not to take advantage of this great deal, can you please return the attached nickel to either store? With a sale this good, every nickel counts . . . call me crazy!"

For this mailing, the envelope was plain but had the address printed in "ink pen blue" in a font that resembled handwritten letters—a sure way to increase the open-rate.

One last point is that the letters were mailed with a first-class postage stamp, again increasing the open-rates.

Result: A successful mailing, a continuing campaign, and increased sales and profits (see Figure 5.4).

Round Tuit

Can you guess from the heading of this example where this one is going? Take another look before reading on.

This mailing piece also used a glued-on token; a real token, it was a wooden "Round Tuit." The other stand-out factor is that the letter is printed on actual yellow, ruled legal paper in "ballpoint blue" as if the whole letter were handwritten, complete with scratch-outs, scribbles, arrows, and other means of emphasis. In this case, Bill Glazer was marketing the marketing system that he sells to other retailers.

His message, tying in to the token, says: "Whatever the reason (referring to not finding the time to respond) *you haven't gotten around to it* . . . Well, at the risk of being a bit silly . . . now you have No More Excuses because I've just given you a "Round Tuit" which is attached to the top of page one of the letter."

FIGURE 5.4	Shiney Authentic Nickel Promotion

Crazy Bill Glazer

Why Is This Menswear Retailer Sending Beth Fitzpatrick A Shiny Authentic Nickel?

your FREE Nickel!

(Has He Finally Gone Crazy!!)

To: Beth Fitzpatrick

001076

Dear Beth,

As you can see, I have attached a shiny, nickel to the top of this letter. Why have I done this? Have I finally gone crazy? Perhaps…but there are two reasons:

1. I have something extremely important to share with you, and I needed to get your attention right was…so…

2. Since what I have to share involves **saving you an incredible amount of money now when you need it the most, right before the holidays,** I thought using a nickel as an "eye catcher" was especially appropriate.

Well, to be perfectly honest with you, there is a third reason:

3. From NOW until December 24th, I am conducting our 1st time ever (and probably never to be repeated again) BUY-1 ITEM, at prices sold elsewhere and, GET-1-FOR-A-NICKEL SALE, and I thought it would be nice to treat one of our best clients to their first nickel item...as my gift to you!

Let me say this once again because I'm sure you will not want to miss out on this opportunity. From now until December 24th, you can take advantage of the Gage "World Class" Menswear's...

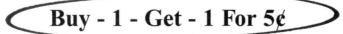

Buy - 1 - Get - 1 For 5¢

That's right!! Choose from our extensive inventory of top quality designer and brand name menswear, including Joseph Abboud Ralph Lauren, Calvin Klein, Tallia, Hugo Boss, Tundra, Bill Blass, Mezlan and Tommy Hilfiger…just to mention a few.

Of course every size is included, from 36 to 60 in regular, short, long, x-long, and portly. Sportswear sizes from small, all the way up to 6x-large. Dress shirts from 14" to 20" neck, with sleeve lengths from 32 to 37 inches. Even pant sizes from 28" to 52" waists. **As you can see, regardless of who is on your gift list...we can probably fit him.**

Just in case there is any confusion, let me say it once again:

Buy ANY Suit and Get a Second for .... **5¢** ✓

Buy ANY Sport Coat and Get a Second for .... **5¢** ✓

Buy ANY Dress Pant and Get a Second for .... **5¢** ✓   Look!...More for 5¢

Buy ANY Outer Jacket and Get a Second for .... **5¢** ✓

CONTINUED

| FIGURE 5.1 | **Shiney Authentic Nickel Promotion** |

Buy ANY Topcoat and Get a Second for .... 5¢ ✓

Buy ANY Leather Jacket and Get a Second for .... 5¢ ✓

Buy ANY Rain Coat and Get a Second for .... 5¢ ✓

Buy ANY Sweater and Get a Second for .... 5¢ ✓

Buy ANY Sport Shirt and Get a Second for .... 5¢ ✓

Buy ANY Tuxedo and Get a Second for .... 5¢ ✓

Buy ANY Pair of Shoes and Get a Second for .... 5¢ ✓

Don't need two items in the same category...NO PROBLEM. You can select ANY two items from ANY category and just pay a nickel for the lower priced one...or if you want, bring a friend with you and each pick out an item.

Whoa Nelly...I'm not done yet. Since this is the season of gift giving, I have a gift for you.

Bring in the enclosed special FREE GIFT insert that is included with this letter and receive a genuine Geoffrey Beene leather wallet, in a handsome gift box, with any purchase you make during the Buy-1-Get-1-For-A-Nickel Sale. Keep the walle for yourself or give it as a gift to a loved one or friend.

Whew! Now I am done...and I've got to get moving to prepare for the avalanche of 'preferred clients' like you who will be taking advantage of this unbelievable savings opportunity.

Dedicated To Making You Look Good,

Bill Glazer

Bill Glazer, Owner

P.S. #1: Just a reminder, the Buy-1-Get-1-For-A-Nickel Sale ends on December 24, 2004

P.S. #2: Don't need two items in the same category. No problem....you can select ANY two items and just pay a nickel for the lower priced one.

P.S. #3: Make sure you remember to bring in the enclosed FREE Gift insert to redeem it for your FREE genuine Geoffrey Beene leather wallet with any purchase during this incredible sale.

P.S. #4: I almost forget to mention it, but our entire Boys Department (Suits, Sport Coats, Dress Shirts, Slacks, etc.) at our Owings Mills Location is also included in the Buy-1-Get-1-For-A-Nickel Sale.

P.S. #5: If you decide not to take advantage of this great deal, can you please return the attached nickel to either store. With a sale this good, every nickel counts...call me crazy!

Downtown - 200 W. Baltimore St.
Across from 1st Mariner Arena
410-727-0763
Mon.-Sat. 9 to 6 & Sunday 11 to 4
Free Parking at Arrow Garage

Owings Mills - 9616 Reisterstown Rd.
Owings Mills in Valley Centre
410-581-5351
Mon.-Sat. 10 to 9 & Sunday 12 to 5

Baltimore's World Class Men's Stores

Verified Checks and Bank Debit Cards

www.gagemenswear.com

The letter spells out more than one way Bill's system is guaranteed; he removes risk in many, unique, attention-getting ways throughout the letter. It is not just stimulating, one-page, handwriting on legal paper, but a four-page sales letter. Yes, it ends with two P.S.'s and is mailed in a standard business-size, white envelope. Double-digit response rates were realized by this mailing; along with an increase in store traffic, customers buying more, and increased profits for Gage Menswear (see Figure 5.5).

Gage Legal-Pad Letter

The previous example presented Bill Glazer's marketing system to other retailers using the handwritten, legal-pad paper approach for the sales letter and the token Round Tuit. A similar approach was used for the actual marketing of the menswear store, this time without the token. This sales letter was five "handwritten," legal-pad pages long. At the end, there were numerous coupons "sketched" out in handwritten fashion. Bill calls them "Shameless Bribe Coupons." Who else do you know who calls coupons bribes. No one. That is the uniqueness of this direct marketing approach.

One very important feature is that each coupon has a different "SKU number" reference on it, which is characteristic of retail inventory items. This isn't really an inventory tracking number for Gage Menswear; it is a tracking mechanism for Bill's marketing! These SKUs keep track of each coupon redeemed and the particular mailer it came from. Bill can then evaluate the effectiveness of each mailing and each offer (see Figure 5.6).

Merchants Savings Bank and Trust Bank Bag

Getting attention in mailings has been emphasized over and over. It has also been said that people respond to three-dimensional mailings. Imagine the surprise and subsequent response when clients of BGS Marketing opened their mail to find an actual Merchants Savings Bank and Trust bank bag. Inside the bank bag was a cassette tape describing the marketing program. You can bet recipients of this unique mailing unzipped the bank bag and looked inside. And maybe they played the tape or looked at the related printed material, complete with offers, guarantees, ways to respond, etc. (see Figure 5.7).

Placemat Sales Letter

Imagine finding in your mail pile a paper placemat from a local eating establishment with a handwritten note on the back. That's what Bill Glazer did to announce one of his popular retail sales for his menswear stores. The place mat looked like it had a handwritten note on it but of course this was a simulation. That's what you have to do when you are mailing out large quantities like Bill does. The simulation was complete with printed "coffee stains" on the placemat and notes pointing to the stains that apologized for them an attempt to get closer to the client with a little bit of humor (see Figure 5.8).

Brown Paper Bag Mailing

Uniqueness in direct mail is only limited by your imagination. Imagination was in high gear when Gage Menswear sent out a sale announcement on a brown paper lunch bag with simulated handwritten notes all over it. This was a sure way to get noticed and get opened. In each of Glazer's examples, there is extreme and abundant use of coupons, offers, guarantees, free gifts, and ways to respond. Copy and messages are some of the most unique in the industry, all in an effort to capture the mind of a direct-mail reader, to stay out of the junk mail pile, and to elicit a response

FIGURE 5.5 Round Tuit

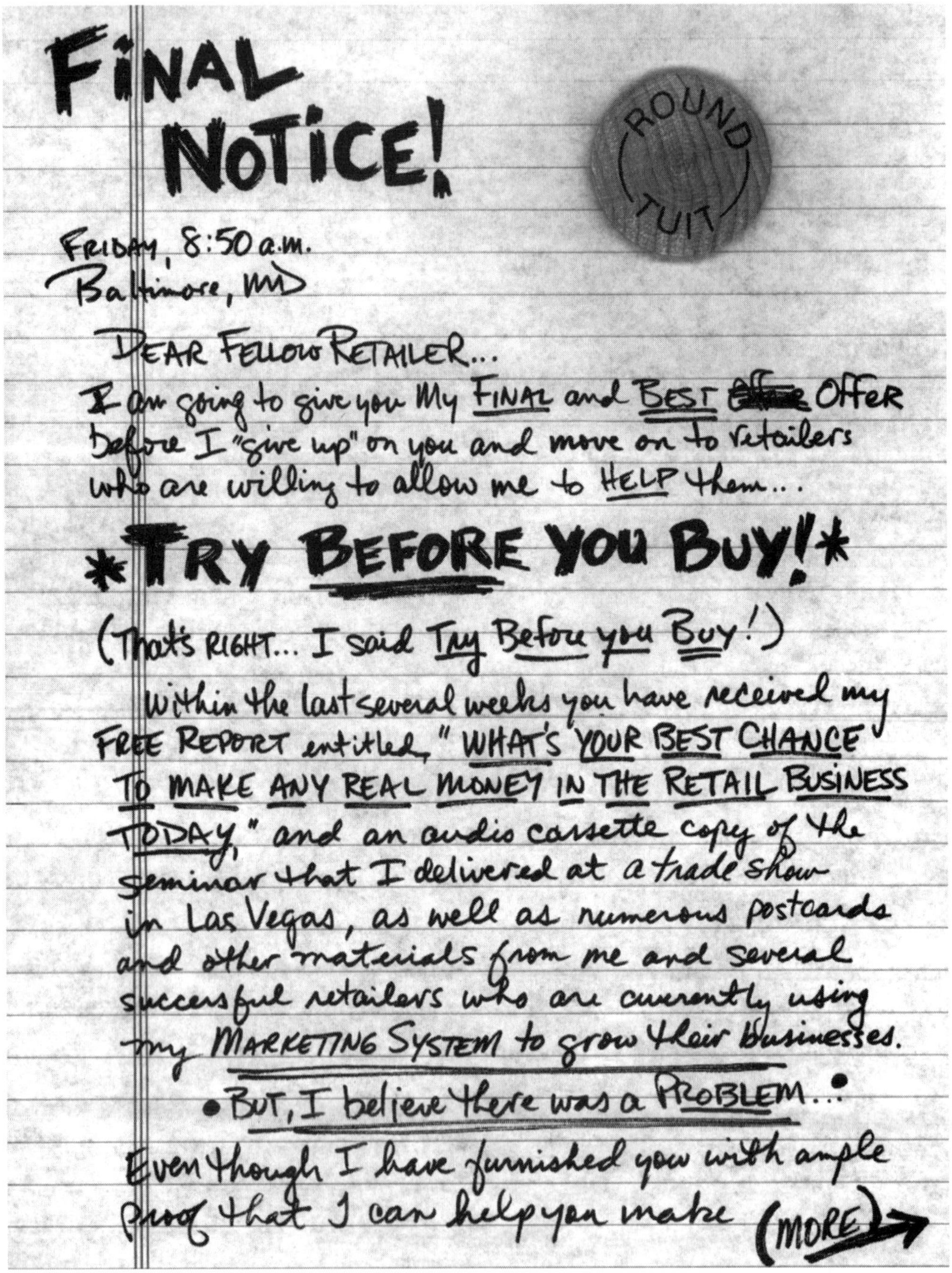

FINAL NOTICE!

FRIDAY, 8:50 a.m.
Baltimore, MD

DEAR FELLOW RETAILER...
I am going to give you My FINAL and BEST ~~offer~~ OFFER
before I "give up" on you and move on to retailers
who are willing to allow me to HELP them...

* TRY BEFORE YOU BUY! *

(That's RIGHT... I said Try Before you Buy!)

Within the last several weeks you have received my
FREE REPORT entitled, "WHAT'S YOUR BEST CHANCE
TO MAKE ANY REAL MONEY IN THE RETAIL BUSINESS
TODAY," and an audio cassette copy of the
seminar that I delivered at a trade show
in Las Vegas, as well as numerous postcards
and other materials from me and several
successful retailers who are currently using
my MARKETING SYSTEM to grow their businesses.

• BUT, I believe there was a PROBLEM...•

Even though I have furnished you with ample
proof that I can help you make (MORE)→

CONTINUED

| FIGURE 5.5 | Round Tuit |

④

* JUST FILL out the enclosed **ENROLLMENT FORM** and **FAX IT BACK** to me before _____ .

For your convenience, I have — for the **FINAL TIME** — included information about my **Business-Building Materials**. So, take a few minutes **RIGHT NOW** and read about my remarkable story and learn why my Marketing System can work so well for you — as it has for me and **800+** retailers ... maybe even _better_ !

But, please remember your opportunity to join our **800+** Retailer Network and use the Retail Marketing System **FREE** for **31-DAYS** before you decide is limited by the Expiration Date stamped in RED at the top of this page.

Please _Enjoy_ the enclosed information.

I look forward to hearing from you soon!

BEST Wishes for your _Success_ ...

Bill Glazer

* P.S.#1 — I've _RUSHED_ the enclosed Report to you... So, please take a few minutes right now to read the information and fax Back the "TRY _BEFORE_ YOU BUY" RISK-Free **ENROLLMENT FORM.**

* P.S.#2 — If you still have questions, give me a call **TOLL-FREE** at **800-545-0414.**

| FIGURE 5.6 | Gage Legal Pad Letter |

FROM: Bill Glazer   6:43 PM
OWNER/Gage Menswear

"SOMETIMES WHEN TIMES ARE
TOUGH — YOU'VE GOT TO DO
SOME PRETTY DRASTIC
THINGS..."

Dear Gage Client and Friend...

I just got this VERY impulsive idea... I had to jump on it and print this handwritten note before I had a chance to give it to my typist and think it all out clearly. So... Before I change my mind — I want to make you this "UNBELIEVABLE OFFER."

I'VE ONLY MAILED A FEW HUNDRED OF THESE letters to PREFERRED CLIENTS LIKE YOU...

Just in case you don't know me, I'm the owner of Gage world class Menstores in Downtown Baltimore & in the Valley Centre Shopping Center in Owings Mills. AND QUITE FRANKLY — I think you are going to be interested in WHAT I'm about to tell you.

So... I apologize for this handwritten NOTE... BUT I must get this off my chest A.S.A.P.!! In fact, right now I'm in New York sitting at the airport waiting for my flight home. Problem is... my business is no different from any other retail business this YEAR... REAL TOUGH. AND I'm worried that I have WAY too much inventory — and in a few weeks, the new fall 2001 stuff is going to START arriving.   (MORE)

If you DO NOTHING ELSE, TAKE A LOOK ON THE LAST PAGE FOR my "SHAMELESS BRIBE" COUPONS!

CONTINUED

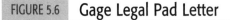

FIGURE 5.6   Gage Legal Pad Letter

⊛ P.S. Don't forget to bring in the "SHAMELESS BRIBE" coupons below... Do it before July 15th, 2001 to get your additional discounts.

⊛ P.P.S. — Plus... if you come in BEFORE July 8th, 2001 Bring in your "SHAMELESS Bribe" coupon for an ABSOLUTELY ✴FREE✴ pair of Designer socks!

> **"SHAMELESS BRIBE" COUPON**
> Take an additional
> **$20⁰⁰ OFF**
> EVERY SUIT!
> (EXP. 7/15/01) SKU:025907

> **"SHAMELESS BRIBE" COUPON**
> Take an additional
> **$10⁰⁰ OFF**
> EVERY SPORTCOAT!!
> (EXP. 7/15/01) SKU: 025908

> **"SHAMELESS BRIBE" COUPON**
> Take an additional
> **$5⁰⁰ OFF**
> EVERY PAIR OF DRESS SLACKS!
> (exp. 7/15/01) SKU:025909

> **"SHAMELESS BRIBE" COUPON**
> FREE
> PAIR OF DESIGNER SOCKS!
> (exp: 7/8/01) SKU: 025910

—⑤—

FIGURE 5.7   Merchants Savings Bank and Trust Bank Bag

FIGURE 5.8   Placemat Sales Letter

that drives sales up. That's the whole direct marketing formula in a nutshell (see Figure 5.9).

The Ink Well Free Marketing Booklets

The Ink Well, a commercial printing and mailing company in Wheaton, Illinois (www.1-800-inkwell.com), has had similar success using a simple flyer with offers and a response mechanism. Remember that information is a good hook, an incentive and offer to generate a response. Figure 5.10 shows one such flyer offering "Free Marketing Booklets." Response rates to this offer also were significantly above average.

FIGURE 5.8   **Brown Paper Bag Mailing**

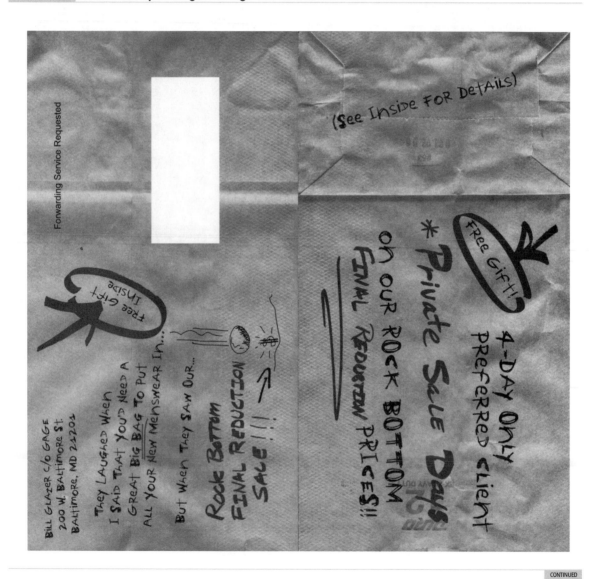

CONTINUED

FIGURE 5.9 **Brown Paper Bag Mailing**

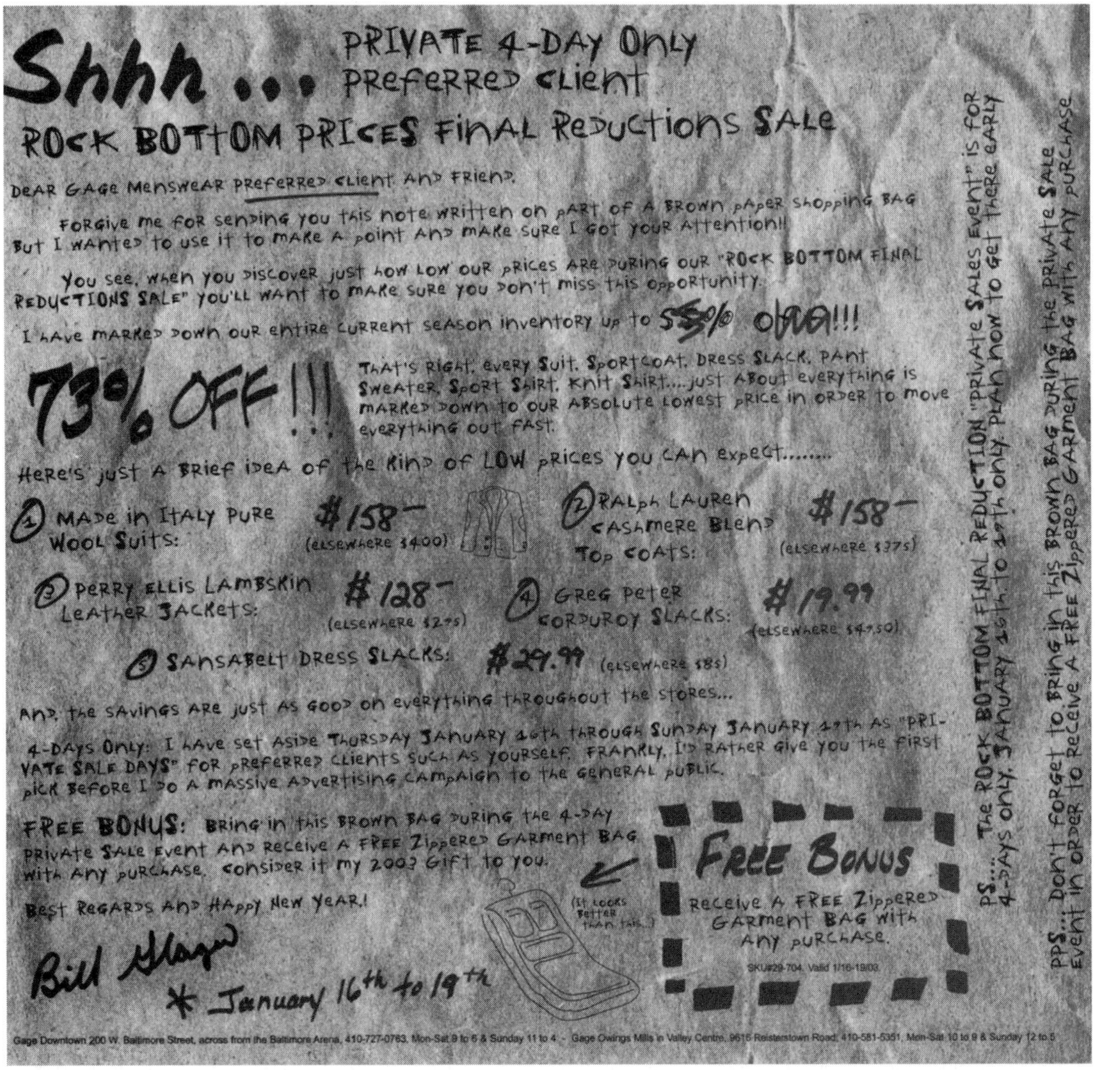

Shhh . . . PRIVATE 4-DAY ONLY PREFERRED CLIENT

ROCK BOTTOM PRICES FINAL REDUCTIONS SALE

Dear Gage Menswear preferred client and friend:

Forgive me for sending you this note written on part of a brown paper shopping bag but I wanted to use it to make a point and make sure I got your attention!!

You see, when you discover just how low our prices are during our "Rock Bottom Final Reductions Sale" you'll want to make sure you don't miss this opportunity.

I have marked down our entire current season inventory up to 55% off!!!

73% OFF!!!

That's right, every suit, sportcoat, dress slack, pant, sweater, sport shirt, knit shirt... just about everything is marked down to our absolute lowest price in order to move everything out fast.

Here's just a brief idea of the kind of LOW prices you can expect........

1. Made in Italy Pure Wool Suits: **$158** (elsewhere $400)
2. Ralph Lauren Cashmere Blend Top Coats: **$158** (elsewhere $375)
3. Perry Ellis Lambskin Leather Jackets: **$128** (elsewhere $275)
4. Greg Peter Corduroy Slacks: **$19.99** (elsewhere $47.50)
5. Sansabelt Dress Slacks: **$29.99** (elsewhere $85)

And the savings are just as good on everything throughout the stores...

4-Days Only: I have set aside Thursday January 16th through Sunday January 19th as "Private Sale Days" for preferred clients such as yourself. Frankly, I'd rather give you the first pick before I do a massive advertising campaign to the general public.

FREE BONUS: Bring in this brown bag during the 4-day private sale event and receive a FREE zippered garment bag with any purchase. Consider it my 2003 gift to you.

Best regards and happy New Year!

Bill Glazer

* January 16th to 19th

(It looks better than this.)

FREE BONUS
Receive a FREE zippered garment bag with any purchase.
SKU#29-704. Valid 1/16-19/03.

PS... The Rock Bottom Final Reduction "Private Sales Event" is for 4-days only, January 16th to 19th only. Plan now to get there early.

PPS... Don't forget to bring in this brown bag during the private sale event in order to receive a FREE zippered garment bag with any purchase.

Gage Downtown 200 W. Baltimore Street, across from the Baltimore Arena, 410-727-0783, Mon-Sat 9 to 6 & Sunday 11 to 4 - Gage Owings Mills in Valley Centre, 9615 Reisterstown Road, 410-581-5351, Mon-Sat 10 to 9 & Sunday 12 to 5

FIGURE 5.10   Inkwell Free Marketing Booklets

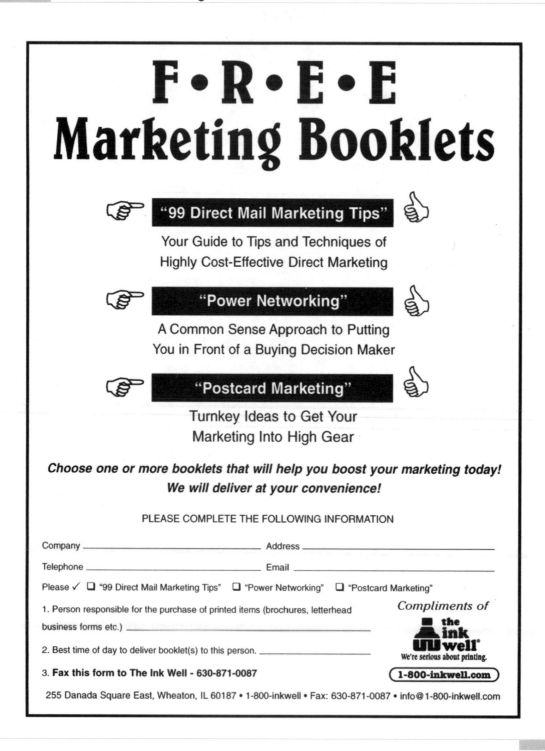

—— **CHAPTER 5 SUMMARY** ——

▶ Just like any other component of marketing, an effective campaign is the result of careful planning. The typical components of a campaign consist of the following:

- Designing a direct mail campaign

- Pinpointing your target/list

- Concept/copy development

- Printing, letter-shop, fulfillment

- Mail prep and processing

- Best postage rates/budget

- Tracking and analyzing results

- Internet/e-mail support

- Follow-up

▶ Managing direct-mail expenses during your campaign is just like managing any other component of your business. You want to control costs and spend as necessary while striving for the highest return on your expenditures.

▶ Turn to professionals when it comes to the printing and production of your campaign components. This will best keep your costs under control and your deadlines met.

The Marketing Message

ONE OF THE FOUR PRIMARY COMPONENTS in direct marketing is the marketing message. Essentially, this is the component that defines what you will say and how you will say it to your targeted prospect.

By now you have read about most of these major direct marketing principles. All are to be considered when crafting your direct marketing message:

- Eighty percent of repeat business comes from 20 percent of your customers.
- A two-time buyer is twice as likely to buy again as a one-time buyer.
- Direct mail success depends, in order of importance, on the list, the offers made, and the copy and graphics.
- Response lists outpull compiled lists.
- Adding one more characteristic to your list specifications will improve response.
- Time-limited offers and offers with a sense of urgency outpull marketing that doesn't have these features.

- Free gift offers outpull discounts in direct marketing.
- Benefits sell, features tell.
- The more copy in your message that is read, the better your chances of a response.
- It is easier to increase the average dollar amount of an order than it is to increase percentage of response.
- Your best prospect is a current customer, past customer, or someone who resembles these two.

DIRECT MARKETING COPY

Direct marketing copy is writing that communicates your marketing message and persuades people to respond or spend money.

David Garfinkle, known as a true copywriting guru and "The World's Greatest Copywriting Coach," says his ability to write killer copy is not because he is a superior writer. He says he is not better schooled than other copywriters nor has he had copywriting jobs in major agencies. He has simply concentrated, focused, and learned how to write what he calls "killer copy."

Goodman Ace, a famed radio personality, once wrote in the *Saturday Review* the 13 most powerful and evocative words in the language: you, save, money, easy, guarantee, health, proven, safety, new, discovery, love, results, and free.

Denny Hatch, editor and Direct Marketing Association Hall of Fame member, takes this a step further and tells us that there are emotional appeals to be considered that will stimulate action and direct marketing response. These appeals are greed, flattery, fear, power, love, revenge, anger, envy, guilt, health and well being, patriotism, eternal life, grief, exclusivity, discovery, and more. Things that look official, appear to be secretive and exclusive, also are part of his set of emotional appeals to consider when writing direct marketing copy.

Yet another guru, Bob Hacker, boils these down to six factors: fear, greed, anger, guilt, exclusivity, and salvation. You can certainly see an appeal to people's emotions in all of these descriptors, appeals, and factors.

Emotion sells. As David Ogilvy has said, "Probably well over half our buying decisions are based on emotion . . . . You cannot bore people into buying." Brilliant copy creates wants and doesn't just fill needs.

One of the keys to writing articles, letters, and marketing messages of any type to go along with the killer copy that David Garfinkle refers to, is to bring in the element of emotion as much as possible. This is especially true with the headline or opening statement. When using e-mail or a web site, this could be a subject line or the top header. When using broadcast, it's the opening words in your script.

Copy has often been described as where the marketing rubber hits the prospect's road. It is what grabs the reader, sells your product or service, and convinces the reader to buy. Copy can do all this even when the design and graphics are inferior.

Engaging Copy

Readers like clear and concise copy. General communication is fine but it assumes so much knowledge on the reader's part. General information informs. You want your direct marketing copy to motivate to action. Many times this motivation requires the writer to change the mind (perception) of the reader. Clear and concise, to-the-point copy wins out when trying to change minds. This the goal. Simple is better. Even though bulleted copy may be preferred by a reader, it is still a conversation or stories that pull a reader into the copy in an engaging fashion.

When striving for engagement, have a conversation with your reader. You can still be persuasive, convincing, and motivating. You can cite reasons for taking action. You can describe the benefits of doing so. You can even communicate details while maintaining a conversational tone.

Making your copy engaging brings readers into it, inspiring them to read further, learn more, and dig deeper. This is the creation of desire in the AIDA formula (Attention, Interest, Desire, and Action) described next.

AIDA

There is a standard formula in all marketing called AIDA—Attention, Interest, Desire, and Action. Some will term this Attention, Interest, then Motivation to Action, but it is essentially the same. I'm not sure of its origin, but I do know it works. It deserves a mention here.

Attention

The first A is attention. The rest of your copy isn't important if you can't get a reader's attention. Without attention, they won't read on.

It is the marketer's job to cut through the clutter of marketing messages you are bombarded with and to stand out. The way to do this is to get attention. YOU NEED TO SCREAM SOMETHING! Maybe it's a strong benefit or something odd and unusual or something controversial or emotional. You can do this with words and/or pictures as well as design. Think EXTREME when trying to get attention! Tune into the reader's point of view when doing this.

Here are some examples of attention-getting, emotional statements or headlines observed recently:

Martha Stewart Lawyer Tells the Real Story

Lose Weight while Eating More

How to Get on any Game Show

Free Airline Tickets Just for Taking a Survey

Interest

Attention starts the communication process. To keep it going, you must be interesting. No one has ever been bored into a sale. Direct marketing is so targeted, you will usually know who your target market is made up of. Because it is narrow and focused, you will generally know what interests your prospects and what doesn't.

The second part, interest, is getting someone interested in what you have written. This is done by making a promise or an offer. You can also make a promise in the headline, but depending on how many words you use up, you can do it secondarily. This is done by providing a visualization of the way things might be (i.e., "Imagine never having to make a cold call again"). This sentence promises or creates a situation that is more desirable than the way things are now, capturing the interest of the reader.

Desire

To create the necessary level of desire that will eventually lead to action requires the use of case studies or proof of the promise, proof of the claim, or proof that things really will be better. Testimonials serve this purpose as well as the bio or resume of the people or person behind the promise. You want your communication to come across as being very believable.

Make them want it, and you've got it sold. This is where appealing to a want comes in to play. It means having just the right offer, the right irresistible offer. A focus on benefits is important when creating desire. When prospects see that what you are offering could and will change their lives, and they want that change, you have scored with desire.

Action

Don't go through all the buildup of attention, interest, and desire and than walk away with nothing. That's what will happen if you don't tell your prospect what to do: what action to take and how easy you've made it to act. This is your opportunity to be as compelling and direct as possible. Action implies results. That's what your prospects want, and that's what you want.

We're talking about killer copy here and leading a reader to the point of action. It's part of our AIDA formula, and it is why you make offers in your direct marketing. Action: Ask the reader to do something. "Call me at my toll-free number." "I would like to meet you at our grand opening." "Call me for your free audit." The more specific your call to action, the more successful it will be in generating response.

One example of applying the AIDA in marketing in a hard-hitting, succinct fashion is the positioning statement for Domino's Pizza: Hot Pizza Delivered Fast. In four short words, Domino's gains attention (HOT), interests pizza lovers (PIZZA), and creates desire through communication of a benefit (DELIVERED FAST). This is usually followed in all their marketing by a call to action to call the local phone number of the nearest Domino's Pizza to place your order or to call a number that is emblazoned all over their coupon sheets.

EMOTIONAL FACTORS IN THE MARKETING MESSAGE

Saying something with "flowery" words or clever clichés, having an entertaining ad, and hoping people remember you does not make for compelling copy, especially in the world of direct marketing.

It all boils down to creating copy that is based on human motivations and focusing on those things that influence people's attitudes and buying decisions. Killer copy appeals to these emotional factors and then presents the benefits that will be enjoyed upon purchasing the service or product.

You need personal contact with your target audience. You need an understanding of how people feel about your products or services, what their emotional hot buttons are, and what motivates them to act. Not only do you need to understand what they need to face their challenges or improve their situations, you have to totally understand their wants as well.

All of this learning, all of this emotional response, and all of these marketing messages focus on your prospects' needs and wants, not on you. This definitely attracts attention.

There is a psychological factor involved when creating copy. You have to satisfy basic human needs with your product or service. Telling how you will satisfy these is the foundation of effective copy.

It all goes back to Dr. Abraham Maslow's hierarchy of needs. For those who need this psychology 101 refresher, Dr. Maslow identified the basic needs of humans as:

- The need for sustaining one's life (food and shelter)
- Safety and security
- Social acceptance and love
- Ego: self-esteem and status
- Self actualization

In writing direct-marketing copy, you need to point out the need that your prospects might not even think about or know that they have. Once this is done, you then point out in your copy how your product or service can satisfy that particular need.

Choosing the right motivating words that prompt your prospect to buy or respond is the goal here.

Certain motivating concepts have been identified as being key to direct marketing copy:

Greed	Security	Health
Fear	Pride	Recognition
Pleasure	Love	Accomplishment
Ego	Intimacy	Exclusivity
Status	Power	Acceptance

These motivators are basically broken down into two groups. One group is positive and relates to pleasure and the improvement of life; the second group relates to the absence of this pleasure or improvement, more specifically, to the alleviation or avoidance of pain.

Good direct-marketing copy is like using ink and paper as your sales person. You already know that direct marketing's job is to sell, not to impress or position.

Studies have shown that the general consumer leans more to the negative side of these motivators—how to protect what they have and not lose it, the avoidance of pain. Turning this into the right copy means describing what might happen to your prospects if they don't respond.

EXAMPLES OF USING MOTIVATORS IN DIRECT MARKETING

Fear

Good: You could be four minutes away from a heart attack and not know it.

Better: Missing the Stock Tip of the Day on our Radio Broadcast could cost you millions, literally.

Even better: There are things your local police department won't tell you about criminals at large in your neighborhood.

Financial

Good: One of our new tax law savings tips will add $398 to your refund, guaranteed!

Better: You can obtain real estate with no out-of-pocket money by following our real estate purchasing plan.

Even better: Now you can legally double your savings deposit interest!

Esteem

Good: You'll be the only one in your neighborhood to know how to do this.

Better: These insider secrets are *not* for everyone.

Even better: This information puts you in a very unique, select group of people.

Praise

Good: You have been preapproved for membership.

Better: Because your credit is good, you are one of the first to hear this news.

Even better: (combination of Financial and Praise) You have been preapproved for a home loan mortgage at 1 percent lower than you are paying now.

BENEFITS

Moving past the emotional hook, you are now ready to add the next major ingredient of good copy, information tied to benefits. Benefits answer your prospect's question, "What's in it for me?" Benefits are what satisfy the human needs discussed earlier. (Benefits sell, features tell.)

▼ FEATURES VS. BENEFITS

Features vs. benefits is not the name of the next boxing card at Caesar's Palace. It is, however, a boxing match in the mind of business owners, as evidenced by their confusion of the two. Today, we will eliminate that confusion and put you on the right track.

A feature is a factual statement about a product or service. Factual statements aren't why customers buy. Benefits are the reason. Features are things that might be included in the "about us" section of a web site.

Factual Statements Called Features

Prospects and customers care very little about a statements. Sorry. Not one of the examples below tells a prospect how their life or business will improve as a result of working with you and your company, or buying your product or service:

- Self-cleaning oven
- 200-CD jukebox
- One-click buying on Amazon
- Live operator on duty 24/7
- 125-page owners' manual included
- In business since 1910
- We have the biggest widget maker.
- Award-winning
- Made with 100 percent recycled product

The latest and greatest equipment means nothing to a prospective buyer unless that feature translates into a benefit of lower cost, quicker delivery, or something else of value. Being established 100 years ago means nothing to a prospective buyer unless that feature translates into a benefit of reliability and a guarantee of being in business in the future.

Now look at the factual feature statements above and translate the value from them into the form of benefits:

- Convenience
- Time savings
- Organization
- Easy access
- Immediate
- Quicker answers
- Immediate access to information
- Fewer resources required
- Reliability

Benefits sell. Benefits clearly answer the customer's question, "What's in it for me?" "What results will I get that will improve my current situation?" "Will it make me healthier, wealthier,

or wise?" Ben Franklin was a benefit kind of guy.

The most compelling benefits are those that provide emotional or financial return. It's not the steak, it's the sizzle—it's not the gift, it's the thought. It's not the price; it's the overall value. Emotional returns are related to making the customer feel better in some way. Financial returns generally save money or make money for a customer.

How do you know if you are touting a benefit or a feature? It's actually easier than you think. Ask the question: "Will this one thing improve the life, finances, health, or well-being of someone?" If the answer is yes, then you have a benefit, a benefit that can be marketed to this someone who represents and is part of your target market. If the answer is no, chances are you have identified a feature. (Source: *Guerrilla Marketing in 30 Days*, Entrepreneur Press, 2005.)

Don't fall into the trap of just telling about features. Your job in direct marketing is to sell a product/service or an offer to be responded to.

Copy-Related Benefits

Coming up with a list of benefits is not a casual exercise. In fact, you should not write one word of copy or start a list without fully understanding your product or service the way that your customer or prospect does. Talk to others. Ask questions to those who buy from you. Understand how the competition sells. Use your own product or service. From this you will then understand the true benefits enough to start constructing your copy and marketing messages. Dig really deep for these. Sometimes a benefit is not obvious.

Jay Levinson, of *Guerrilla Marketing* fame and coauthor of *Guerrilla Marketing in 30 Days* (www.gm30.com), talks about driving many extra miles to a particular bookstore just because it had the best carrot cake in its bookstore café. You can bet when the bookstore came up with its list of benefits, it did not include carrot cake. But might have, if the store had talked to customers or had done some deeper investigation.

List your benefits and then start crafting your selling points. Sometimes this takes longer than the actual copywriting that follows. Don't hold back on this step. Some possibilities are:

- Save money.
- Save time.
- Be more safe and secure.
- You will feel better.
- You will look better.
- Your knowledge will increase.

Understanding benefits is really understanding your market. What are you really selling and who is it being sold to? This is like selling in person except you are using printed direct mail material or electronic material to substitute for your sales pitch and spoken words.

Addressing the benefits that you offer or at least what your customer wants in your copy is a promise you are making to them. The quicker your prospect notices and reacts to this, the more attention your copy has earned from them. This is very advantageous in leading them through the AIDA cycle as well as your selling process or your process to evoke a response from your direct marketing.

In your direct marketing copy, and parallel to AIDA, you should:

- Know as much as you can about your prospects.
- Be able to describe all the characteristics that relate to them.
- Have an irresistible offer.
- Share as many benefits and "need satisfiers" as you can.

- Explain why they should buy from you.
- Get a response; have the prospects take action.

Killer copy fills in around each of these with triggers, emotions, sound bites and attention-getting images.

THE IMPORTANCE OF COPY

In all of marketing, regardless of the vehicle, it is often said that copy is king. Without the copy, how else can a prospect understand your offer, understand your product or service, or understand the benefit of doing business with you? By definition then, effective copy commands higher response rates in direct marketing.

Copy can be made more effective by doing the following:

- Present copy in small bite-size sound bites or chunks. A sound bite is a short, sweet, to-the-point statement that you might hear on a 30-second radio or television commercial, thus the association with sound, a bite-size chunk. Use bulleted information and lists. Readers like headlines and subheadlines. Bold text and underlined text highlight important points. White space is a good thing. Don't worry about filling a page full. Only tell what's important to your prospect/reader, not what's important to you.

ONLINE COPY TIP

Don't worry about having your readers scroll one long web site page or e-mail page. Just make sure you have calls to action and purchase or response links readily available and clearly visible.

- Make sure that call to action appears early in your copy. Some prospects are convinced right away and want to respond before reading all the available copy. This is especially true with online copy. Tell your prospects to respond. It can be that simple.
- Emphasize benefits throughout. Features tell, benefits sell. Write benefits first, at the beginning of paragraphs.

Example of Benefits First

Focus on selling the offer, not necessarily the product. Sure, if all your direct marketing only sold product and you got 100 percent response rates, you would only focus on selling. Unfortunately, prospects and consumers don't behave in 100 percent fashion. Research shows that direct marketing is effective using an offer to respond to and then a follow-up to close the sale.

Right: Save time by having a professional marketing firm, Market for Profits, write your press release.

Wrong: Those who have Market for Profits write their press release, save time.

Example of a Focus on Selling the Offer

Talk about "what's in it for me, the prospect," not all about your company. So many marketers want to jump right in and tell their story. Prospects don't care. They're coming to you to see how you can help them. Your copy should talk about "you" (meaning them), not "me" (meaning the marketer).

Right: Visit our web site to discover the money-saving, timesaving tips that will make your mailings more efficient.

Wrong: Visit our web site for a free download of a report on how our company can help you.

Example of "What's in It for Them"

Use a logical flow in your copy, leading the reader:

- Ask a question, relate to pain, cite a challenge, and/or present an opportunity.
- Start explaining your benefits as an answer to those pains and challenges.
- Jump right to a call to action.
- Restate the benefits and make an offer.
- Repeat the call to action.
- Instill a sense of urgency related to the call to action.
- Mention the product or service with more benefits.
- Provide an incentive for responding to the offer *now*.
- Close with another call to action.
- If a letter, use a P.S. that is benefit-laden and action-oriented.

Right: You will save time and money by working with us.

Wrong: Our services are second to none and will help you in your business.

CRITICAL COPY COMPONENTS

Powerful headline/ opening statement	Get the attention
The basic story	
The proposition/offer	Let them know what you are.
Guarantee	
Call to action	Develop your offer and state why they should act now.
Name/location	Tell them how and where to act upon your offer.

Unique selling proposition	Explain why they should buy from you.

comparable knowledge among readers. You still have to inform in such a way that the reader desires more, to the point of taking some kind of action.

CREATING GREAT COPY

Here are some ways to create great copy:

- Start with a complete and comprehensive creative brief/plan that pulls together all information available for your subject. This will serve as the foundation and sometimes the outline of your copy.
- Writing, revising, and making changes over and over creates good copy. It's almost like brewing good coffee or making fine wine. It takes time. Rushing through copy development is a sure violation of good copywriting.
- Write from the reader's perspective. The writer typically knows the subject matter so well that he or she makes an assumption of

More Tips to Consider for Writing Great Copy

- Dig deeply for every benefit and possible selling point.
- Aim your copy at the most likely group to respond not the general population.
- Speak your prospect's language.
- Make a promise with proof it can be delivered.
- Make the promise immediately within the copy.
- Identify your competitive advantages.
- Determine the single best selling point.
- Craft a headline around this point.

FIGURE 6.1 Copy Checklist

- ❑ Do you have a strong and clear offer?
- ❑ Is your offer clearly something of value?
- ❑ Is your headline big, bold, and attention getting?
- ❑ Does your first paragraph pull the reader into your copy?
- ❑ Are benefits pointed out and emphasized?
- ❑ Do you restate the challenges and suggest that there is a solution available?
- ❑ Do you have short, readable paragraphs?
- ❑ Does the copy flow logically from point to point?
- ❑ Is your language understandable, without assuming too much knowledge on the part of your readers?

- ❑ Have you included the high-impact words and emotional appeals?
- ❑ Is your copy written as if you are having a conversation with just one person?
- ❑ Do you have a call to action that will generate a response?
- ❑ Is it clear what action you want your prospect to take?
- ❑ Do you make it easy for your prospect to respond?
- ❑ Do you have a deadline to respond by or some other sense-of-urgency copy?
- ❑ If using a letter, do you have a hard-hitting P.S. with benefits and some value restated?

- The headlines and lead paragraphs are specific to the selling proposition.
- Copy is concise and compelling.
- Copy is logical, clear, and flowing.
- Your message is enthusiastic and this enthusiasm is sincere and believable.
- There is a true sales orientation to your copy.
- Appeal to human needs and wants in your writing (remember the key words of what people want most).

HEADLINES

John Caples, the famed advertising guru and coauthor of the direct marketing classic *Tested Advertising Methods*, said that the best headlines are those that appeal to a reader's self-interest. The second-best headlines are those that give news, state benefits, or motivate action.

Caples was a pioneer in copy testing. An author of four direct-marketing classics, Caples discovered the do's and don'ts of creative direct-marketing copy over a career that spanned 58 years—56 of them at the advertising agency of Batten, Barton, Durstine and Osborn.

He won countless awards, among them election to the Copywriters Hall of Fame in 1973 and to the Advertising Hall of Fame in 1977. Today, the world's most prestigious creative award for marketing is the John Caples International Award.

Headline Rules

Advertising legend David Ogilvy said that on average, five times as many people read the headline as read the body copy. It follows that, unless your headline sells your product or service, you have wasted 90 percent of your money.

This statistic, underscores the importance of writing headlines that work:

- Short and sweet
- Enclosure within quotation marks draws attention to it.
- Very effective when posed as a question or challenge
- A teaser
- A thought-provoker
- An attention getting-device
- Shock

The job of a headline is to grab attention, communicate benefits, appeal to the reader, set the marketing tone, and introduce you immediately. You want the headline to motivate, regardless of whether it generates excitement or fear; as long as it generates some emotion that motivates the reader to continue reading, it's doing its job. Headlines are the first impression you make on a prospect, and all to often the only impression.

There are many techniques to writing headlines, but they all usually come back to copy that is benefit-oriented and aimed at satisfying one of the human needs identified earlier. Advantages play a part as well in headlines. The benefit that you offer that no one else does is your competitive advantage. Trumpet this to the world. Use headlines to do your best communicating. Think of headlines as what you would say if you knocked on a prospect's door and you had to say something before he slammed it shut.

Don't just think of print ads or letters as a place for headlines. Headlines are just as effective in brochures, inserts, envelopes, and other direct marketing.

In addition to these three most powerful headline words/phrases—"How To,, "Free," and "You" —others to consider are:

- Quick
- Discover

- Now
- Exclusive
- Announcing
- Protect
- Save
- New
- Safeguard
- Suddenly
- Only
- Easy
- Do You?
- Secrets
- Inside information
- The Truth
- Love
- On sale
- Introducing

Listen for these the next time you recognize a direct-marketing radio or TV commercial. You will definitely hear them in a David Oreck commercial.

The Headline Test

To determine if your headline is doing its job and doing it as effectively as possible, ask the following questions:

- Does this headline stop browsers from scanning, capture attention, and trigger emotions enough to make people want to read more of what I have to say?
- Does my headline beg for the attention of the reader while arousing enough curiosity to cause emotional feelings to happen?
- Does the headline really cater to the needs of my target audience?

If you can answer yes to these questions, you have passed the headline test. If there is any doubt as to any one of these outcomes related to your headline, go back to the drawing board and

dig deeper, reword phrases, and harvest more benefits.

Types of Headlines

Problem/solution. You are selling something because you have a solution to a challenge or problem that your customer or prospect has. Addressing it right away will grab them and encourage them to keep reading or immediately respond.

"Are You Too Busy to Work Out Every Day? We Have a No-Exercise Solution for You!"

Testimonial. Provide proof that if it works for someone else, it will work for your prospect. This headline is making a major claim about your product or service. Make the claim with significant impact.

"I was always overweight and on and off diets until I started the No-Exercise Workout program. It works!"

Credibility. Here you will make a claim to increase the credibility of your product or service. Crest Toothpaste made this type of headline famous when they started off their commercials and print advertising with:

Four out of five dentists recommend Crest Toothpaste for the prevention of cavities.

Provocative question. Challenging your prospect group with a provocative question about a situation leads readers and listeners into your sales message.

"Do you have all the customers that you could possibly handle in your business?"

Hook or extreme statement. Nothing grabs attention like extremes. Saying something extreme in a headline when your reader least expects it is effective and attention-getting and creates curiosity.

> *"Four Things Your Local Police Won't Tell You About the Crime Rate in Your Neighborhood."*

There is much written about the subject of headlines. These few points will help make your direct marketing effective. Headlines can't be produced by a formula. They require the marketer to dig deep, think about in terms of the prospect, and grab. Most headlines fail because they don't make a strong promise backed up by proof. These concepts and suggestions have been proven and tested, and are as effective today as they were in the early days of direct marketing and advertising.

Tips for Writing Headlines

Because of its importance, you want to write a headline that works and does its job. Here are some tips to make your headline read stronger and more compelling.

- Think of your headline as being news.
- Use words that sound important and valuable.
- Use quotation marks around the headline.
- Use upper and lowercase letters; not caps.
- Use benefit- and action-oriented words.
- Be extreme and outrageous yet compelling.
- Pique curiosity.
- Move the reader to the body copy.
- Reveal mistakes.
- Be short and sweet in the number of words in your headline.
- Use numbers to quantify your promise and to convince and emphasize.
- Highlight an advantage.
- Make an appeal to an emotion.
- Make a comparison.

- Reveal a secret or insider information.
- Relate to your products and services.
- Ask a question.
- Identify your prospects' biggest challenge or area of pleasure, and address it.
- Make a promise or recommendation that addresses challenge or desire.
- Use emotional motivators.
- Converse with the prospect in a one-on-one conversational tone.

Don't Make These Headline Mistakes

If you want your headlines to capture attention and lead readers into your sales message, there are a few mistakes that you want to avoid at all costs. Here are the most critical ones:

1. *You can be extreme and provocative but remain serious and not kid around.* Don't

---

IMPROVING A HEADLINE: GOOD, BETTER, BEST

Good: How to Save a Lot of Money Clipping Coupons

Better: How to Make Your Bank Account Overflow by Spending 30 Minutes with Your Daily Newspaper.

Best: How to Save $27,395 for Your Next Spring Break Vacation Just by Clipping a Few Coupons, 30 Minutes A Day, Just Like I Did.

These headlines make you want to read the rest of the piece or letter to find out how you can get these same benefits and have your needs satisfied in the same way that the headline is suggesting.

overuse comedy in your headlines. There is a place for using humor; your headline is not one of them. Humor typically does not grab attention or encourage further reading like other types of headlines.

2. *DON'T SHOUT.* Using all capital letters is the equivalent of SHOUTING in print. It has been determined that capital letters do not increase the effectiveness of headlines. All caps are not conducive to easy reading. If something is difficult to read, readers will skip over it.

3. *Don't over-punctuate!!!!!!!!* Avoid hype of all types. Hype will turn off a prospect very quickly, and your message will be ignored. Too many exclamation points, too many underscores, and other crazy punctuation defeat the purpose of a headline.

4. *Let the headline be the attention-getter.* Don't let illustrations, graphics, or photos compete with the headline for attention. The headline's job is to grab attention. All other copy components support the headline and the message. The headline is the most important part.

5. *One-on-one communication.* Just as with body copy, focus on your target as if you were having a one-on-one conversation. You can't get everyone's attention every time with every headline. Aim your headline at those who have the greatest probability of responding to your offer. Remember, you are targeting—not creating mass appeal.

6. *Don't let the Company Name dominate the headline.* You don't know yet if your prospect is interested in your company or even your company name. You want the headline to focus on something they're interested in—a benefit they want to enjoy or a problem they'd like to solve. A company name or logo doesn't do this unless the company name is also a benefit like Cost Cutters Hair Cutting.

Now that we have reviewed the most effective kinds of headlines, suggested powerful words to use, and warned about mistakes to avoid, you are armed with all you need to create effective headlines for your direct-marketing messages. See Figure 6.2 for the Headline Checklist.

Headline Examples

Victor O. Schwab was one of the most famous direct marketing copywriters of all time. His work for Dale Carnegie's "*How to Win Friends and Influence People*" made it a bestselling book in the 1930s.

In his series of five articles "How to Write a Good Advertisement," that appeared in the 1941 *Printers' Ink*, Schwab introduced a five-step copywriting formula:

1. Get attention.
2. Show people an advantage.
3. Prove it.
4. Persuade people to *grasp* this advantage.
5. Ask for action.

He later developed these ideas further in his own book of the same title, *How to Write a Good Advertisement* (Wilshire Book Company, 1985). In this "short course in copywriting," he also showcases some of the best headlines of all time.

Here are a few winners from his list of 100:

- A little mistake that cost a farmer $3,000 a year
- The child who won the hearts of all
- Are you ever tongue-tied at a party?
- Why some foods "explode" in your stomach
- You can laugh at money worries—if you follow this simple plan.
- When doctors "feel rotten" this is what they do.

How I improved my memory in one evening

- Discover the fortune that lies hidden in your salary.
- Thousands have this priceless gift—but never discover it!
- They laughed when I sat down at the piano—but then I started to play!

Here are other headlines that grab attention:

- Create the Same Financial Results as Enron, Legally
- How your Government Can Spend More With No More Tax Revenue
- 1,237 Ways to Make Money in the Stock Market
- Seven Mistakes People Make While Closing On a House
- Stocks to Own to Pay for Your Child's College Tuition
- How to Make a Million Dollars and Pay No Taxes, Legally

> ## ▼ THE USE OF A USP IN YOUR MARKETING COPY
>
> Figure out the Unique Selling Proposition of a product or service; find out what makes it the one and only, why it is so different and desirable, and communicate it over and over in your marketing messages.

- Donald Trump's Real Estate Secrets That You Must Know
- College Tuition On a Shoe String Budget
- How the Pros Profit from Inside Trading Legally
- Why You Will Be Out of Business in Two Years
- How To Acquire a Company for $10
- How To Sell Your Home in Less Than One Week

FIGURE 6.2 Headline Checklist

- ❏ What product or service are you marketing?
- ❏ What are the main benefits of what you are marketing?
- ❏ Dig deep; think of one or two benefits that aren't as obvious.
- ❏ What incentives or special offers are you providing?
- ❏ What claims can you make that your competition can't?
- ❏ What is your single most competitive advantage?
- ❏ Write five rough-draft headlines using different types.
- ❏ Find synonyms of power and impact that express your benefits.

- ❏ Add a curiosity factor to your headline.
- ❏ Compress headline phrases into one sentence.
- ❏ Edit your sentences for clarity and impact.
- ❏ Narrow your headlines down to your top three and prioritize.
- ❏ Ask others for their impression of your top three headlines.
- ❏ Test your favorite headline and measure the results.

SALES MESSAGES

Much is written on writing effective sales copy. In direct marketing, the following guidelines apply, even though you are selling an offer more often than selling a product:

- Use an attention-getting headline.
- State believable claims without exaggeration.
- Use testimonials from satisfied customers.
- Motivate your prospect to action with a compelling offer.
- Eliminate risk by offering a strong and clear guarantee.
- Take advantage of the popularity of a P.S.
- Instill a sense of urgency to respond now.

Copy Components in Sales Messages— Examples

Providing credibility. ". . . over the past ten years, these three have helped thousands of businesses— and more recently female business owners, to learn new methods and create their own new ideas."

Demonstrating a return on investment. "Just one idea implemented from the hundreds presented here will return ten times what you pay for this package."

Appealing to an ego. "Can you afford to appear behind the times to your clients, customers, vendors, associates, and employees? You aren't yet an expert in everything. Is it important to you to be perceived as successful, savvy, and with leading with a purpose and living with a passion?"

The guarantee. "If, for any reason, you are not delighted with your purchase, return it for a full refund—no hassles, not strings, no hard feelings. You won't find this with many other information products."

Association and identification. "Do you plan the payroll, talk to customers, and then rush home to fix meals, wipe runny noses, and wash and spin dry a few items, only to have five whole minutes left to yourself . . . in the bathroom?"

Bonuses. "Free with this purchase, enjoy your bonus data CD. Some people make the purchase more for the freebie than the rest of the product."

An expiration. An expiration will help increase response rates. Consider these:

- For a limited time only
- Only for the month of December
- While supplies last
- Reply by midnight tomorrow
- For the next three days only

Incentives. Incentives also increase response rates. Consider these:

- Premiums and gifts
- Free shipping
- Discounts
- Free trial/samples
- Buy two, get one free.

Sales Letter Length

In direct marketing, the question of how long a sales letter should be is debated daily, especially with the proliferation of online marketing. The true answer, and the one the pundits agree on, is "as long as it needs to be to get results."

The question is asked of all marketers: "Do people read long copy?" The answer is clearly yes. People will read something for as long as it interests them. Just look at the way you read the newspaper. You scan headlines. When you find one of interest, you start reading. If the story is interesting, you keep reading. If it doesn't have the appeal you thought it did when you spotted the headline, you stop reading. Prospects receiving direct mail letters read the same way. An uninteresting one-page letter can be too long. A skillfully woven four-page letter can hold the reader all the way to the end and, if successful, persuade him or her to respond. A letter should be long enough to cover the subject adequately, and short enough to sustain interest. Finding this happy medium is done by testing.

Long copy is OK. If you have something to say and you say it well, it is better than short copy. The key is saying it well.

The longer the letter, the more important it is that a few fundamental techniques are followed: lead paragraphs, the same attention-getting techniques used in direct marketing ads, closure and closings, and the famous P.S. Make the letter easy to read, somewhat scannable, and with subheads, quotations, underlines, italics, bulleted information, and color. Don't overload the letter with these, but use them to accomplish your purpose. And don't go overboard to the point that it is quickly mistaken for just another junk mail sales pitch and discarded.

The debate of length goes on and on especially when you consider the online sales letter where a page can be scrolled endlessly. The real answer of "as long as is necessary, to get results" is so true and becomes evident to you in each and every case through extensive testing. Did you expect any less of an answer in the world of direct marketing?

A Johnson Box is short, terse copy that summarizes the main benefits, positioned in a box above the salutation in a letter.

Letter Writing Formula

- Open with benefits as fast as you can. Place the most compelling one first and the rest in order of importance to the prospect. You can even do this in headlines.
- Once you hit on that most important benefit, expand on it, communicate it relentlessly, and sell it hard.
- When making an offer, you are making a promise. Be specific about this, and tell readers exactly what they are going to get.
- Have as many testimonials and endorsements as you can to convince the reader that you will deliver on your promise.
- Tell readers what they will be missing if they don't take you up on your offer.
- Close by telling more about the benefits, even at the risk of repeating them.
- Ask the reader to take action. Tell them what to do.

THE DIRECT MAIL PACKAGE

While a targeted list and offer are two important parts of a direct mail package, most marketers will spend more time on the creative component of package design.

The package is the physical format, the appearance, the look, the use, the way it is posted and sealed, as well as all paper, copy, design, and layout.

Idea

It all starts with an idea. Marketing of all kinds is made up of idea—ideas of messages, design, clever headlines, products, services, and offers. Generating these is the start of all marketing.

Ideas are born of your core mission and how you wish to convey and deliver this to a customer base. You not only need to think from your own perspective during idea generation but also from a customer and prospect's perspective.

Don't discard ideas without proper thought and testing. What worked once may not work again, and vice versa. Times change. Customer demands change. Technology changes. Ideas change as a result. Finding the right idea is achieved through testing, formally and informally.

Type Style

Your words are key to your direct marketing message. How these words "look" is the key to how well they sell for you. Pleasing, presentable, and easy-to-read will win out every time over fancy, cluttered, and distracting. Typeface has everything to do with readability.

Typeface is often like the referee in a basketball game—not noticed but doing a great job. You don't want your words to point to every reader and say, "Hey! Look at the typeface I used here." You want type style to do its job but not dominate. You want people to be aware of the words, not their shapes or arrangement. Readability is the goal of type style. Using abstract, unusual, or funky typefaces scares away readership and should be avoided entirely.

There are literally thousands of typefaces to choose from. They generally fall into two classifications: serif and sans-serif.

Serif type has small projections at the end of each part of a letter, just like the type style used in this book. Sans serif typefaces do not have these projections. In most cases you should use a serif-style in the body copy of your marketing. This has proven to produce better responses than sans serif.

Try not to be dazzled by all the typefaces available. Be prudent in their use, and don't think that you have to use a large variety. Mixing type styles is all right, but don't overdo it. Typefaces

> **U**ntil recently, it was always recommended that you give your direct marketing letters the typewriter look, the look that your letters were freshly typed on a typewriter. The type style that approximates this look is Courier. This notion still plays today and is popular. Readers do feel a bit nostalgic, but it subliminally sends the idea that "this is a letter; better read it."

may be mixed for emphasis, but readability is still the overriding consideration. The general rule of thumb is to limit type style to no more than two to three varieties per marketing piece. If you want to add more dash, consider using italics and bolds. You don't want the different typefaces vying for the reader's attention. Type should never call attention to itself. This is a distraction and takes away from your marketing purpose.

Today when the typewriter look isn't used, Times New Roman is the more popular style. It's OK that everybody else uses it, too; your goal is readability, not uniqueness here.

Most body copy is best read in 10- to 12-point type size. Larger is OK too, but usually no smaller. Headlines and subheadings are larger.

Photos/Illustrations

When the eye sees a direct marketing piece, a postcard, a letter, or an ad, the first things noticed are the photos, graphics, and illustrations. In attempting to grab a reader's attention, photos and illustrations increase the time to do that from a few seconds to several. Several seconds could mean the difference between response and no response.

Graphics and pictures in direct mail can also move attention in an opposite direction and be a

> The purpose of design is not to make direct marketing prettier. The purpose is to support your message and make it effective.

distraction to the reader. Graphics in direct mail should get people to read your copy. Remember, copy is king in direct marketing. Copy sells, but design sells the copy. The longer you keep your prospect reading, the higher your response will be. Some of the most effective direct marketing is done without photos and illustrations.

The experts will tell you that photos "have direction." This "direction" should be used to direct the reader to your copy. It's best to consult with a graphic designer to determine your photo's direction.

People and action shots have proven the most effective in direct marketing. Illustrations that clarify, reinforce, or tie in with the text are most effective. Photos of people using your products help to sell, lead, and sustain the interest of a prospect. The weight loss companies effectively use before-and-after photos to reinforce their message. Photos may also be used to demonstrate benefits. If you are promoting a product that will withstand the weight of ten elephants, show a picture of ten elephants on your product.

Captions under photos are among the most frequently read items in direct marketing; therefore, make them hard-hitting and benefit-oriented. Your direct marketing message is not a news story with an accompanying photo; it's a message you want noticed, read, and responded to. Use captions to help make this happen.

If you use illustrations, make sure they are there to tie in with your products and services, or at least with your headline. They are not to be used to make things look prettier unless they can also support copy and message.

Design

Desktop publishing and advances in computer technology have made "graphic designers" out of many people and turned them into do-it-yourselfers. While this is fine, especially when trying to hold down costs, you still need to evaluate your time investment in doing your own design versus doing what you do best in that same amount of time.

The purpose of design is to bring an idea forward to communicate a reality without distorting it. You have something to communicate in your direct marketing. Design helps you do that efficiently and effectively.

Visual images are very powerful. Use them to your advantage, but don't overwhelm your direct marketing with them. Your copy still has a job to do.

Design leads your reader through your marketing, creating interest, curiosity, and desire to the point of taking action. Copy is still king and does the selling in direct marketing but it's the design that sells the copy. It is the designer's job to make sure the copy gets read. One way to do this is to avoid designing direct marketing that could be perceived as junk mail.

If you stop and think about why you open some direct mail and not others, you're taking the first step in understanding successful design in direct mail. What appeals to you, what catches your eye or attention, or what strikes you as intriguingly different are questions that can be answered to further your design understanding.

Creating direct mail that gets results, of course, is the ultimate goal. You don't just want to create a fancy, glamorous, entertaining piece.

After all, it is creative design that makes direct mail so successful for marketers. Use design to help your marketing cut through the clutter. Look at all the marketing messages you are bombarded with every day, including what's in your mailbox. People like to get mail that isn't just a bill to be paid.

The words of David Ogilvy, in *Ogilvy in Advertising:* "I do not regard advertising as entertainment or an art form, but as a medium of information. When I write an advertisement, I don't want you to tell me that you find it creative. I want you to find it so interesting that you buy the product." The same goes for direct marketing design.

Direct mail that is three-dimensional, colorful, oddly shaped, or with samples starts the selling process even before the mail is opened. That puts the *direct* in direct mail or direct marketing. Add to this the many ways a message can be conveyed, crafted, or created and the possibilities for creative direct-mail messages and design are endless.

The job of direct mail is to attract and hold the recipient's attention and communicate a message very clearly. When sending direct mail to businesses, you have the additional challenge of getting the message in front of a decision maker. Intriguing, exciting, extreme, unusual, and different are all qualities and descriptors that can help make this happen.

There are other design principles related to direct marketing. You probably know some of them, but a professional can help you with all of them. The following are some design considerations to keep in mind:

- One thing dominates the page. Don't confuse the reader with two main points.
- Use consistent typefaces; minimize font variety.
- White space is OK; it contributes to readability.

- Fonts with serifs make for easy-to-read text.
- Illustrations are good if they help make your point.
- Don't let your logo overwhelm your message; a consistent identity is OK.
- Always use a call to action; more than one is effective also.
- Make the piece graphically pleasing and hard to ignore.

Getting Noticed

Direct mail and other direct marketing has to get noticed. Maybe the headline, the shape, the color, or a picture will do this. Something has to take the lead role in getting your prospect's attention. The driving force behind any of these components is design. *Webster's Dictionary* tells us that to design is to create, fashion, execute, or construct according to plan; to conceive and plan out in the mind; to devise for a specific function. Every one of these descriptors applies to the design phase of direct marketing and direct mail. And that "specific function," referred to in *Webster's* definition, is to get noticed.

Just like other aspects of marketing, design is built upon a number of principle components:

- Lively copy
- Headlines
- Borders
- Photos
- Graphics
- White space
- Shapes
- Colors

The Design Process

The process of designing your marketing piece follows this basic course:

- Review marketing objectives, including the target.
- Brainstorm layout, shape, flow, and positioning of all elements.
- Sketch and/or produce a thumbnail mock-up.
- Submit to graphic designer.
- Get design proof.
- Create the mock-up, including folds, perforations, die cuts, etc.
- Transmit electronic artwork to printer.

There are four main elements to consider when designing a direct mail piece or a direct response ad:

- Headline
- Photo/Graphic/Drawing/Illustration
- Body copy
- Other elements for response: coupon, company identity components (logo, tone, feel, look), white space

Other Elements

There are other design elements that will help spark interest in your reader. Your goals as a direct marketer are many, but converting disinterested scanner of your material into an interested reader is one of them. You want your

POSTAL SERVICE MAIL PIECE DESIGN REQUIREMENTS
(as reprinted from www.usps.com)

The United States Postal Service has basic allowed sizes and shapes for cards, letters, and envelopes—essential information for any U.S. direct mail. The following links are provided for the Postal Service's mail piece design requirements. They will help you design mail pieces that qualify for postal discounts and conform to mailing regulations. These links are for all of those who are involved with direct marketing design, specifically direct mail design.

Business Reply Mail Templates: http://pe.usps.gov/mpdesign/mpdfr_brm_intro.htm

These Business Reply Mail (BRM) templates are perfect for standard business sizes of letters and cards. Just download the template you need, input your address, unique ZIP + 4 and corresponding barcode, and BRM permit number and you will have a perfect finished proof in just minutes.

The Postal Service has designed these templates to meet all spacing and positioning requirements if used for the correct-size mail-piece. Caution: You must know your assigned, unique ZIP + 4 Code and permit number for Business Reply Mail before you proceed. You will also need to create and import the corresponding barcode for your ZIP+4 Code. Barcodes can be created from a number of commercially available programs. Use the MDA locator to contact your local MDA to confirm these numbers and to arrange for a review of your proof before printing.

Courtesy Reply-Mail Templates: http://pe.usps.gov/mpdesign/mpdfr_crm_intro.htm

These Courtesy Reply Mail (CRM) templates are perfect for standard business sizes of letters and cards. Just download the template you need, input your address, ZIP + 4 Code and corresponding barcode, and you will have a perfect finished proof in just minutes. Barcodes can be created from a number of commercially available programs. Use the MDA locator to contact your local MDA to confirm these numbers and to arrange for a review of your proof before printing.

Mailpiece Quality Control (MQC) Program: http://pe.usps.gov/mpdesign/mpdfr_mpqc_view.htm

The MQC program is the Postal Service's certification program for mailpiece design. Recently revised, the program is all new for a new millennium. The course is designed for individuals responsible for creating mailpieces for entry into the U.S. Postal Service's mailstream. After completing this course, you will better understand the acceptance requirements of the USPS as they relate to mailpiece design.

The program incorporates a self-study guide in which you learn at your own pace. When you're ready, send away for the final exam. If you pass, you'll receive a certificate recognizing you as the "Mailpiece Quality Control Specialist" for your company. This course will give you the confidence that your mailpieces will qualify for postal discounts and meet all relevant standards for mailing at the rate and class you desire.

Mailpiece Design Analyst: http://pe.usps.gov/mpdesign/mpdfr_mda_intro.htm

Mailpiece Design Analysts (MDA) are postal employees specially trained to answer your questions regarding mailpiece design. These employees provide advice and issue rulings regarding acceptability for automated rates. MDAs provide technical assistance on mailpiece design to envelope manufacturers, printers, advertising agencies, and graphic designers.

Mailpiece Design Analysts are available for:

- Testing paper and actual mailpiece samples for acceptable thickness, background color, flexibility, rigidity, and barcode print tolerances.
- Assigning unique ZIP + 4 for Business Reply Mail (BRM) mailpieces.
- Providing camera-ready artwork for the proper Facing Identification Marks (FIM) and barcodes for Business Reply Mail (BRM) and Courtesy Reply Mail (CRM).
- Reviewing artwork prior to printing.
- Review and approval of vendor-prepared "privately printed" forms for USPS special services.
- Analysis of Optical Character Reader (OCR) readability and automation compatibility of prospective or actual mailpieces.

Additional Resources: http://pe.usps.gov/mpdesign/mpdfr_addl_all.htm

The Postal Service provides plastic templates and numerous informative publications concerning mailpiece design. This link provides online access to these valuable resources. These publications and templates can be used by themselves, or as resources for the Mailpiece Quality Control (MQC) program.

design to pull the reader in to your material. Along with graphics, illustrations, and headlines, you can do this with things like a table of contents, charts, graphs, captions under photos, text on a slant, quotes, handwritten notes, and bulleted lists and text. Use these other elements to your advantage. Don't use them to clutter up your marketing! Consider using the following as well:

- Personalized envelopes
- Copy teaser
- Odd sizes and shapes
- Involvement: scratch-offs, tokens, stickers

Design Tips

The direct marketing world is full of graphic designers, ad agencies, and marketing professionals who make their living in design. Here is just a sampling of techniques and tips to consider when conferring with a professional or designing on your own.

Color. Color sells. The last thing you want to happen is for your recipient to pick up a black-and-white mailing piece, think that it is an unassuming copy of something less than professional, and discard it. Color can be used in paper, print, and text. Consider using colored type in the headlines to make them stand out. Consider color print in the form of borders or accents. Don't overdo, but use color to make your marketing look professional and impactive.

Sizes. Consider something other than the standard letter size of 8.5" by 11". Both larger and smaller sizes work. Be mindful of budget constraints when doing anything nonstandard. Depending on your objectives, your message, and your products and services, you might want more space for communication and marketing. "Less is more" is especially true when your marketing

piece is standing out from the flurry of other people's marketing.

Type style. The goal for your marketing is to get it noticed and to get it read. It is very important that you keep these goals in mind when determining typeface. Readability is your primary consideration. People must be able to absorb your message quickly by scanning. Unreadable type that's unconducive to scanning is more a contributor to deletion or complete avoidance. Serif fonts around 11 or 12 points in size are best for readability. Make sure that spaces between paragraphs and lines are ample as well.

Bullet the points. Attention spans are not what they used to be. People will look at graphics, headlines, bullet points, and then text, in that order. Use bullets to break up text. This is a good place to highlight benefits or to show lists. Readers will notice this material and probably comprehend it much more readily than boring text paragraphs.

Bolds and italics. Don't overuse the bold and italic features of your word processor. Using italics and bolds to highlight key words and ideas is appropriate. See how they are used in this list.

Clip art looks like clip art. This statement is increasingly relevant as more and more consumers become computer savvy. Unless your piece of clip art absolutely and positively reinforces some major point in your copy, use a real photograph or no art at all. Clip art looks like clip art. Stock photography looks like stock photography.

Noncompeting design. Many people want to emblazon their company name or logo all over a design piece. This goes for tag lines and product placements as well. If appropriate, use them, but don't overuse them to the point of competing with headlines, graphics, key concepts, and related copy. Clutter is not good. White space can be your friend. Let your piece work for you: don't work the piece.

Postage-friendly. Different mail piece designs fall into different rate categories according to size (shape) and weight. This requires knowledge of the rates and rules from the USPS. Making the designed piece easy to go through processing automated equipment will keep postage down.

MESSAGE TESTING

Everyone reading this book, at one point or another in their life, took a test. You either passed or failed it. You took tests in school. You took a driving test. You may have had your eyes tested for correct vision. Why all this testing? It was done to find out if something was learned, or if something was working well. Did you learn the right lessons in school? Did you learn the rules of

the road and how to handle a car? Testing provided the answer to these questions.

Recent surveys point out that the measurement of marketing by companies, entrepreneurs, and professionals is generally not done, done very little, or not done well. Minimal testing is done, and simple testing methods are not used or applied.

In this book, it is stressed that over half of the success of a direct-marketing campaign is due to having the right target, targeting the right audience, and using the right list. The more you learn about this most important component, the more chance you have for a successful campaign. And the only way to "learn" more is through testing.

The use of testing is based on the fact that you can accurately predict what could happen on a larger scale by looking at a "representative sample" that was tested.

Testing is the foundation of direct marketing—unlike traditional marketing and advertising. Testing is one of the things that makes direct

FIGURE 6.3   **Design Checklist**

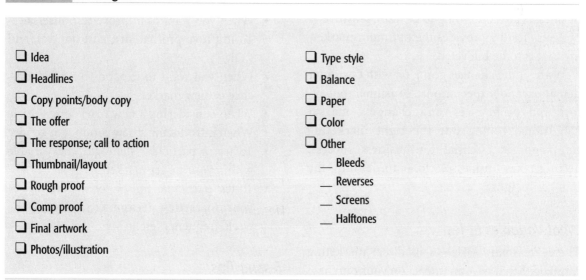

- ❏ Idea
- ❏ Headlines
- ❏ Copy points/body copy
- ❏ The offer
- ❏ The response; call to action
- ❏ Thumbnail/layout
- ❏ Rough proof
- ❏ Comp proof
- ❏ Final artwork
- ❏ Photos/illustration

- ❏ Type style
- ❏ Balance
- ❏ Paper
- ❏ Color
- ❏ Other
  - __ Bleeds
  - __ Reverses
  - __ Screens
  - __ Halftones

marketing different from traditional marketing and advertising. Because of its quantitative nature, direct marketing and its elements are very conducive to testing.

David Ogilvy, author of *Ogilvy on Advertising* and founder of Ogilvy and Mather, said: "General advertisers and their agencies know almost nothing for sure, because they cannot measure the results of their advertising. They worship at the altar of creativity, which means originality—the most dangerous word in the lexicon of advertising."

Why Test?

Testing is done to learn what works and what doesn't work with your respective target markets. It is when two or more variations of one variable are compared to one another simultaneously with all other variables the same.

Testing your direct marketing in small groups will help you determine which variables will lead to the greatest success. Once testing is complete, you can roll out your entire campaign based on the most successful test results.

In today's more competitive environment, businesses are continuing to be more sensitive to budgets. Testing provides the optimum marketing that is to be budgeted.

With all the changes going on with customer demands and expectations, consumer behaviors and preferences, and changing market conditions, rolling out the right marketing campaigns is essential for business success. Testing takes businesses closer to defining the best campaigns.

What Variables to Test

There are many variables in direct marketing campaigns that have an impact on your purchase and response rates:

- *The format of the marketing vehicle.* Should you mail out a postcard or a letter, or invest in an infomercial?
- *The offer.* Are you offering a premium conditional upon a sale, something for free, or other value in exchange for a purchase and/or response?
- *The target.* Are you delivering your marketing to the right audience?
- *Color and design.* Does one set of creative artwork and design get more response than another? Do certain colors induce more response than others?
- *Subject line of an e-mail.* This is the most logical place to start the testing of a direct-e-mail marketing message.

These are only some of the variables to test in your direct marketing. Add to this list any variable that will impact response or purchase.

Understanding these variables can also help you troubleshoot your marketing when things might not be working according to your plans or expectations.

When to Test

- When you want to improve response/sales
- To improve profitability, cost control, and ROI
- When you want to expand to a new audience or new market
- When considering a new marketing vehicle
- When introducing a new product or service
- To test a particular demographic variable within your target market
- To test particular timing for the delivery of your marketing (seasonality, day of the week, frequency, etc.)

Testing Tips

- Keep track of your testing.

- Keep testing methods simple.
- The larger the test sample, the more reliable the results.

Testing of Direct Mail

Because direct mail is one of the primary methods of direct marketing, let's look at the different variables to test in a direct mail campaign:

- Postcard vs. letter
- Folded letter vs. open letter in a larger, flat envelope
- Hand-stamped vs. presorted permit
- Headline on the envelope vs. blank envelope
- Handwritten note vs. mass-printed note
- Toll free number response mechanism vs. visit this web site
- Send in an order form versus fax an order form
- List suppliers—one vs. the other
- Conventional vs. nonconventional (e.g., for someone in the high-end home accessory business testing a list of custom home builders vs. subscribers to *Architectural Digest*)
- Frequency—every two weeks vs. four weeks or quarterly.

These tests generally fall into the categories of the message (copy, headlines, creative), the vehicle (format and design), timing and frequency (day of the week, time between mailings), and the target (demographics).

Testing is something that can happen quickly relative to a total direct-marketing campaign. The USPS states that, as a rule of thumb, you will receive about 25 percent of your responses within one week, 50 percent within two weeks and 75 percent within four weeks. The last 25 percent trickle in, if at all, over the next few weeks. From this, the appropriate test results can be evaluated, conclusions may be drawn, and adjustments to campaigns and roll-out can be made.

Testing does need to be factored in to your campaign budget. Purchasing lists, new designs and creative concepts, and different formats and printing all incur costs. Devising your test while developing your budget will help you determine the quantity of testing. Don't become a compulsive tester of direct marketing. Do enough to make the necessary conclusions for improvement, and then act upon them.

Remember, the goal of testing is to learn. If you have optimized your learning, i.e., tested and learned all you can afford, then you are ready to launch your campaign.

The bottom line is that testing can save you money, can improve upon what you are already doing, and totally take the guesswork out of marketing. On top of marketing conditions and budget pressures, the availability of alternative marketing vehicles is growing. Testing helps choose the optimum vehicle for the respective direct marketing campaign.

Not knowing what works and what doesn't is like throwing mud or spaghetti against the wall and seeing what sticks. Some might and some might not depending on several variables. The fact is, when it comes to direct marketing, there is no guessing.

TROUBLESHOOTING YOUR DIRECT MARKETING

Troubleshooting marketing is almost the reverse of planning your marketing. Think of all those things you would do in marketing your business, products, or services, itemize them, and analyze each one to see whether they are working or not. Once you understand these components, they can be isolated, changed if necessary, and retested for contribution significance.

The Message

Although sometimes subjective, you must check to make sure that the message is clear, concise, and attention-getting to your audience. Does it create interest and desire, and is there a call to action? Does the message relate to you, your company, product or service, or does it relate to the challenge that you are offering the solution to? If all is in order and the message is convincing or purposeful, consider one of the other components. Sometimes there are one or more messages that are ideal for the given marketing situation. It is still OK to test messages. Testing always is a trade-off to what's working now. If the message you have is working now, it may be reaching your goal and you may decide not to mess with it.

The Vehicle

The definition of a vehicle is something that takes you somewhere. This component has already been described in this book. If it is not taking you somewhere you want to go, you need to change vehicles. The same thing applies to your marketing. You may be using a nice letter in an envelope that appears as promotional in nature and is yet automatically discarded by the receiver when a postcard would do the job and be more effective. You might be trying to use television advertising when radio would be better. This is common in the business-to-business market. Another vehicle that sometimes is ineffective is a salesperson with poor appearance, poor demeanor, or poor selling skills. That would be the wrong vehicle to carry your marketing message to your customer/prospect. In today's world of technology, different audiences require a different medium in contrast to the marketing of yesterday. This all has to be considered. If it's not working and you know you have the right mes-

sage for the right audience, change the vehicle, test its effectiveness, and make the necessary corrections to optimize your marketing.

Related to the message itself is the consistency of the message. This mostly has to do with the frequency your message is communicated to your target audience. Someone once said to me, "I tried direct mail once and didn't get any business." There are all kinds of statistics on how many times someone must be exposed to you or your message before they take action. Once is certainly not ideal. Most will say six to eight times while others say even higher. This being the case, did you give your message a chance before you stopped or changed it?

Usually the person who tires of the message first is the marketer him/herself. Usually the target audience doesn't remember in the same way as the sender, and it may still have potential for response when receiving the message. Does this mean you should communicate your marketing message once a day? Usually not, but sometimes you see or hear something related to consumer brands daily, e.g., Coca-Cola. This must be measured against audiences tiring of your contacts and message.

In the case of direct mail, once per month is probably optimal. In the case of direct sales, it depends on the sales cycle, the stage of the relationship, and the magnitude of the sale. Different audiences will require different frequencies of messages. Each must be evaluated as to optimum effectiveness. If it's not enough, change it. If it's too much, change it. Consistency and frequency are just two more components to be evaluated when trouble shooting your marketing.

The Target Audience

It's already been said in the second section of this book that you could have the best marketing message ever, the best vehicle sent out over and over. If the right potential buyer doesn't receive your message, nothing gets marketed; no one acts. Putting yourself in front of a potential buyer is the key to marketing and selling. No potential buyers? No selling. The right target audience might be the right segment, the right niche within a segment, or the right people within a niche. If you are marketing to banks, are you marketing to the bank president or the branch manager? If you are marketing to manufacturers, are you marketing to the operations department or the purchasing department? All this has to do with having the right target audience for your marketing.

Just as a side note, don't forget about current customers as part of your target audience. Even breaking up current customer segments into different targets may be more effective for your marketing. Find the people to populate the forest, and let the trees fall.

If all the above is in order and deemed effective, don't fix anything.

Troubleshooting is not only trying to find out what the problem is, but what the problem is not.

With these four components outlined, you can differentiate what is working and what is not.

When your direct marketing is in trouble is not the only time to test. Testing is appropriate, and a passion of direct marketers, when you want to improve upon the performance of your marketing. Because of this, testing is always done against a control. The control in direct marketing testing is usually the best campaign you've run in the past. Beating the control means finding something better than your previous best, continuous improvement at its best, always yielding better results.

Important: Only test one variable at a time. Testing more than one doesn't tell you which variable worked and which one didn't. If you're going to test your offer, then you test two marketing packages that are identical except for the offer. If you are testing a postcard vs. an envelope and letter, all copy, the target, and frequency of mailing should remain identical for the two tests. The only thing that should change during this single-variable test is the physical format.

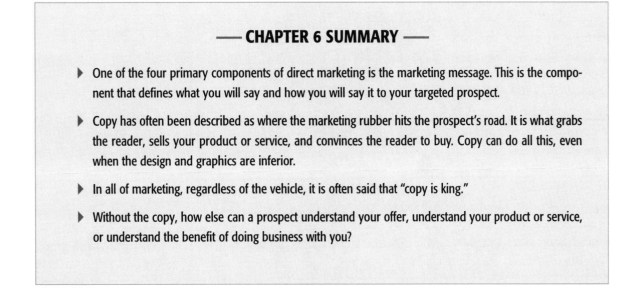

—— CHAPTER 6 SUMMARY ——

▶ One of the four primary components of direct marketing is the marketing message. This is the component that defines what you will say and how you will say it to your targeted prospect.

▶ Copy has often been described as where the marketing rubber hits the prospect's road. It is what grabs the reader, sells your product or service, and convinces the reader to buy. Copy can do all this, even when the design and graphics are inferior.

▶ In all of marketing, regardless of the vehicle, it is often said that "copy is king."

▶ Without the copy, how else can a prospect understand your offer, understand your product or service, or understand the benefit of doing business with you?

- ▶ The job of a headline is to capture attention, communicate benefits, appeal to the reader, set the marketing tone, and introduce you immediately.

- ▶ You want the headline to motivate, regardless of whether it generates excitement or fear; it simply has to generate some emotion that motivates the reader to read on.

- ▶ Headlines are the first impression you make on a prospect, and many times they will be the only impression.

- ▶ In direct marketing, the question of how long a sales letter should be is debated daily, especially with the proliferation of online marketing. The true answer, and the one professed by the pundits, is "as long as it needs to be to get results."

- ▶ The purpose of design is to bring an idea forward and to communicate a reality without disrupting it.

- ▶ You have something to communicate in your direct marketing. Design helps you do that efficiently and effectively.

- ▶ Testing is the foundation of direct marketing (unlike traditional marketing and advertising).

- ▶ Testing is one of the things that makes direct marketing different from traditional marketing and advertising. Because of its quantitative nature, direct marketing and its elements are very conducive to testing.

Message Offers and Responses

I N THE WORLD OF DIRECT MARKETING, THE message to the intended target is paramount. The message in *any* marketing communication is paramount. The message in direct marketing is intended to elicit a response from a prospect or customer. Because response is the objective, the direct marketing vehicle needs to provide a mechanism for response. I'm not talking about an order for a product or service every time. You want a response. You will take an order or purchase, but that is not the only type of response.

A response is involvement and interaction. Involvement, interaction, and a response of any kind indicates interest. Response shows an interest by the prospect in exploring your offer more, which leads to exploring your product or service more. Exploring provides information. Informed customers and prospects will be the ones who buy your product or service. Uninformed customers and prospects don't get to the purchasing point.

CONSUMERS ARE SAVVY

Good marketing, over the years, has made consumers and prospects very savvy. They have grown to know when they are being marketed and sold to and when something of true value and interest to them is being presented.

Consumers and prospects now know that when they're offered a "free consultation" or the opportunity to receive your brochure, it is nothing more than a disguised sales call.

They know a brochure will be promotional in nature and, of course, will project a positive, nonobjective light on the company, product, or service. People get plenty of brochures unsolicited. Most will not take the time to request one in response to a direct marketing offer. Prospects are inundated by sales calls and requests for appointments. Requesting another one in response to a direct marketing offer happens only on a limited basis.

Now, if the offer is something different, a little more substantial and not "salesy," it has a higher probability of being responded to. That is why many companies offer white papers, special reports, checklists, or articles to prospects. Information is a good hook, especially free information. Information can benefit a prospect, making them more interested in your company, product, or service. The information offered is unique and is perceived to be of value—all valuable considerations when constructing an offer.

MESSAGE EFFECTIVENESS

There are many things that can be done to get more response from any marketing message. Most of these apply to direct mail as much as they do to traditional advertising, awareness marketing, and e-marketing. The following are tips for increasing the response from direct mail:

▼ THE IDEAL REPLY YOU CAN MAKE TO A PROSPECT'S RESPONSE

- Thank you
- Acknowledge
- Restate the offer
- Fulfillment of the item you promised in your offer
- Benefits of your product or service
- Reasons to do business with your company
- Up-selling, reasons to buy again
- A promise to keep in touch
- In today's world of privacy rules, an opportunity to "opt-out" of the list and to end any further communication

---

- *Emphasize and highlight the offer.* Put it in the headline, make it big and bold, make it a different color, or circle it. Do anything to highlight the offer.
- *Include a sense of urgency with the offer.* Use a deadline or an even better offer if responded to by a certain date; use the words "for a limited time only"; say how many are left before inventory will be depleted or how you will be out of capacity for a particular item, product, or service.
- *Smother your communication with benefit points.* Benefits sell, features tell. Direct mail is direct marketing that needs to sell. That means use benefits. Benefits in headlines work, too, and reinforce them. How are you going to improve your prospect's life? The answer to that is benefit marketing.
- *P.S.* If your prospects scan your letter or message, they will first notice the graphics, headlines, and the P.S. Make it benefit-laden with high impact, and take advantage of the way your prospect will read and notice your marketing.
- *Personalize your direct mail.* As mentioned in the description of P.S., seeing your own name in a direct mail piece will catch your eye and probably make you read further. This certainly increases the propensity to act. Personalization also means communication of something just for your recipients. They feel like you are talking just to them. If they like a certain type of music, for example, and you are a music store, sending an announcement of the latest CDs of their favorite music type will increase response rates to your marketing.
- *Repetitive mailings.* Repetition helps to break through the clutter and also increases the chance that your timing will coincide

with theirs. It certainly helps with the top of mind awareness that eventually will help facilitate a direct response.

- *Make it easy to respond to you.* The use of a business reply card or pre-addressed, stamped envelope makes it easy for a prospect to drop something in the mail. When the prospect spots these easy-to-use response mechanisms, they immediately think direct response.

- *Make exclusive.* Explain that you are only presenting your offer to a select few. Make the offer as high a perceived value as possible and as exclusive as possible.

- *Lumpy mail.* Always call the enclosure, or "lump," a "free gift."

- *Use odd shapes and sizes for the physical format of your mailing.* Remember your goal is to stand out from all the other direct mail in a recipient's pile. Different shapes and sizes do this.

- *Emphasize the call to action.* Prospects usually will only do what you tell them to. These are calls to action: "Visit our web site," "Call our toll-free number," "Send in for information," "Come by our location." These are the responses you are proposing in return for your offer.

MORE WAYS TO INCREASE RESPONSE

You just read some of the very fundamental ways to increase message response. Here are additional ways to increase response that apply specifically to direct marketing:

- Use envelope teaser copy.
- Appropriately use (and not overuse) the word "free."
- Focus on the offer and getting a response, not necessarily the product and getting the sale first.

- Offer more than one way for a prospect to respond to your offer (toll-free number, web site, BRC, etc.).
- Focus on your competitive advantage, that benefit you offer that your competition does not.
- Consider segmenting your database even more and creating even more targeted messaging.
- Put your headlines in bold, large print and enclose them in quotation marks. Studies show that headlines in quotes draw more attention.
- Suggest forwarding your marketing to a more appropriate person, if your recipient is not the right one.
- Select a few recipients and follow up by phone. Depending on results, consider a formal telemarketing follow-up program.
- Create a sense of urgency by stating a deadline, how many are left, or an expiration date. Also, consider this on the front of an envelope as part of your teaser copy.
- Always use a guarantee that has as few strings attached as possible; use minimal or no small print.
- Do something extreme; print a message upside down, put your picture on the envelope, use 37 one-cent stamps instead of one 37-cent stamp.
- Make it easy to respond to you and pay you.
- Have a clearance sale even if your intentions are not to clear out inventory.
- Use a Business Reply Card or Business Reply Envelope (BRC or BRE).
- Remind customers of their last purchase and the length of time since then.
- Thank people in advance of their order.
- Use photos to create relationships with people; use photos of products to help prospects visualize.

THE USE OF COLOR IN DIRECT MAIL

An envelope with any color on it many times appears to the general public to be mass mailed and screams "advertising" to the recipient. If the recipients are averse to receiving advertising through the mail, your mail will fall into their junk mail category and not reach its intended target.

Why then is there so much use of color in direct mail? The easy answer is that color sells. Even with the possibility of being recognized as potential junk mail, there still is a percentage that reaches its intended target and is responded to and responded to more often with the use of color. Color in direct mail increases the desire by a recipient to act on an offer, respond, or purchase something by about 30 percent.

Using color in printing and direct mail can affect budgets though. Significantly. You will find this as you obtain price quotes for various printing formats. The options and their likely impact need to be considered before the creative process begins or the production planning starts.

THE OFFER

Some have referred to the offer as "the deal." It is the specific proposition that causes the prospect to respond, purchase, or act as you hope they will. It is essentially the commitment required from your prospect. The offer is an incentive to generate a response. The prospect has to take a particular action to receive the incentive or the deal.

Offers take many forms. The key is to make the offer as compelling as possible so the recipient has a sense of urgency to respond, act, or accept the offer.

Differences between direct marketing and traditional advertising and marketing have been discussed, the key difference being the solicitation of a response with direct marketing. This solicitation is often referred to as the offer. The offer is the mechanism to drive the response. An offer in direct marketing is really a request in disguise—a request to respond somehow, some way.

After you attract the attention of a prospect (with a headline, a graphic, or something extreme), the offer is one of the most important components of direct marketing. A great offer can succeed even if all the supporting copy is only mediocre. Excellent supporting copy, however, cannot make a poor offer succeed.

Direct marketing focuses on getting people to do things. That's where the offer comes in.

Direct marketers rely heavily on offers. The right offer accomplishes the direct marketing objectives of standing out from all other direct marketing, holding attention, creating interest, and motivating interested prospects all the way to action.

According to Claude Hopkins, a famous advertising guru of the 1920s and '30s said, "The right offer should be so attractive that only a lunatic would say no."

WHAT MAKES A GOOD OFFER?

First and foremost, an offer should be something of value. Consumers and prospects are savvy enough to see right through an empty offer. Tangible offers are better.

Any offer that can be tied to your competitive advantage and other benefits will increase your response rates.

One of the most important elements of an offer is the perceived value to the recipient. Information-based offers capitalize on perceived value very well. The cost to develop a white paper is negligible compared to the help or knowledge a prospect or reader could gain from requesting and reading it.

The offer should be important to your prospect. The question to ask is, are your benefits important to your target audience?

The more specific the offer, the higher the response. For example: "Free Direct Mail Report" is not as specific or perceived as valuable as "A free 301-tip filled booklet, providing insider secrets to improve your direct mail campaign."

Think "priceless." If you can offer a prospect something money can't buy, your offer will get response. Examples of this are "backstage concert passes," "dinner with the speaker," or "a seat in the dugout."

Make offers that are relevant to your products and services. Don't offer free chocolate sundaes if you are selling vitamins. Don't offer Disney products as part of a mountain-climbing vacation package.

Items to Consider When Creating Your Offer

Creating an offer is more than just communicating benefits and asking a prospect to try or purchase your product. Sure, benefits are very important and the call to action is, too. But the prospect has to be courted. There are a number of considerations to take into account that help this courtship create the interest and desire necessary to generate a response from a prospect. Take a look at a few of these considerations:

- *A good price.* Before a consumer makes a purchase, he or she most generally looks at how much something costs. In the case of direct mail offers, a prospect will mentally evaluate whether a price is justified by the value of the product or service offered. This is done almost instantaneously, but has to be considered when developing your offer.
- *Free shipping and handling.* This is seen in many offers as a standout headline. It is very popular in direct mail offers and has been shown to work. Consumers know that if they have to pay shipping and handling it increases the price they will pay. Free shipping and handling is a very appealing offer to a consumer. Prospects don't want to have to calculate additional pricing and use it in comparisons. Making it free increases the value of an offer immensely.
- *Attractive bundling.* Can an offer be more valuable if a consumer receives two for the price of one, three for the price of two, buys two and gets one free, or is offered some other bundling that creates value? Free bonuses and gifts added onto a unit of one provide value in an offer as well. Anything to make it more than a particular price in exchange for one thing makes an offer more appealing.
- *Add-ons/options.* Car dealers made these famous by adding options to a base price to increase the average selling ticket price. Options can be upgrades of many types, additional colors, and things like personalization, gift cards, and reminder services.
- *Continuous recurring programs.* A recurring program is basically an offer of something for free if you buy subsequent items at regular price. Columbia House made this famous by its offer of 12 records for a penny if you agreed to buy one at regular price for each of the next five months, or some form of that. This type of offer proved to be very profitable for Columbia House and one that a whole business was built on.
- *Financing options.* Credit cards made this a popular offer consideration. "Ninety days same as cash," installment payment programs, and "no payments for a year" are other popular financing considerations in

direct marketing offers. With price a huge consideration, anything that affects cash changing hands is an equally important consideration.

- *Incentives.* This offer consideration exists in many forms and is covered in more detail below. Free gifts, discounts, and free bonuses are incentives to get recipients to respond to offers. More and more offers are being made with free bonuses. The more free bonuses, the more enticing the offer. Some will order or respond just to get the free bonuses.

- *For a limited time only.* Many offers have built-in time limits. The goal of direct marketing is to get a recipient to act and to act now. Putting a time limit on the offer encourages more response quicker than offers without a time limit. Anything that can be done to instill a sense of urgency in a prospect will increase the effectiveness of an offer.

- *Quantity limits.* Communicating a finite quantity available encourages response. Time-limit offers can be in the form of limited editions for collectibles, signed and numbered items (usually for art or autographed items), "limit two per customer," and the basic "while supplies last."

- *Guarantees.* Even though this is last on the list, it is not last in importance. It is one of the most considered items in offers by both direct marketers and offer recipients. Always offer a guarantee with your product or service, or offer with no strings attached. The more unconditional it is, the better your response will be. More on this below.

There are many considerations when developing a direct marketing offer. Understand what your prospects will respond to most, and offer accordingly.

Another offer idea is to give the prospects a "taste" of what they would experience if they did business with you or purchased from you. The offer should aid in the "visualization" or the "touch" of what the product or service would "look" or "feel" like once it was in hand. Appealing to the senses, and not just the thought processes, is one more step to a sale, one more step in furthering a customer relationship, or a step toward a positive experience delivered by you. The offer of the taste is important and must be something that the customer/prospect "wants," which takes us back to the interest factor that prompted a prospect's response initially.

Visualization is critical. Visualization connects your prospect's emotion to your product or service. Once you get to the point and communicate compelling benefits, your prospect starts thinking about life without your product or service and actually starts selling to himself/herself. That's the ultimate point you want to reach with all direct marketing messages.

To create the strongest direct-response marketing, your marketing message should concentrate on selling the offer, whether or not it contains your product or service information. Remember, the primary purpose of direct marketing is to get a response of some type from an interested prospect. Do not oversell the product in the marketing message. Sometimes marketers can be so passionate about a product or service that they oversell to the point of overshadowing the very mechanism designed to elicit the response—the offer. Offers can be overpowered and hidden by copy that is too product- and service-oriented and not offer-oriented.

The orientation of the marketing message and the offer should be toward the prospect or customer, a benefit orientation and a clear statement of "what's in it for me, the prospect?" The offer should be: "Here is something for you, not me, but you. You can have it if you respond to me." Consider this as the generic description of an offer.

Components of a Good Offer

Once you have considered all those things that will appeal to your customers and prospects, it's time to create your offer. Remember the purpose of the offer. There are some components that are vital to every offer. The following components are essential as you review the rest of the offer considerations:

- Offering something of value
  - Free report: white paper or other information
  - Discount
  - Sample/trial
  - Two-for-one or other pricing
  - Special financing
  - A "deal"
- Guarantee
  - Take the risk out of your offer for the prospect.
  - You many times are making the offer before you have earned the trust and gained the confidence of the prospect, so anything you can do to hasten this will increase response.
- Sense of urgency
  - Your offer won't last forever; state it and reinforce it.
  - Your goal is to get prospects to respond now, not linger, not take their time to think about what you are offering.
  - Don't overlook the risk that they will forget about you or lose interest.

Planning Your Offer

Understanding your prospect and customer as well as your product or service will help you optimize your offer. Working through the following questions will provide the information you need to do this:

- What are the benefits of your product or service?
- Why should the prospect buy from you?
- Why should the prospect buy from you now?
- What is the objective of your direct marketing?
- What is the competition doing?
- What is the objective of your offer?
- Direct purchase
- Renewal
- Loyalty
- Step one of a two-step sales process

Communication of the Offer

The most successful offers actually use the attention-getter (headline or graphic) as a lead in to the offer. The ensuing copy and marketing message then is usually support for the offer.

A key component to any offer is that it should be crystal clear, specific, and leave nothing to the prospect's imagination.

Incentives Used in Offers

The whole foundation of direct marketing, getting a prospect to respond to an offer, depends on the types of offers just discussed. Incentives play a big role in the effectiveness of the offer. Not only must you precisely hit the wants and needs with benefits, you need to provide the proper incentive to make prospects act, and act now. Here are different types of incentives to consider when crafting your offer:

Information. You are probably an expert in something. This affords you the opportunity to write an article, a report, a top-ten list, a checklist, or a white paper. The only cost of this premium is your time to develop the information. This incentive is also easy to offer online in digital form. Information offered by an expert will be responded to by an interested target market.

Merchandise. A "free gift" sounds enticing. Many in your target audience would respond to a free gift. Gadgets, trinkets, useful tools, and accessories of all types are offers of value that can generate a satisfactory response. Merchandise has to be fulfilled, shipped, and delivered, which adds a logistical component to your offering, but still is a good incentive.

Trial offers. When you want your prospect to experience your product or service, you present a trial offer. This is an actual product sampling. You see this a lot in service industries when they offer free consultation.

Those with a physical product many times will offer a shipment of a product without requiring payment until the prospect decides whether to keep the merchandise or not. This is a sure way to offer experience with your product to a prospect and increases your chance for a direct sale or subsequent response.

David Oreck uses a trial offer for his vacuum cleaner:

> *Just look at the offer for the Oreck vacuum cleaner: Take the 15-day challenge. Let me send you my eight-pound Oreck XL. Then vacuum your floor with your current vacuum and go over it with the Oreck. You will find dirt in the bag, guaranteed, or your money back.*

Discounts. Discounts are offers that will generally increase response rates. Playing with price can sometimes be like playing with fire, however. Some prospects will expect the discounted price

on an ongoing basis. Retailers are challenged by this as they always offer sales. There are ways around it. You can offer an "introductory" price indicating that the discount is a one-time offer. You can also bundle products or offer free shipping and handling as other discount mechanisms.

Frequent buyer loyalty. The airlines do it every day. The term "frequent flyer miles" is commonplace today. Credit card companies have jumped in the action, offering "reward points." Frequent flier miles and frequent buyer points are examples of loyalty programs in which the offer is points redeemable later for products and services. As a loyalty marketer, be prepared for the tracking and fulfillment that goes along with these types of offers.

An incentive can be as simple as a statement such as: "Respond to this _____ and get this _____ in return for your response." It's the proverbial offer/response formula for direct marketing.

Offers That Work and That Have a High Perceived Value

Tool kit. Tools imply that something is available to make the work easier. Subliminally, they also suggest that something will get done. In many cases, the tools are information-based: a how-to checklist, an audio CD, a workbook, articles, a directory, etc. Associate it with a benefit, e.g., "increased response direct mail tool kit."

Workbook. Just like people need to be told what to do in the form of a call to action in your direct marketing, they like to be led through a process in their work. A workbook will do this. A workbook tells how to put one foot in front of the other (in a matter of speaking) as you progress through your work plan in logical fashion. A workbook also serves to record answers for reference later. Prospects are much more likely to answer questions in workbook style than come up with ideas on their own and develop them. A workbook has a high perceived value. A study guide is another name for the workbook that might work better for those prospects who are averse to work.

Audit. An audit is simply an offer to look at your business or situation and identify areas of opportunity or challenges that lead to an offer of a solution for those challenges or a way to take advantage of the identified opportunity. Many will associate an audit with an accounting or financial function. This is a very narrow view. An internet service provider can offer a network security audit. A printing company can offer a forms audit. A personal performance consultant can offer a productivity audit.

White paper/position paper. A white paper refers to information offered by an expert. The term came into use because there were no fancy graphics, just black-and-white (usually) paper, much like a research paper. The goal of a white paper is to provide useful, meaningful information, research findings, trend information, predictions, and positions. This puts the company offering the white paper in the classification of expert and many times as a leader in its industry.

Special report. A special report is an article full of information that is of interest to your prospect. You call it a special report because you wrote it especially with your prospects and their challenges in mind.

Critique. A critique is close to an audit. A critique evaluates something that has already been done and suggests improvement. A web site developer can offer a web site critique. A copywriter can offer a sales letter critique.

Evaluation. An evaluation is the first half of a critique. It implies that the evaluator will assess a situation and report on it. This is usually where an evaluation stops. Solutions are not presented with this type of an offer.

Survey/survey results. When you are stating opinions or positions, prospects like to know that they are based on facts or research. A survey is good, current research, usually unique to the target market. An offer of a survey is an offer of what's going on in a market or what people are thinking now. It also is current information that could aid in decision making for a prospect. Survey results have a high perceived value and work well as an offer.

Sweepstakes. An imaginative and creative sweepstakes can be a valuable offer. The key is to make the prize something that interests your prospect and compels them to enter. Think deeply on this one. You might be surprised at what your prospect would be interested in winning.

Offers You Can Use

- Free teleseminar
- Paid teleseminar
- Free seminar
- Paid seminar
- Meet-and-greet session
- Free report
- Free CD audio
- Free consultation
- Free product
- Checklist/guide
- Bundled products for discount
- P.S. double bundle
- Tickets
- Anniversary gift
- Handbook
- Free kit

Care package
- Savings certificate
- Save 67 percent and receive four free gifts
- I'll pay half of your _____ bill, to gain you as a new customer.
- Newsletter
- First month free
- Audit/critique

Offers That Don't Work

- Offers with a long deadline
- Free information with no details
- An offer that has no benefit to your prospect; too much *you* and not enough *them.*
- Something that is hard to get or hard to figure out how to get.

Direct Response Offers

Without the offer, your marketing falls back into the category of traditional marketing. Without the offer, your marketing becomes awareness- and brand-oriented, and the response you really want from a prospect may never happen or may take a really long time to happen. The offer then, is one of the key components to direct marketing and direct mail.

The offer is one of the variables in direct marketing that is easily tested. As long as all other variables remain the same, sending out direct mail with different offers can generally tell you a lot about what your target market will respond to. That is the beauty of testing in direct marketing: It can usually be done quickly and effectively, so that you can roll out the optimum offer for your entire campaign.

Offering the Actual Product or Service

Listed in offer types above were the actual products and services, or a sample of them.

Although a purchase is the ultimate goal, it is not always easy to make that happen directly with one contact. It does happen, but many times you must rely on a response other than a direct purchase. Consumers and prospects don't like to feel pressured into buying things. Many times they want to "look around" before buying and kick a few tires. Creating an offer that isn't just the product or service for sale allows for that looking around to happen. Usually this is done with no obligation to the consumer or prospect. Now, of course, you want them to look around with enough interest and desire to act or buy at some point.

Presenting just the product or service as your offer can, however, sometimes backfire. Prospects can get overwhelmed with copy-heavy product offers and get completely turned off. In this case, focusing on an offer that isn't the product or service, overcomes this problem and generates a higher response.

An offer must be something of value. Prospects and consumers are generally savvy and aware. They can spot a fake promise, empty offer, or an exaggerated claim a mile away. They can also spot true value. True value turns these prospects into paying clients and lifetime customers.

Guarantees

Prospects want a risk-free offer as well. In our list of offer ideas above, a guarantee was listed.

Guarantees reduce prospects' risk of taking action. Naturally, this will increase response rates and action taken. Many times there is a want or a need, but they can't experience the product or service associated with it. They can't touch it, see it, or experience it in some way. If that is the case, the prospect is generally slow to act because of the risk involved. Removing this risk increases response rates. That's exactly what guarantees do.

Guarantees also build customer loyalty. Although this is not the primary goal of your direct marketing, it is a nice side benefit.

Most reputable companies guarantee their product or service. If something doesn't work or goes wrong, the product is returned and a refund is usually given. If done ethically, respectfully, and reasonably, you will generally get the refund.

What may not happen as much is telling your prospects and target market about your guarantee. Whatever form it takes, tell the world. Shout it loud and clear in your copy. Make it big and bold. Make sure your prospect can't miss it. In addition, make it as simple as possible, no small print. Leave the lawyers out of this. You don't want to confuse your prospect or let any doubt or suspicion enter their mind.

The simplest guarantee is the one that Lands' End offers. On the front of its catalog, web site, order forms, retail stores, outlet stores, etc., its guarantee is emblazoned in big bold letters: Lands' End—Guaranteed, period.

▼ A NOTE ON FREE CONSULTATIONS AS AN OFFER

People like anything free as an offer. Early on, offers consisted of "Free Consultations" as a way to entice a prospect further. This offer was once considered impressive by prospects and had a relatively high response rate. Today's consumers recognize that a free consultation is nothing more than a glorified sales call. In a world of do-not-call, spam, and intruding and offensive salespeople, free consultations don't have the luster they once did.

Examples of Offers

Gevalia Kaffee offers a premium that is worth more than the initial product shipment. In this case, Gevalia Kaffe promotes the premium heavily in its offer. Other components that make its offer smart are:

- Low introductory price on the first shipment
- More freebies in the future
- A full guarantee on unwanted product shipped in the future
- Other premiums

Actual offers in today's newspapers, magazines, and web sites:

- Get four full weeks of the Journal for free!
- Order your free mutual fund select list today!
- $2.00 off 1 adult admission—good any day
- Earn $150 for your time!
- Order now in time for Spring and save 15 percent!
- Join now for free!
- Buy one phone, get one for free!
- Free estimate!
- Visit our web site for a complete schedule of events and enter for a chance to win two free tickets to the show.
- $1,000 off
- Receive a free gift card when you open an account.
- Zero down, low interest rates available.

Direct Marketing Sampling

Sampling in the world of direct marketing is simply offering a sample of your product or service for use by a targeted recipient. You see samples mailed every day even when not asking for a direct response. There are cereal samples included in the plastic wraps of newspapers on the driveway, toothpaste samples handed out by your dentist, and chicken bit samples cooked and passed out at the end of your grocery store aisle. Sampling is used every day in many forms of marketing. The thought is that if you sample a product or service, you might purchase it.

Free consultations are nothing more than a sampling technique. The offering of service samples is less costly than product samples. A massage therapist can offer a 15-minute stress-relief massage, a marketing consultant can offer a critique on marketing-communication pieces, and so on. Demonstrations one-on-one is a form of sampling that also works. Whatever your choice of sampling is, make it part of your offer.

Call to Action

The action associated with the offer is referred to in marketing as the call to action. It is an invitation for your prospects and customers to do something. It is what your expectation of the prospect is. This invitation or call to action should be specific, clear, and easy to carry out. Prospects generally like someone else to make their decisions for them or help them as much as possible. This includes helping them decide what to do next, what action to take.

Note: A message that doesn't include a call to action actually makes the recipient more suspicious of the legitimacy of the message. You want to prevent the reaction, "Why did I receive this and what am I supposed to do."

Postscripts

It has been proven by direct mail pundits, associations, and direct marketers that the first thing read in a personalized letter is the recipient's name. People like seeing their name in print, even if it's a salutation in a letter. The second thing most often read is the post script.

Whether it's the curiosity factor or the way the human eye/mind works, many people go straight to the P.S. In view of this, craft your P.S. as hard-hitting and benefit- and action-oriented as possible.

Don't worry about a long postscript. It will get read. Pack it full of information. The P.S. also represents one more area to personalize. More is not necessarily better. Don't go overboard with P.S.S., P.S.S.S., etc. This usually is a tip-off that your mailing is a mass, nontargeted mailing, which is the definition of junk mail.

Involvement

Involvement keeps a prospect's attention and encourages response. Things like Yes and No stickers, membership cards, certificates, rub-offs, and contests are a few examples of how to create the appropriate involvement.

Make It Easy to Respond To

Just as many businesses are committed to being easy to do business with, direct marketing offers should offer the same value and be easy to respond to. Whether online or offline, the attention spans and patience of prospects are growing shorter and shorter.

A suggested action that is difficult to carry out almost always results in no response at all.

Consider, for example David Oreck's vacuum cleaner marketing. All of it, including print, broadcast, and direct mail use a toll-free 1-800 telephone number. This makes it easy for the customer to make a purchase or request the famous 15-day trial—both acceptable responses for any direct marketing. It also allows Oreck to direct an interested prospect to the nearest dealer if they want to see and touch the product. That still is a response generated by Oreck's direct marketing.

INCREASING THE EFFECTIVENESS OF DIRECT MAIL/DIRECT MARKETING

Managing direct mail expenses during your campaign is just like managing any other component of your business. You want to control costs, spending only what is necessary while striving for the highest return on your expenditures.

Here are considerations for your bottom line:

- *A clean, efficient mailing list.* Whether you compile your own list or purchase one from a list vendor/broker, there will be turnover. People move and companies change, causing mailing lists to be less than 100 percent accurate. Accept this because it is inevitable and direct marketing is a numbers game. Inaccuracies figure into the probabilities and returns. Getting rid of these inaccuracies and making your list as deliverable as possible is one way to increase your probability of response and subsequent returns.
- As you receive change-of-address notifications and returned mail, update and change your list/database. You can also use a company that offers National Change of Address capabilities as a licensee of the USPS.
- Remove duplicate addresses as you find them. Pay particular attention to duplicate addresses with slightly different names:

> R. Smith, 123 Cross Village Dr.
> Robert Smith, 123 Cross Village Dr.
> Bob Smith, 123 Cross Village Dr.

These are all probably the same person, but show up as three different addressees. Deleting two of these saves postage and the cost of the marketing piece sent, increasing the efficiency of your list. Pay particular attention to this as you merge lists from different vendors or sources.

WAYS TO IMPROVE YOUR DIRECT MAIL RESPONSE

- Increase the frequency of your mailings.
- Use a P.S. on every direct mail letter. The P.S. is second in importance only to the headline.
- Continually thank your customers for their orders by enclosing a message with the orders.
- Enclose another merchandise offer with the thank-you message.
- Vary your mailing format. Use self-mailers, different envelope formats, catalogs, etc., so that prospects don't get in the habit of recognizing your mailing piece and automatically discarding your offer.
- Ride on the coattails of current events (energy crises, elections, cold winters, etc.). When inflation rises, have an "inflation-cutting" special, etc.
- Include more than one offer in your direct mailing package at a time.
- Think about using simulated handwriting for emphasis in your letters and on the front of your envelopes.
- Try an unusual shape, size, or color that you've not used before.
- Stimulate off-season business by sending out more direct mail. If you normally have a summer slump, have a special "summer sale" mailing in the summer.
- Present more value by offering a baker's dozen instead of a regular dozen, 110 instead of 100, or a super-size.
- Make your envelope smell the way your product does.
- Offer the opportunity to use MasterCard or Visa.
- Use multiple windows on the face and back of your envelope to encourage "sneak peaks."

- Use stamps, coupons, early bonuses, etc.
- Include a sample in your mailing.
- Be extreme. Use a tiny letter with a tiny pencil accompanying it or a jumbo letter in a jumbo envelope, format that will be exciting to prospects and clients.
- Use a wraparound band on your catalog. It gives you two cover surfaces to market with instead of one.
- Use teaser copy on your outer envelope and test it vs. a blind envelope.
- Make it easy to buy from you by giving the inquirer a return envelope to send an order back in.
- Use the expertise of your printing company partner. It knows shortcuts that you don't.
- Resend your mailing to just your best customers three to four weeks later. You'll do 60 to 75 percent as well on the second mailing as you did on the first.
- State your guarantee in the strongest possible terms and state it often.
- Spotlight your benefits in your headline.
- Put distinctive differences in your catalog and point them out to increase interest.
- Stimulate action by featuring a time limit or some other sense-of-urgency message at the top of your letter.
- Use full-view envelopes to display attractive literature.
- Have offers directed exclusively to customers.
- Dramatize big news by using a big format to present your message.
- Try a massive display of stamps on the outside of your envelope to emphasize a fact.
- A reply envelope plus loose stamp might be more effective than a BRE.
- Try using the space on the inside of your mailing envelope to sell your product.
- Make sure your free gifts are really free.

NATIONAL CHANGE OF ADDRESS (NCOA)

The USPS reports that over 40 million Americans change their address annually. Imagine what this does to the quality of mailing lists if they are not kept up. This contributes to the estimated 8 percent of all undeliverable mail that is due to incorrect addresses. The National Change of Address is a program that helps direct marketers identify changes to addresses before they process their mail.

Updated change-of-address information is provided by the USPS to certified and licensed private sector licensees. The whole process involves the direct marketer processing their mail with one of the NCOA licensees. The licensee then matches the standardized addresses with a change-of-address file of over 156 million records. This file is compiled from those change-of-address order forms that everyone fills out when they move and relocate. As the matches are made with old addresses, the licensee then updates the mailing with the new addresses. NCOA licensees receive change-of-address information on a weekly basis to update the whole NCOA database. Costs for these services generally range from $2 to $6 per thousand addresses processed.

The NCOA network is made up of approximately 18 commercial licensees. For a list of certified NCOA licensees, visit the web sites:

www.usps.com./ncsc/ziplookup/vendorslicensees.htm

or

www.usps.com/ncsc/addressservices/moveupdate/changeaddress.htm

The USPS reports that since 1986, this system has saved millions of dollars in postage and production costs.

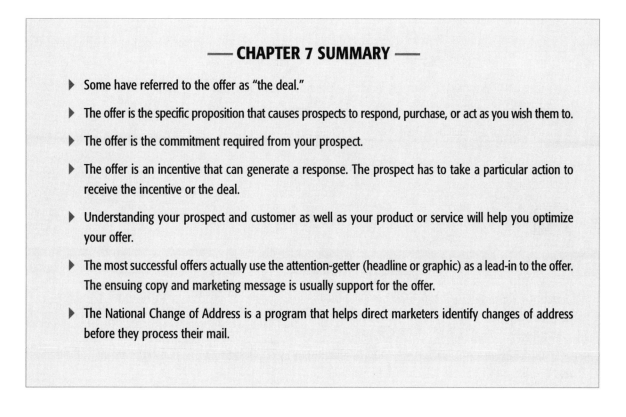

— **CHAPTER 7 SUMMARY** —

▶ Some have referred to the offer as "the deal."

▶ The offer is the specific proposition that causes prospects to respond, purchase, or act as you wish them to.

▶ The offer is the commitment required from your prospect.

▶ The offer is an incentive that can generate a response. The prospect has to take a particular action to receive the incentive or the deal.

▶ Understanding your prospect and customer as well as your product or service will help you optimize your offer.

▶ The most successful offers actually use the attention-getter (headline or graphic) as a lead-in to the offer. The ensuing copy and marketing message is usually support for the offer.

▶ The National Change of Address is a program that helps direct marketers identify changes of address before they process their mail.

Timing and Frequency

WHETHER YOU ARE CONSIDERING ON-line or offline direct marketing, it takes repetition and consistency to achieve your marketing goals. You first must get your message noticed, read, absorbed, and understood enough to moti-vate a reader to take action. It's only natural some people will respond immediately, on the first message, to a direct marketing offer. Others will need to see the message more than once and probably many more times before responding.

Direct marketing and direct sales studies have shown that the highest probability for a sale occurs during the follow-up process. Now that might sound like common sense and apple pie, but it is not common practice. This follow-up process must be done right away with consistency in order for it to be effective. Jim Rohn, the famed personal development motivator, points out, "Without a sense of urgency, desire loses its value." Correspondingly, without consistent

follow-up and attention, prospects and cus-tomers lose desire. Collection agencies and debt collectors prove this every day with their collection letters and warnings.

In the world of direct marketing, the process of consistent follow-up mailings and communication is known as sequential mar-keting. I first heard it called this by Dan Kennedy, the famed direct marketing guru. Many entrepreneurs speak of low response (less than 1 percent) for a one-time first mail-ing, but higher responses (1 to 10 percent) the second and third time the same mailing to the same audience is received. Here is what a three-part sequential mailing might look like:

- *Letter #1.* A direct sales letter is sent with a time-sensitive special offer and a chance to enter a sweepstakes drawing for a "valuable" prize.
- *Letter #2.* Two weeks after the first mail-ing a second letter is mailed to those not responding, with copy that contains

phrases like: "We've missed you." "We're concerned that we haven't heard from you." "Maybe you did not see this the first time…" There are also more mentions of free trials and bonus add-ons, along with more emphasis on many calls to action, giving the prospect more ways to respond to an offer.

- *Letter #3.* Usually about a month after the first mailing a third letter is sent with lots of headlines, often including the words to "last chance" and "act now before this offer expires." This letter more than the other two, emphasizes the sense of urgency even more. An additional incentive, not given in the first two, is also offered. Pointing out negative outcomes if no action is taken is also a tactic in a final mailing of a sequence like this one.

The beauty of this sequence is that each step makes the offer more valuable. Repetition in this case emphasizes the importance and value of the offer. Its value makes the communication more understandable and reinforces the sense of urgency about acting now; it's a classic direct marketing approach that turns unresponsive prospects into paying clients.

Should you stop your sequence at three contacts? No. This is just an example. If it takes six to eight times to get prospects into a purchase-ready frame of mind, three mailings may still not reach the full potential of your target market.

SUBCONSCIOUS DECISION MAKING

Jay Levinson of *Guerrilla Marketing* fame and my coauthor of *Guerrilla Marketing in 30 Days* says that 90 percent of purchase decisions are made with the subconscious mind. Copywriter Joe Sugarman puts this number closer to 95 per-

cent. Words are communicated consciously, but the information is processed subconsciously.

The way to access that subconscious process is through repetition, which is why sequential mailings return higher response rates than single mailings.

Bill Gallagher, Ph.D., also a fellow guerrilla marketer, sees the human mind as organized in layers, much like an onion. As marketers, people need to penetrate the outer layers and get the message through to the subconscious where all buying decisions are made. Saying your message over and over again consistently is the key to marketing successes. Repetition cuts the groove.

You've read it here before and in other places that people are bombarded daily with over 3,000 marketing messages. This is enough to numb the mind. Which ones do you remember? You remember the ones you have heard over and over, repeated consistently.

A good example of this process is the simple e-course that you sign up for online as an interested prospect. If it's a seven-day e-course, you have opted for one message day for a week. At the end of that week, you've witnessed the value of the offer being made each day as part of the e-course. The probability of your buying or responding to the offer goes up dramatically in this case.

USING THE ELEMENT OF TIME TO YOUR ADVANTAGE

When looking at the total picture of timing and frequency, there are essentially three ways you can make the element of time work to your advantage.

1. Choose which day of the week, time of the month, and time of day to send your mail. This primarily relates to the timing of e-mail because it is almost instantaneous.

2. Manage the timing of multiple communications to create a sequential mailing.
3. Add a time constraint, deadline, and sense of urgency to your offer.

Integrating these three components into your direct marketing timing, whether online or off, will increase your chances for success and the resulting return on marketing dollars.

Times of the Day

In all kinds of marketing, there may be certain times of the day, days of the week, or months when a prospect is more receptive to your message.

Business-related mailings are generally most responded to during the heart of the business day. This starts at around 10 A.M. after many fires have been put out, the morning meetings are over, and the crises are managed and brought under control. Some have described this period as being after the "inbox glut." This window of opportunity extends to about 3 P.M., when the workday starts winding down. This is the period when people start to mentally check out.

If the mailing is consumer-oriented, then the best time is from 6 P.M. to 9 P.M. This is when personal e-mails are most likely to be read and when direct mail piles are sorted. These times are ideal for e-mail communication, but it is difficult to pinpoint exactly when people actually sort and read their offline direct mail pieces.

Days of the Week

The same goes for the days of the week. Tuesdays through Thursdays work well for the same reasons. Monday-morning fires are out and thoughts about the upcoming weekend haven't affected the work mind yet. On the other hand, consumer-related and personal communications are read from Friday to Monday, away from the workplace and outside of the workweek.

You can target days; you can't target the time of day, however. Some people look at e-mail constantly all day long while others check mail sporadically, usually throughout the day. The same goes for traditional offline direct mail. Mail can sit in an inbox and not be read for a period of time that you cannot predict or control. Something might be glanced at and set aside for a later review. That's why some direct mail campaigns show a response even after the campaign is over.

Months-of-the-Year Timing

Businesses of all types face timing challenges with particular months of the year.

In August, many people are on vacation, away from their businesses, squeezing in family activity before the start of the school year.

In December, you've got the overrun of holiday activity. This may or may not be good for your business communication. If you are a retailer, the holiday gift-buying season bodes well for your communication. If you are not a retailer, the fight for mind-share is definitely on during this time.

Likewise, in direct-response newspaper advertising, there are two major newspaper direct response advertising seasons. The fall mail-order season begins roughly in August and runs through November. The winter season begins with January and runs through March.

One to two weeks before a holiday also presents similar timing challenges. Marketing during this time competes with the preholiday mindset. This applies to the less commercialized holidays like Presidents' Day, Memorial Day, Indepen-dence Day, Easter, Yom Kippur, Rosh Hashanah. Take note that that of these last few occur on different dates each year.

The other thing about holidays is that they influence not only accessibility to e-mail as people take time off from their jobs and computers, but also how e-mails are read upon their return from the holidays. E-mails sent during holiday time stand to get lost in the flood of holiday e-mails and may be deleted en masse when your recipient returns to this flood. The same thing can happen to traditional direct mail, but to a lesser extent.

Timing Tied to Events

Timing can also be tied to events. Plow and Hunter, an online catalog offering products for the home and garden, realized success by offering a two-day, online sale. The offer was timed to an impending winter snowstorm predicted for the whole East Coast. This geographical area made up a large portion of its target list. The offer was an invitation to shop from the comfort of home without having to go out and shovel the driveway. The success was in the sense of urgency built in to the "two days" of the sale.

Because this campaign was tied to an event (a snowstorm), the campaign was successful. Without the tie-in, the response rates would have been much lower, according to Plow and Hunter's testing.

HOW MANY TIMES DOES IT TAKE?

In 1885, Thomas Scot of England posted for the advertising world of his day how many times it would take for a particular marketing message to prompt action. His list approaches 20 times. Here is his posting:

Thomas Scot—London

1885

The first time a man sees an ad or receives a mailing, he:

1. Doesn't see it.
2. Doesn't notice it.
3. Is conscious of its existence.
4. Faintly remembers having seen it.
5. Reads the ad.
6. Turn up his/her nose at it.
7. Says, "Oh brother" or "Right."
8. Says, "Here's that confounded thing again."
9. Wonders if it amounts to anything.
10. Asks his neighbor if he's tried it.
11. Wonders how the advertiser makes it pay.
12. Thinks it might be a good thing.
13. Thinks it might even be worth something.
14. Remembers that he wanted such a thing for a long time.
15. Is tantalized because he cannot afford to buy it.
16. Thinks he will buy it someday.
17. Makes a note about it.
18. Swears at his poverty.
19. Counts his money carefully.
20. He buys it!

Jay Levinson, the father of guerrilla marketing, says that his number is six to eight, but if two out three messages are ignored, the number is closer to what Thomas Scot was saying. Amazing that not much has changed in over 120 years. The lesson to be learned here is that sometimes you have to continually touch prospective buyers

▼ CONSISTENCY IS KEY

The most successful marketing programs are sent out on a regular, consistent basis. Send too many messages and you fall into an annoyance category. Send too few and you lose out on being at the "top of mind" of your prospects' and customers' awareness.

and even customers in your target market before you get the response you want. Jay also says that the familiarity that comes with consistent and frequent communication breeds confidence in you and it is this confidence that is the springboard to sales.

PLANNING AHEAD BY SENIOR LEVEL EXECUTIVES

Karen Gedney of Karen Gedney Communications, an award-winning creative director and copywriter, observes that as a rule, the more senior the executive who is being targeted with marketing, the further in advance you must start your communication process. This could even amount to up to a year in advance for the highest C-level officers of a company. It's hard to do direct marketing with this type of time lag unless you consider "saving the date" a response to your call to action. The true response comes after subsequent communications leading up to the point of intended action. Even though direct marketing works in these cases, people, especially busy executives, still like to plan ahead.

INTEGRATED COMMUNICATIONS

Varying the types of communication increases the overall effectiveness of a direct marketing campaign. This includes online and offline communication. The key is not to vary it to the point of "camouflaging" frequency. Mix up the communication too much, and each communication is like starting over. Use consistent and common threads throughout. These commonalities can be a particular vehicle like e-mail, a branding or identity component, or a consistent offer and response mechanism. You can still run an integrated campaign effectively.

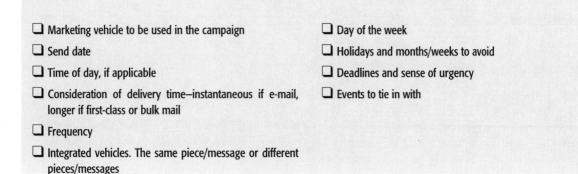

FIGURE 8.1 **Timing and Frequency Checklist**

- ☐ Marketing vehicle to be used in the campaign
- ☐ Send date
- ☐ Time of day, if applicable
- ☐ Consideration of delivery time—instantaneous if e-mail, longer if first-class or bulk mail
- ☐ Frequency
- ☐ Integrated vehicles. The same piece/message or different pieces/messages
- ☐ Day of the week
- ☐ Holidays and months/weeks to avoid
- ☐ Deadlines and sense of urgency
- ☐ Events to tie in with

—— CHAPTER 8 SUMMARY ——

▶ Whether you are considering online or offline direct marketing, it takes repetition and consistency to achieve your marketing goals.

▶ You first must get your message noticed, then read, absorbed, and understood enough to motivate a reader to take action.

▶ Direct marketing and direct sales studies have shown that the highest probability for a sale occurs during the-follow-up process.

▶ Ninety percent of purchase decisions are made in the subconscious mind. Words are communicated consciously, but the information is processed subconsciously.

▶ One way to impress the subconscious mind is through repetition, which is why sequential mailings return higher response rates than single mailings.

▶ Business-related mailings are generally most responded to during the heart of the business day.

▶ Tuesdays through Thursdays work well for of the same reasons. Monday-morning fires have been put out and thoughts about the upcoming weekend haven't yet affected the work mind.

▶ Varying the types of communication increases the overall effectiveness of a direct marketing campaign. This includes both online and offline communication.

▶ The most successful marketing programs are sent out on a regular, consistent basis. Send too many messages and you fall into an annoyance category. Send too few and you lose out on being at the top of mind of your prospects' and customers' awareness.

Bibliography

THERE IS ALWAYS NEW TECHNOLOGIES AND methodologies, but the subject of direct marketing is not new. Many of the forefathers of direct marketing left as their legacy the many books, ideas, and teachings that are still in use today. Some of their most fundamental discoveries and applications are the foundation of much of direct marketing that is in use today. Many of these sources were relied here on for the proper direction, the technicalities, and the foundations of these many experts. This bibliography cites those as well as many of the resources that have been offered on the subject of direct marketing. The notables are here; the up and comers are also cited. This book provides a comprehensive volume and this bibliography offers other sources to round out the trade. Many of these books were used in the writing of this one; others are cited for your reference. The bibliography alone helps to make this book the *Ultimate Guide to Direct Marketing*.

Allen, Margaret. *Direct Marketing*, (Kogan Page, 1997)

Andrews, Les. *The Royal Mail Direct Mail Handbook*, (Exley Giftbooks, 1989)

Arnold, Peter. *Making Direct Mail Work for You: How to Boost Your Profits with Effective Direct Mail Promotion*, (How to Books, 1999)

Bacon, Mark S. *Do-It-Yourself Direct Marketing: Secrets for Small Business*, (John Wiley & Sons, 1997)

Baier, Martin. *Elements Of Direct Marketing*, (McGraw-Hill, 1984)

———. *How to Find and Cultivate Customers Through Direct Marketing*, (McGraw-Hill/Contemporary, 1996)

Baines, Adam, and Shelia Lloyd (editors). *The Handbook of International Direct Marketing: An Essential Country-by-Country Guide and Directory*, (Kogan Page, 1995)

Baker, Sunny, and Kim Baker (contributor). *Desktop Direct Marketing: How To*

Use Up-to-the-Minute Technologies to Find and Reach New Customers, (McGraw-Hill, 1994)

Basye, Anne, and Jim Kobs. *Opportunities in Direct Marketing Careers,* (McGraw-Hill, 2000)

Beitman, Hartford. *Aggressive Investment Marketing! What Every Financial Services Sales Person Should Know About Advertising and Direct Mail,* (ARS Enterprises, 1985)

Benson, Richard V. *Secrets of Successful Direct Mail,* (Benson Organization, 1987)

Berry, Mike. *The New Integrated Direct Marketing,* (Gower Publishing Company, 1998)

Bird, Drayton. *Commonsense Direct Marketing,* (Kogan Page, 2000)

————. *How to Write Sales Letters That Sell,* (Kogan Page, 2003)

Bird, Drayton, and Anne Knudsen (editor). *Commonsense Direct Marketing,* (Kogan Page, 2000)

Blum, Sandra J. *Designing Direct Mail That Sells,* (North Light Books, 1999)

Bly, Robert. *Business to Business Direct Marketing,* (McGraw-Hill, 1998)

————. *Business to Business Direct Marketing: Proven Direct Response Methods to Generate More Leads and Sales,* (National Textbook, 1992)

————. *Complete Idiot's Guide to Direct Marketing,* (Alpha, 2001)

————. *Internet Direct Mail: The Complete Guide to Successful E-Mail Marketing Campaigns,* (McGraw-Hill, 2000)

————. *The Perfect Sales Piece; A Complete Do-It-Yourself Guide,* (Wiley, 1994)

Power-Packed Direct Mail. How to Get More Leads and Sales by Mail, (Henry Holt, 1996)

————. *Start and Run a Profitable Mail-Order Business,* (Self-Counsel Press, 1997)

Bodian, Nat G. *Direct Marketing Rules of Thumb: 1,000 Practical and Profitable Ideas to Help You Improve Response, Save Money, and Increase Efficiency in Your Direct Mail,* (McGraw-Hill, 1995)

————. *NTCs Dictionary of Direct Mail and Mailing List Terminology and Techniques,* (NTC/Contemporary Publishing, 1990)

————. *The Publishers Direct Mail Handbook The Professional and Editing* (Series), (Oryx Press, 1987)

Bolden, Tonya. *Mail Order and Direct Response* (No Nonsense Success Guide), (Longmeadow Press, 1994)

Bond, William J. *Home-Based Catalog Marketing: A Success Guide for Entrepreneurs,* (McGraw-Hill, 1990)

Brady, Regina. *Cybermarketing: Your Interactive Marketing Consultant,* (Contemporary Publishing, 1997)

Brann, Christian. *Direct Mail and Direct Response Promotion,* (Kogan Page, 1971)

Broderick, Amanda, and David Pickton. *Integrated Marketing Communications,* (Financial Times/Prentice Hall, 2005)

Brondmo, Hans, and Geoffrey Moore. *The Engaged Customer: The New Rules of Internet Direct Marketing,* (Collins, 2000)

Brown, Herbert E., et al. *Cases in Direct Marketing,* (NTC Publishing, 1996)

Brown, Herbert E., and Bruce Buskirk. *Readings and Cases in Direct Marketing,* (NTC Business Books, 1988)

Burnett, Ed. *Complete Direct Mail List Handbook: Everything You Need to Know About Lists and How to Use Them for Greater Profit*

Burstiner, Irving. *Mail Order Selling: How to Market Almost Anything by Mail,* (Prentice-Hall, 1982)

Burton, Mary T., and Donna Whitfield. *Insider's Guide to Direct Marketing,* (Zweig White & Associates, 1995)

Caples, John. *How to Make Your Advertising Make Money,* (Prentice Hall, 1983)

———. *Making Ads Pay,* (Dover Publications, 1957)

Caples, John and Hahn, Fred E. *Tested Advertising Methods,* (Prentice Hall, 1998)

Carrey, Dixieann W. *First Impressions: A Guide to More Profitable Direct Mail Advertising,* (Dixeann W. Carrey, 1978)

Clark, Sheree and Wendy Lyons. *Creative Direct Mail Design: The Guide and Showcase,* (Rockport Publishers, 1996)

Clemente, Mark N. *The Marketing Glossary: Key Terms, Concepts and Applications in Marketing Management, Advertising, Sales Promotion, Public Relations, Direct Marketing,* (Clemente Books, 2002)

Cohen, William A. *Building a Mail Order Business: A Complete Manual for Success, 4th edition,* (John Wiley& Sons, 1996)

———. *Direct Response Marketing: An Entrepreneurial Approach,* (John Wiley & Sons, 1984)

Collins, Joyce. *Direct Mail Marketing for Scholarly Publishers: A Beginner's Guide,* (ISI Press, 1983)

Collins, Thomas L., and Stan Rapp. *Maximarketing: The New Direction in Advertising, Promotion and Marketing Strategy,* (Plume Books, 1989)

———. *The Great Marketing Turnaround: The Age of the Individual and How to Profit,* (Prentice Hall Trade, 1990)

———. *The New Maximarketing,* (McGraw-Hill, 1995)

Cone, Arthur Lambert. *How to Create and Use Solid Gold Fund-Raising Letters,* (Taft Group, 1940)

Cossman, E. Joseph. *How I Made $1,000,000 in Mail Order,* (Fireside, 1993)

Crippen, John K. *Successful Direct Mail Methods,* (Garland Publishing, 1985)

Cronin, Blaise. *Direct Mail Advertising and Public Library Use,* (British Library Lending Division, 1980)

Cross, Richard. *Customer Bonding: Pathways to Lasting Customer Loyalty,* (NTC/Contemporary Publishing Company, 1994)

Davies, John M. *The Essential Guide to Database Marketing,* (McGraw-Hill, 1992)

Delphos, William A. (editor). *Direct Marketing in Canada: A Strategic Entry Report,* 1997, (Icon Group International, 1999)

Direct Marketing Creative Guild. *Direct Marketing Design,* (PBC International, 1985)

Dobkin, Jeffrey, and Michelle Axelrod. *Uncommon Marketing Techniques,* (Danielle Adams Publishing Co., 2003)

Dobkin, Jeffrey W. *How to Market a Product for Under $500!: A Handbook of Multiple Exposure Marketing,* (Danielle Adams Publishing, 1995)

Doscher, Robert, and Richard Simms. *The Dialamerica Teleservices Handbook,* (McGraw-Hill, 2000)

Drozdenko, Ronald, and Perry Drake. *Optimal Database Marketing: Strategy, Development and Data Mining,* (SAGE Publications, 2002)

Duncan, George. *Streetwise Direct Marketing,* (Adams Media, 2001)

Dworman, Steven. *$12 Billion of Inside marketing Secrets Discovered Through Direct Response Television Sales,* (Steve Dworman Enterprises, 2003)

Edwards, Dianna, and Robert Valentine. *Catalog Design: The Art of Creating Desire,* (Rockport Publishers, 2001)

Eicoff, Al, et al. *Direct Marketing Through Broadcast Media, TV, Radio, Cable, Infomercials, Home Shopping and More,* (NTC Business Books, 1995)

Eicoff, Al. *Eicoff on Broadcast Direct Marketing,* (NTC Business Books, 1987)

Evans, Poppy (compiler). *Direct Mail Marketing Design,* (Rockport Publishing, 1994)

Fendi, Liz. *Successful Direct Mail.* (Barron's Educational Series, 1997)

Fisher, Peg. *Successful Telemarketing: A Step-By-Step Guide for Increased Sales at Lower Cost.* (Dartnell, 1985)

Fiumara, Georganne. *How to Start a Home-Based Mail Order Business, 2nd edition,* (Globe Pequot, 1999)

Floyd, Elaine. *Marketing With Newsletters: How to Boost Sales, Add Members & Raise Funds With a Printed, Faxed or Web-Site Newsletter,* (Newsletter Resources, 1996)

Fraser-Robinson, John. *The Secrets of Effective Direct Mail,* (McGraw-Hill, 1992)

Gasteiger, Stacy, and Tracy Emerick. *Desktop Marketing with the Macintosh,* (Brady, 1992)

Geller, Lois K. *Direct Marketing Techniques: Building Your Business Using Direct Mail and Direct Response Advertising,* (Crisp Publications, 1998)

Geller, Lois K. *Response!: The Complete Guide to Profitable Direct Marketing,* (Touchstone, 1999)

Gnam, René. *René Gnam's Direct Mail Workshop: 1001 Ideas, Tips, Rulebreakers and Brainstormers for Improving Profits Fast,* (Prentice Hall Trade, 1989)

———. *The Business of Direct Mail,* (KET, 1984)

Godwin, R. Kenneth. *One Billion Dollars of Influence: The Direct Marketing of Politics,* (Chatham House Publishers, 1988)

Goldberg, Bernard A. *Lead Generation Handbook,* (Direct Marketing Publishers, 1992)

Goldberg, Bernie, and Tracy Emerick. *Business-to-Business Direct Marketing,* (Direct Marketing Pub, 1999)

Goldsmith, Richard. *Direct Mail for Dummies,* (IDG Books, 2002)

Gosden, Freeman F. Jr. *Direct Marketing Success: What Works and Why,* (John Wiley & Sons, 1985)

Graham, John W., and Susan K. Jones. *Selling by Mail: An Entrepreneurial Guide to Direct Marketing,* (Scribner, 1985)

Grantenbein, Douglas, and Grantenbein. *Smart Business Solutions for Direct Marketing and Customer Management,* (Microsoft Press, 1999)

Grensing, Lin. *Small Business Guide to Direct Mail: Build Your Customer Base and Boost Profits,* (Self-Counsel Press, 1991)

Griffith, Roger M. *What a Way to Live and Make a Living: The Lyman P. Wood Story,* (In Brief Press, 1994)

Gross, Martin. *Direct Marketers Idea Book,* (Amacom Books, 1989)

Hahn, Fred E., and Kenneth G. Mangum (contributor). *Do-It-Yourself Advertising & Promotion: How to Produce Great Ads, Brochures, Catalogs, Direct Mail, and Much More,* (John Wiley & Sons, 1997)

Hallberg, Garth, and David Ogilvy (contributor). *All Consumers Are Not Created Equal: The Differential Marketing Strategy for Brand Loyalty and Profits,* (Wiley, 1995)

Harper, C. Rose. *Mailing List Strategies: A Guide to Direct Mail Success,* (McGraw-Hill, 1986)

Hatch, Denny (Denison). *Method Marketing,* (Bonus Books, 1999)

———. *Million Dollar Mailings,* (Bonus Books, 2001)

Hatch, Denny, and Jackson, Donald R. *2,239 Tested Secrets for Direct Marketing Success,* (McGraw-Hill, 1999)

Hicks, Tyler G. *How I Grossed More Than One Million Dollars in Direct Mail & Mail Order Starting with Little Cash & Less Knowhow.* (International Wealth Success, 1993)

Hodgson, Richard. *Direct Mail and Mail Order Handbook,* (Probus Publishing, 1988)

———. *Successful Catalog Marketing: How to Plan, Create, Merchandise, and Market to Sell More Products,* (Dartnell, 1991)

Hoge, Cecil C. *The Electronic Marketing Manual/ Integrating Electronic Media into Your Marketing Campaign,* (McGraw-Hill, 1993)

———. *The First Hundred Years Are the Toughest: What We Can Learn from the Century of Competition Between Sears and Wards,* (Ten Speed Press, 1988)

Hollan, James Francis. *The Catalog Handbook: How to Produce a Successful Mail Order Catalog,* (Hippocrene Books, 1991)

Hopkins, Claude. *My Life in Advertising and Scientific Advertising,* (McGraw-Hill, 1966)

Hughes, Arthur M. *The Complete Database Marketer,* (Probus Publishing, 1991)

———. *The Complete Database Marketers: Second-Generation Strategies and Techniques for Tapping the Power of Your Customer Database,* (McGraw-Hill, 1995)

———. *Strategic Database Marketing: The Masterplan for Starting and Managing a Profitable, Customer-Based Marketing Program,* (Probus Publishing, 1994)

Huntsinger, Jerry. *Fund Raising Letters: A Study Guide to Direct Response Marketing,* (Public Service Materials Center, 1984)

Imber, Jane. *Dictionary of Advertising and Direct Mail Terms,* (Barron's, 1987)

Jackson, Donald R. *151 Secrets of Insurance Direct Marketing Practices Revealed,* (Nopoly Press, 1989)

Jackson, Donald R., and Irwin Lowen. *Winning: Direct Marketing for Insurance Agents and Brokers,* (Financial Sourcebooks, 1992)

Jacobs, Ron, and Stone Robert. *Successful Direct Marketing Methods,* (McGraw-Hill, 2001)

Jay, Ros, and Iain Maitland. *Profitable Direct Marketing,* (International Thomson Business Press, 1998)

Jefkins, Frank. *Sell Anything by Mail: The Fool-Proof, Step-By-Step Guide That Shows Anyone How to Sell Anything by Mail,* (Adams Media, 1990)

Jones, Susan K. *Creative Strategy in Direct Marketing,* (McGraw-Hill, 1997)

Jutkins, (Rocket) Ray. *Direct Marketing: How You Can Really Do It Right,* (Rockingham-Jutkins Marketing, 1990)

Jutkins, Ray. *Power Direct Marketing: How to Make It Work for You*, (McGraw-Hill, 1999)

Kachorek, Joseph P. *Direct Mail Testing for Fund Raisers: What to Test, How to Test, How to Interpret the Results*, (Precept Press, 1994)

Katzenstein, Herbert, and William S. Sachs. *Direct Marketing, 2nd edition*, (Prentice Hall College Division, 1992)

Kazuo, Abe (editor) et al. *Direct Mail Graphics, Vol. 1*, (PIE Books, 1994)

Keller, Mitchell. *The Krc Collection of Direct Mail Fund Raising Appeals*, (The Council, 1981)

Kennedy, Dan. *The Ultimate Marketing Plan*, (Adams Media, 2000)

Kern, Russell. *S.U.R.E.—Fire Direct Response Marketing*, (McGraw-Hill, 2001)

———. *Managing Business to Business Sales Leads for Bottom Line Success*, (McGraw-Hill, 2001)

Keup, Erwin J., et al. *Mail Order Legal Guide* (Psi Successful Business Library), (Oasis Press, 1993)

Knapp, Stephen. *Direct Mail Design*, (Rockport Publishing, 1997)

Kobilski, Kathy J. *Advertising Without an Agency: A Comprehensive Guide to Radio, Television, Print, Direct Mail, and Outdoor Advertising for Small Business, 3rd edition*, (Entrepreneur Press, 2005)

Kobs, Jim. *Profitable Direct Marketing*, (McGraw-Hill, 1991)

———. *Profitable Direct Marketing: How to Start, Improve, or Expand any Direct Marketing Operation . . . Plus 11 Detailed Case Studies of Prominent Direct Marketing Companies*, (Crain Books, 1979)

Kordahl, Eugene B. *Telemarketing for Business: A Guide to Building Your Own Telemarketing Operation*, (Prentice Hall, 1998)

Kratz, Bernd. *The Special Demands on Logistics Derived from the Direct Mail Order Trade: An Analysis from a Technical and Economical Viewpoint*, (Centaurus-Verlagsgesellschaft, 1992)

Kremer, John. *The Complete Direct Marketing Sourcebook: A Step-By-Step Guide to Organizing and Managing a Successful Direct Marketing Program*, (John Wiley & Sons, 1992)

Kuniholm, Roland E. *Maximum Gifts by Return Mail*, (Taft Group, 1989)

Lautman, Kay Partney, and Henry Goldstein. *Dear Friend: Mastering the Art of Direct-Mail Fund Raising*, (Fund Raising Institute, 1991)

Law, Merry. *Guide to Worldwide Postal Codes and Address Formats*, (Worldvu, 2004)

Lewis, Herschell Gordon. *Catalog Copy That Sizzles, 2nd edition*, (McGraw-Hill, 1999)

———. *Direct Mail Copy That Sells*, (Prentice Hall Press, 1984)

———. *Direct Marketing Strategies and Tactics: Unleash the Power of Direct Marketing*, (Dartnell, 1993)

———. *More Than You Ever Wanted to Know About Mail Order Advertising*, (Mason National Publications, 1980)

———. *Open Me Now*, (Bonus Books, 1995)

———. *Sales Letters That Sizzle: All the Hooks, Lines, and Sinkers You'll Ever Need to Close Sales*, (McGraw-Hill/Contemporary, 1999)

Lewis, Herschell Gordon, and Carol Nelson, (contributor). *World's Greatest Direct Mail Sales Letters*, (McGraw-Hill/Contemporary, 1996)

Lister, Gwyneth. *Building Your Direct Mail Program*, (Jossey-Bass, 2001)

Lumley, James. *How to Sell More Real Estate by Using Direct Mail*, (John Wiley & Sons, 1982)

————. *Sell It by Mail: Making Your Product the One They Buy,* (John Wiley & Sons, 1986)

Lumpkin, James R., et al. *Direct Marketing, Direct Selling, and the Mature Consumer,* (Quorum Books, 1989)

MacPherson, Kim. *Permission Based E-mail Marketing,* (Dearborn Trade, 2001)

Maitland, Iain. *How to Plan Direct Mail,* (Cassell, 1997)

Majure, Dave. *Direct Hit: Real-World Insights & Common Sense Advice from a Direct Marketing Pro,* (Irwin Professional Publishing, 1994)

Mallory, Charles, and Elaine Brett, (editor). *Direct Mail Magic,* (Crisp Publications, 1991)

Manna, John S., and Herbert Katzenstein. *The Global Legal Environment of Direct Marketing in the 21st Century,* (Legas, 1992)

Martin, Tony. *Financial Services Direct Marketing,* (McGraw-Hill, 1991)

Masser, Barry Z. *How to Make $100,000 a Year in Home Mail Order Business,* (Prentice Hall Press, 1992)

Maysack, Donald R. *Direct Mail Fund Raising: The Art and the Science,* (University Press, 1991)

McCorkell, Graeme. *Advertising That Pulls Response,* (McGraw-Hill, 1990)

————. *Direct and Database Marketing,* (Kogan Page, 1997)

McDonald, William J. *Direct Marketing: An Integrated Approach,* (McGraw-Hill, 1997)

McElhone, Alice Powers, and Edward B. Butler. *Mail It! High-Impact Business Mail from Design to Delivery,* (Benchmark Publications, 1996)

McLean, Ed. *Using Direct Mail to Increase Sales and Profits,* (Caroline House Publications, 1980)

Mersereau, Larry. *Post Card Power,* (Promopower Publishing, 2004)

Miller, Richard N. *Multinational Direct Marketing: The Methods and the Markets,* (McGraw-Hill, 1995)

Morgenstern, Steve. *Grow Your Business with Desktop Marketing,* (Random House Information Group, 1996)

Mueller, Walter. *Direct Mail Ministry: Evangelism, Stewardship, Caregiving,* (Abingdon Press, 1989)

Muldoon, Katie. *How to Profit Through Catalog Marketing,* (NTC Business Books, 1995)

Nakazawa, Tomoe, and Uda Masatoshi (editors). *Successful Direct Mail Design,* (PIE Books, 1997)

Nash, Edward L. *Database Marketing: The Ultimate Marketing Tool,* (McGraw-Hill, 1993)

————. *Direct Marketing: Strategy, Planning, Execution, 4th edition,* (McGraw-Hill, 2000)

Nash, Edward L. (editor). *The Direct Marketing Handbook, 2nd edition,* (McGraw-Hill, 1992)

Nelson, Carol. *The New Road to Successful Advertising: How to Integrate Image and Response,* (Bonus Books, 1991)

Nicholas, Don. *Secrets of Successful Subscription Marketing,* (Dartnell, 1997)

Nicholas, Ted. *The Golden Mailbox: How to Get Rich Direct Marketing Your Product,* (Enterprise Publishing, 1992)

Ogilvy, David. *Confessions of an Advertising Man,* (Southbank Publishing, 2004)

————. *Ogilvy on Advertising,* (Vintage, 1985)

O'Malley, Lisa. *Exploring Direct Marketing,* (Thomson Business Press, 1998)

Osborne, G. Scott. *Electronic Direct Marketing,* (Prentice Hall Trade, 1984)

Quimok, John. *Targeting for Success: A Guide to New Techniques for Measurement and Analysis in Database and Direct Marketing,* (McGraw-Hill, 1993)

Pearson, Stewart. *Building Brands Directly: Creating Business Value from Customer Relationships,* (Palgrave Macmillan, 1999)

Peppers, Don, and Martha Rogers. *The One to One Fieldbook: The Complete Toolkit for Implementing a 1 To 1 Marketing Program,* (Currency, 1999)

————. *The One to One Future: Building Relationships One Customer at a Time,* (Judy Piatkus Publishers, 1996)

————. *Enterprise One to One: Tools for Competing in the Interactive Age,* (Currency, 1999)

Posch, Robert, Jr. *The Direct Marketer's Legal Advisor,* (McGraw-Hill, 1982)

Poynter, Dan. *Direct Mail for Book Publishers,* (Para Publishing, 1997)

Qubein, Nido. *How to Market Through Direct Mail,* Audio Cassette (Nightingale Conant, 1992)

Ramsey, Dan. *The Upstart Guide to Owning and Managing a Mail Order Business,* (Upstart Publishing, 1995)

Raphel, Murray, and Ken Erdman. *The Do-It-Yourself Direct Mail Handbook,* (Marketers Bookshelf, 1986)

Rapp, Stan, and Thomas L. Collins. *Beyond Maximarketing: The New Power of Caring and Daring,* (McGraw-Hill, 1993)

Ratner, Bruce. *Statistical Modeling and Analysis for Database Marketing: Effective Techniques for Mining Big Data,* (Chapman & Hall/CRC, 2003)

Reitman, Jerry I. (editor), and James G. Oates. *Beyond 2000: The Future of Direct Marketing* (McGraw-Hill/Contemporary, 1994)

Research and Education Association. *How to Create Catalogs That Sell,* (Research & Education Association, 2002)

Retzler, Kathryn. *Direct Marketing: The Proven Path to Successful Selling,* (Scott, Foresman, 1988)

Roberts, Mary Lou. *Internet Marketing: Integrating Online and Offline Strategies,* (McGraw-Hill/Irwin, 2002)

Roberts, Mary Lou, and Paul D. Berger (contributor). *Direct Marketing Management,* (Prentice Hall College Division, 1989)

Roman, Ernan, and Anne Knudsen (editors). *Integrated Direct Marketing,* (McGraw-Hill, 1995)

Rosenfield, James R. *Financial Services Direct Marketing: Tactics, Techniques and Strategies,* (Financial Sourcebooks, 1991)

Sackheim, Maxwell. *Maxwell Sackheim's Billion Dollar Marketing: Concepts and Applications,* (Towers Club USA Press, 1996)

————. *My First Sixty Years in Advertising,* (Prentice-Hall, 1970)

Schmid, Jack. *Creating a Profitable Catalog: Everything You Need to Know to Create a Catalog That Sells,* (McGraw-Hill, 2000)

Schmid, Jack, and Alan Weber. *Desktop Database Marketing,* (McGraw-Hill, 1998)

Schultz, Don E. *Essentials of Advertising Strategy,* (National Textbook, 1988)

————. *Sales Promotion Essentials: The 10 Basic Sales Promotion Techniques and How to Use Them,* 3rd edition, (McGraw-Hill, 1998)

Schultz, Don, and Beth Barnes. *Strategic Advertising Campaigns,* 4th edition, (NTC/Contemporary Publishing, 1994)

Schultz, Marilyn Smith. *Mail Order on the Kitchen Table,* (Tribute, 1988)

Schwartz, Eugene M. *Breakthrough Advertising: How to Write Ads That Shatter Traditions and Sales Records,* (Boardroom Classics, 1984)

———. *The Brilliance Breakthrough: How to Talk and Write So That People Will Never Forget You,* (Instant Learning, 1994)

———. *Mail Order: How to Get Your Share of the Hidden Profits That Exist in Your Business,* (Boardroom Classics, 1983)

Scroge, Maxwell. *The United States Mail Order Industry, 2nd edition,* (NTC Publishing Group, 1994)

Services Industries Research Group. *Direct Mail Marketing in China: A Strategic Entry Report, 1997,* (Icon Group International, 1999)

Shaver, Dick. *The Next Step in Database Marketing: Consumer Guided Marketing: Privacy for Your Customers, Record Profits for You,* (Wiley, 1996)

Shaw, Robert. *Computer-Aided Marketing and Selling: Information Asset Management,* (Butterworth-Heinemann, 1991)

Shepard, David. *The New Direct Marketing: How to Implement a Profit-Driven Database Marketing Strategy,* (Irwin Professional Publishing, 1994)

Sheppard, William E. II. *Fund-Raising Letter Collection Vol. 1, 2nd edition,* (Fund Raising Institute, 1988)

Sherr, Leslie, and David J. Datz. *Design for Response: Creative Direct Marketing That Works,* (Rockport Publishers, 1999)

Shimp, Terence. *Advertising, Promotion and Supplemental Aspects of Integrated Marketing Communications, 4th edition,* (Harcourt Brace, 1996)

Shrello, Don. M. *A Vocabulary of Common Terms for Direct Marketing of Training Programs, 2nd edition,* (Schrello Direct Marketing, 1985)

Silverstein, Barry. *Business-To-Business Internet Marketing: Seven Proven Strategies for Increasing Profits Through Internet Direct Marketing, 4th edition,* (Maximum Press, 2001)

———. *Direct Marketing Lessons You Shouldn't Have to Learn the Hard Way,* (Directech, 1989)

Spiller, Lisa and Martin Baier. *Contemporary Direct Marketing,* (Prentice Hall, 2004)

Sroge, Maxwell. *How to Create Successful Catalogs,* (McGraw-Hill/Contemporary Books, 1995)

———. *Inside the Leading Mail Order Houses, 4th edition,* (NTC/Contemporary Publishing, 1997)

———. *101 Tips for More Profitable Catalogs,* (NTC Business Books, 1990)

Stein, Donna Baier, and Floyd Kemske. *Write on Target: The Direct Marketer's Copywriting Handbook,* (Glencoe Division Macmillan/ McGraw-Hill, 1997)

Sterne, Jim. *Advanced E-Mail Marketing,* (Lyris Technologies, 2003)

Stewart, Marilyn. *The Canadian Direct Marketing Handbook II: Building Customer Relationships,* (Canadian Marketing Association, 1998)

Stimolo, Bob and Lynn Vosburgh. *Introduction to School Marketing,* (School Market Research Institute, 1989)

Stockwell, John, and Henry Shaw. *Direct Marketing Checklists,* (McGraw-Hill, 1993)

Stone, Bob, and John Wyman (contributor). *Successful Telemarketing: Opportunities and Techniques for Increasing Sales and Profits,* (National Textbook, 1992)

Stone, Bob, and Anne Knudsen (editor). *Direct Marketing Success Stories: . . . and the Strategies That Built the Businesses,* (McGraw-Hill/ Contemporary, 1995)

Stone, Merlin, and Derek Davies. *Direct Hit: Direct Marketing with a Winning Edge Financial Times,* (Prentice Hall, 1995)

Sugarman, Joseph. *Advertising Secrets of the Written Word: The Ultimate Resource on How to Write Powerful Advertising Copy from One of America's Top Copywriters,* (Delstar Publishing, 1998)

———. *Marketing Secrets of a Mail Order Maverick,* (Delstar Publishing, 1998)

Sugarman, Joseph, and Dick Hafer. *Television Secrets for Marketing Success,* (Delstar Publishing, 1998)

Throckmorton, Joan. *Winning Direct Response Advertising, 2nd edition,* (NTC Business Books, 1997)

Toffler, Betsy Ann, et al. *Dictionary of Marketing Terms, 2nd edition,* (Barron's Educational Series, 1994)

Vernon, Lillian. *An Eye for Winners,* (Harper Business, 1996)

Vitale, Joe, and Jo Han Mok. *The E-Code,* (Wiley, 2005)

Vogele, Siegfried. *Handbook of Direct Mail,* (Prentice Hall Trade, 1969)

Warwick, Mal. *How to Write Successful Fundraising Letters,* (Jossey-Bass, 2001)

———. *Revolution in the Mailbox: Your Guide to Successful Direct Mail Fundraising,* (Jossey-Bass, 2004)

———. *Testing, Testing, 1, 2, 3: Raise More Money with Direct Mail Tests,* (Jossey-Bass, 2003)

Weintz, Walter. *The Solid Gold Mailbox,* (John Wiley & Sons, 1987)

White, Sarah. *Streetwise Do-It-Yourself Advertising,* (Adams Media, 1997)

Wilbur, Peter. *How to Make Money in Mail-Order,* (John Wiley & Sons, 1990)

Wunderman, Lester. *Being Direct: Making Advertising Pay,* (Random House, 1997)

Glossary

Accordion fold. Foldings in a mail-out that are at opposite ends of the paper, so that it folds in on itself like an accordion.

Account executive. Also known as advertising account executive. An AE functions as the link between the client and the advertising agency. Prepares presentations to win new business and serves the clients' needs by planning, organizing, and monitoring ad campaigns.

Actives. People on a list who have recently bought merchandise.

Additions. People whose contact info is to be added to a list.

Address correction requested. Instructions on the outside of a mail-out requesting that that the post office update you as to the correct address.

AIDA. The acronym for Attention, Interest, Desire, and Action—a marketing formula.

Airtime. The live time that a radio or television commercial is broadcast on the air.

Alternative print media. Magazines outside the mainsteam.

Artwork. Graphic images that illustrate copy.

Attendee list. A list of people who will be attending a given event.

Average order. The average amount that a respondent to a direct marketing campaign buys or orders.

Banner ads. Large ads placed on web sites that resemble banners.

Bar codes. A coding device on all products sold in America.

Benefits. Improvements brought about by products or services.

Bill-me. A plan by which a respondent can put in an order now and be billed for the cost of the order.

Bindery. The post-production term for converting; the place where converting is done in a printing plant.

Bingo cards. A business reply card inserted into a publication. It is used by readers to request material or products from companies wthat either advertise or are mentioned in the magazine; also referred to as a reader service inquiry card.

Bleed. Printing that flows off the edge of a sheet of paper.

Blind mailing. A direct marketing mail-out to everyone for whom you have contact info; the mail equivalent of a cold call.

Blow-ins. Direct marketing business reply cards inserted into the pages of a magazine.

Boldface type. Type that is thicker and darker than regular type.

Booklet. A short, multi-page pamphlet.

Border. Typically perforated to include a coupon with an offer of some kind.

Bounce back. An offer that is enclosed with a customer order.

Break-even. The amount of revenue needed to meet the expenses of a direct marketing campaign.

Broadcast e-mail. An e-mail message sent to a large audience all at once.

Broadcast media. Radio and television.

Brochure. A glossy piece of copy illustrated with graphics. Tells the reader about the product or service. Often multipage or folded over.

Broker. A person who buys from the original vendor and sells to the end customer.

Buck slip. What results from cutting a letter-sized sheet of paper into thirds, or roughly the size of a dollar bill, or "buck".

Bulk mail. A discounted mailing rate for mailing out many identical pieces at once.

Bullet. Lists of items set off by bullet points. Typically used in direct marketing material because they help break up long copy and are more interesting to the eye.

Business reply card (BRC). A postcard included for the purpose of responding to a direct marketing campaign. It has postage paid, so it doesn't cost the respondent money to reply.

Business reply envelope (BRE). Similar to a BRC, but in the form of a regular sized envelope, with postage paid.

Business to business. Also known as B2B. Businesses that sell exclusively to other businesses.

Call to action. Copy that asks or tells the reader to do something, such as buy product.

Campaign. An organized direct marketing strategy with targeted respondents.

Card decks. Stack of direct marketing postcards all mailed at once to an intended target audience.

CASS. Coding Accuracy Support System within the U.S. Postal Service processing.

Catalog. Printed material, that lists a company's products or services along with prices, descriptions and photos.

Catalog buyer. A customer who buys from a catalog.

Catalog request. A potential customer's request to be sent a catalog.

Cheshire. Pieces of paper that have printed names and addresses that can be mechanically placed individually on each mailing piece. Types of paper include fanfold, accordion fold, and others; most often referred to as labels.

Chromalins. Color printed proofs that are intended to simulate a finished printed product.

Circulars. Advertising brochures that are one page; also referred to as fliers.

Click-through rates. Measures how many readers clicked on links embedded in an e-mail or web site.

Cold lists. Lists of potential customers, none of whom have ever bought from you before.

Collate. To arrange copies in proper page order; take a stack of page ones, page twos, and page threes and arrange them in three-sheet sets or one by one according to page numbers.

Commercial envelope. An envelope used for business mail.

Compiled list. A list of names and addresses that can be compiled from various sources, like newspapers, directories, public records and retail sales slips, that identify groups of people with things in common.

Compiler. The person or company that assembles names and related data into a list.

Consumer list. A list of consumers and their contact info.

Contact. A person who handles communication.

Contributor list. A list of people who have written articles or editorials for a publication.

Controlled circulation. Publications, usually free, that have a restricted distribution.

Conversion. Making a sale.

Conversion rate. The number of sales that are made from a finite, measurable group of prospects.

Co-op mailing. A situation wherein two or more organizations combine to make separate offers within the same mailing, thus sharing the mailing cost and each other's target audience.

Copy. Written text that induces readers to buy.

Coupon. An offer of a discount by redemption.

Creative. New, fresh, original; the art and copy concept of marketing.

Cyberspace. The internet or World Wide Web environment.

Data card. The precursor to an individual entry in a database. An index card with data on a potential respondent.

Data overlay. A means of culling sub-populations from a database, such as finding out who's had a baby in the last year, who's moved in the last six months, people with certain income levels, geographic locations, etc.

Database. A system for keeping track of potential customers and respondents. The database can track multiple variables; system for keeping track of customers and their various characteristics.

Decoy. A trackable, false name to monitor mailing list usage, and determined by a list purchaser.

Deduplication process. Finding all names and entries on a list that are duplicated, then removing them.

Demographics. Various characteristics of a group of customers, such as age, income level, and geographic location.

Dimensional mailing. A three-dimensional direct mail package.

Direct mail. Advertising and marketing communication sent directly to the potential consumer through the U.S. Postal Service.

Direct mail advertising. Sending copy that may interest readers in buying goods or services

Direct mail package. An assortment of direct marketing materials sent to a potential customer.

Direct marketing. Marketing products and services directly to the consumer, soliciting a direct response and being directly measurable.

Direct Marketing Association (DMA). An association that promotes direct marketing.

Direct response. When a customer contacts a marketer in response to a solicitation.

Direct response TV. Commonly known as infomercials, and television advertising, usually longer in length than other direct marketing and with the purpose of soliciting a direct response by the viewer at the time of airing.

Directories. Categorized lists of people, companies, and organizations.

Donor list. A list of people who have donated to a charity.

Double postcard. Two postcards connected by a perforated border. One is addressed to the respondent, the other is a business reply postcard with the respondent's info printed on it. It makes responding easy.

Doubling day. A mailing's point in time when exactly 50 percent of the returns for it can be expected to have been received.

Drop date. The date of a scheduled mailing.

Dummy. A name that is inserted into a list to verify how the list is being used, or a preproduction printed mock-up of the copy showing how the finished product is likely to look.

Dummy name. The actual name that is inserted into a list to see how the list is being used; see decoy.

Duplicate. A copy of something.

E-mail etiquette. A system of customs and courtesies for e-mail communication.

E-mail marketing. Sending out e-mail solicitations.

E-mail signature. An electronic tag line listing your name and contact info and other marketing information that signs off the e-mail you send.

Envelope stuffer. Someone paid to stuff copy into envelopes and send it out; an inserted printed piece stuffed into an envelope.

Envelope teaser. Catchy copy on the outside of an envelope that interests the respondent in opening it.

Ezine. Electronic magazine or newsletter communication online.

First-class postage. Postage paid on direct mail.

Flat. A tray of mailing pieces bundled, trayed, and strapped for the post office.

Frequency. How often direct mail for a certain product or service is sent out.

Fulfillment. Sending merchandise to a customer that has been ordered.

Guarantee. Pledge that the customer will be satisfied, while removing all risk of purchase.

Handling charge. A charge for the time involved in packaging an order to be shipped.

Hard copy. A printout of copy onto paper.

Headline. A sentence that tops a story or article, usually set off in large letters to grab the attention of the reader.

Hotline names. Names of potential respondents that have come onto the database within the last 30 days or 60 days, depending on the list. They are the most recent names in the file, and normally pull at higher rates than the core list. Thus, they cost more.

House list. A list composed of your customers. Who have bought something from you at least once. They're familiar with your company and your product, and satisfied with them. A list of current customers, subscribers, or members.

House organ. An inhouse newsletter or newspaper within a company.

Hurdle rate. The percentage of customers who have a certain minimum activity level for "recency", frequency, and monetary value. It's the percentage of customers who have bought

X, Y times, within Z months, and spent D number of dollars.

Indicia. The printed mailing permit on a direct mail piece.

Insert. Pages of copy that are inserted into magazines or newspapers.

Institutional advertising. Used mainly by large businesses or by small ones that want to seem large. Does not include a call to action, just builds image.

Junk mail. Direct mail that was of no interest to the recipient; that missed its intended target; unwanted solicitation mail.

Key words. Words provided in a web search for a one or more relevant web pages.

Lead generation. Finding those who are interested in buying from you.

Lettershop. A company that processes letters and other direct mail pieces for the purpose of bulk mail or mass distribution of direct mail.

Lifetime value of a customer. How much that customer will buy over his or her lifetime.

Lift note. A short paragraph at the end of a solicitation that asks for the respondent's business.

List broker. A specialist who sets up the arrangements for a company to make use of another company's list. The broker's services might include research, selection, recommendation, and evaluation.

List buyer. Someone who buys a list from another company or organization.

List count. The number of entries on a list conforming to a set of list specifications.

List criteria. Criteria for a person's name being on a list.

List maintenance. The process of keeping a list up-to-date with regard to customer characteristics.

List manager. The person whose job it is to maintain the list; also involved in the selling of the list.

List owner. The company or organization that owns the list.

List rental. The authorized and paid use of another company's list.

List vendor. The person who sells the list; may be the original owner or a broker.

Mail order. An order sent in through the U.S. Postal Service.

Mail prep. Preparing a mail-out by of addressing and processing in conformance with U.S. postal regulations.

Mailing house. A company that processes mail for mailing in accordance with U.S. postal regulations; see lettershop.

Mailing list. A list, usually kept in database form, that provides contact info for potential respondents.

Membership list. A list of members of a special club or offer group.

Merge/purge. A program designed to reduce undesired redundancy in a direct mail campaign, such as duplicates sent to the same household.

Monarch envelope. A 7" by 5" envelope.

National change of address. A program offered by the U.S. Postal Service that corrects undeliverable addresses.

Niche market. Segment of the market having specific demographics that are typically tighter in description than a target market.

Nixie. Direct mail letter returned to sender because the address was wrong. Also, any undelivered piece of mail. Nixies are commonly used to correct a list.

Offer. A product or service that a direct marketer puts out for response.

One to one marketing. When one marketer contacts one potential customer personally.

Opt-in list. A mailing list that respondents have to be on the list in order to get on.

Orders. Agreements to purchase products or services.

Paid circulation. Nonfree published material; the customer who reads it either pays to subscribe or buys it at a newsstand.

Paid circulation. The number of readers of a publication who pay to receive it.

Permission marketing. Also known as "opt-in." The customer is asked for and grants his or her permission to receive direct marketing solicitations.

Personalization. Putting a person's name on a piece of direct mail, as in "Dear Joe Smith."

Piece rate. Rate charged per piece.

Poly-bag mailing. Mail-outs that go out in a poly plastic bag.

Postcard. A small mail-out that costs less postage than a letter, tand is usually a card that measures 4¼" by 6" or larger.

Premium. A reward or bonus given to those who respond by a certain date or who are among a set number of first-respondents. ("Act now and you'll receive . . ." or "Be among the first 100 to reply and you'll get . . . .")

Premium sheet. A sheet of something that may have value to the respondent, such as return address labels or stickers.

Presort. Mail that has already been sorted into ZIP codes and/or carrier routes in accordance with U.S. postal bulk mail requirements.

Privacy. The boundary beyond which you should not push; customer-set limits on contact and list/information usage.

Rate card. A card that lists advertising or direct marketing rates.

Recency frequency monetary (RFM). Database models that directly link the future value of a customer with the customer's behavior. The more recently someone has done something, and the more frequently, and the more money they've spent, the more likely they are to continue to purchase.

Record. An entry or a name on a list.

Response. An answer that a customer sends in response to a direct mail campaign.

Response list. A list of the respondents to a direct mail campaign.

Response rate. The number of responses received compared to the number sent—usually expressed as a percentage.

Return postage guaranteed. A guarantee that postage will be paid for a return.

Rollout. The beginning of a campaign.

Second class. A less expensive form of U.S mail than first class.

Segmentation. Dividing up markets into clusters or portions with common characteristics.

Select. This refers to various characteristics that identify segments or sub-groups within a database list.

Self-mailer. A self-contained mailing piece designed to take the shape of an envelope when folded. Thus, it doesn't require a separate outer envelope.

Self-mailer. Self-contained mail-out that can be mailed without a separate outer envelope.

Sic. Exact text, even with misspellings; common in legal depositions.

Signature. A subset grouping of pages to be bound into a discrete group to make a book, booklet, guide, or other bound publication.

Solo mailing. A mailing that only promotes one product or service.

Spam. Unwanted, unsolicited e-mail. May carry legal penalties.

Split run. Representative samples from the same list, used for package runs and testing.

SRDS. The Standard Rate and Data Service is a reference for all direct marketers.

Statement stuffers. Advertising copy stuffed into the same envelope as a customer's statement.

Subheads. Subheadings such as smaller titles over blocks of copy.

Subject line. Header line of an e-mail that describes in a single line what the e-mail message is about.

Tabloid. An inexpensive magazine typically sold at supermarket checkouts. Often runs lurid stories.

Tag line. A marking on a record using definitive criteria so the record can either be used or avoided in the future.

Target market. The exact demographic segment that a direct marketing campaign is aimed at.

Tear sheet. A sample of an ad that ran in a magazine, created by literally tearing the relevant sheet from a copy of the magazine.

Teaser campaign. A direct marketing campaign in which little hints of what is to come are disseminated one by one.

Telemarketing. Calling people on the phone to sell products and services.

Test. The use of a focus group to gauge how well a proposed new campaign will work.

Testing. The act of determining feasibility; comparison of variables.

Text. The copy itself, the words.

Third-class mail. Cheapest way to send U.S. mail other than book rate or bulk mail.

Trade advertising. Advertising in niche markets to groups that share certain commonalties. For instance, putting an ad for tires in a car enthusiast's magazine.

Trade name. A special name that is trademarked with the U.S. Patent Office.

Trademark. A special design that is trademarked with the U.S. Patent Office.

Undeliverable. The post office could not locate the intended recipient of mail.

Unique selling proposition. The one set of benefits that separate you from the competition that will make a prospect or customer want to buy.

Viral marketing. Marketing in which customers tell other customers about a product or service. Often referred to as word-of-mouth marketing.

Web site. Internet site or page on the World Wide Web.

ZIP + 4. ZIP code with four digits added to pinpoint a location.

ZIP code. A five-digit code used in the United States to indicate a geographic region.

ZIP code sequence. Sorting and arranging presorted/bulk mail in ZIP code order for the purpose of increasing post office efficiency, therefore entitling the mailer to a discounted postage.

About the Author

AY LEVINSON ONCE DESCRIBED AL LAUTENslager as a true guerrilla marketer with a passion for marketing that is second to none. He went on to describe how Al's strong desire and uncanny ability to share his knowledge and experience with others usually results in their success.

Al Lautenslager is an award-winning marketing/PR consultant, speaker, author, and entrepreneur who has helped hundreds of business owners succeed in their own businesses. He is the coauthor of *Guerrilla Marketing in 30 Days* and a featured business coach on Entrepreneur.com, the online version of *Entrepreneur* magazine. He is the principal of Market for Profits, a Chicago-based marketing consulting firm, as well as president and owner of The Ink Well, a commercial printing and mailing company in Wheaton, Illinois.

Al may be heard every year on the radio as a marketing expert reviewing Super Bowl commercials. He has also appeared on TV.

Al has started up businesses and closed them down. He has walked the walk of a guerrilla marketer. He is a multiple-winner of Business of the Year awards from various organizations. His articles may be seen on over 20 online sites.

His leadership has extended to his involvement in the community as a member of the board of directors of numerous nonprofit organizations, including two chambers of commerce. A member of *USA Today's* small-business panel and a certified Guerrilla Marketing Coach, Lautenslager is also a much-in-demand speaker on the subject of marketing. He speaks to audiences wanting to learn more about building their businesses through low- or no-cost marketing tactics, including direct marketing. Many in his audience gain strategies and tactics they can use the very same day.

In 2004, *Fast Company* magazine announced that Lautenslager was a finalist for its annual Fast 50, "ordinary people doing extraordinary things" as "leaders, innovators, and technology pioneers." He can be contacted through his web site, www.market-for-profits.com or e-mail al@market-for-profits.com.

Al lives with his wife, Angela, and their daughter, Allison, in Naperville, Ilinois.

Also by Al Lautenslager

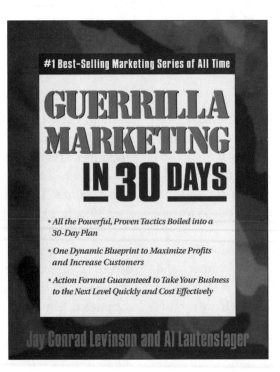

Index